THE COMPLETE POETICAL WORKS OF THOMAS CHATTERTON

VOLUMES I & II

By

THOMAS CHATTERTON

First published in 1906

Read & Co.

Copyright © 2020 Ragged Hand

This edition is published by Ragged Hand,
an imprint of Read & Co.

This book is copyright and may not be reproduced or copied in any way without the express permission of the publisher in writing.

British Library Cataloguing-in-Publication Data
A catalogue record for this book is available
from the British Library.

Read & Co. is part of Read Books Ltd.
For more information visit
www.readandcobooks.co.uk

O Chatterton! how very sad thy fate!
Dear child of sorrow — son of misery!
How soon the film of death obscur'd that eye,
Whence Genius mildly falsh'd, and high debate.
How soon that voice, majestic and elate,
Melted in dying numbers! Oh! how nigh
Was night to thy fair morning. Thou didst die
A half-blown flow'ret which cold blasts amate.
But this is past: thou art among the stars
Of highest heaven: to the rolling spheres
Thou sweetly singest: nought thy hymning mars,
Above the ingrate world and human fears.
On earth the good man base detraction bars
From thy fair name, and waters it with tears.

JOHN KEATS.

Sonnet to Chatterton, 1848

I thought of Chatterton, the marvellous Boy,
The sleepless Soul that perished in his pride;
Of Him who walked in glory and in joy
Following his plough, along the mountain-side:
By our own spirits are we deified:
We Poets in our youth begin in gladness;
But thereof come in the end despondency and madness.

WILLIAM WORDSWORTH.

AN EXCERPT FROM
Resolution and Independence, 1807

With Shakespeare's manhood at a boy's wild heart,—
Through Hamlet's doubt to Shakspeare near allied,
And kin to Milton through his Satan's pride,—
At Death's sole door he stooped, and craved a dart;
And to the dear new bower of England's art,—
Even to that shrine Time else had deified,
The unuttered heart that soared against his side,—
Drove the fell point, and smote life's seals apart.
Thy nested home-loves, noble Chatterton;
The angel-trodden stair thy soul could trace
Up Redcliffe's spire; and in the world's armed space
Thy gallant sword-play:—these to many an one
Are sweet for ever; as thy grave unknown
And love-dream of thine unrecorded face.

Dante Gabriel Rossetti.

Poem of Thomas Chatterton,
Five English Poets, Ballads and Sonnets, 1881

THE COMPLETE POETICAL WORKS *of* THOMAS CHATTERTON

VOLUME I

CONTENTS

VOLUME I

ACKNOWLEDGED POEMS

AFRICAN ECLOGUES:—
    The Death of Nicou 1
    Heccar and Gaira 5
    Narva and Mored 8

THE REVENGE: A BURLETTA 11

SONGS IN 'THE REVENGE':—
    A Bacchanalian — 'Bacchus, ever smiling power' 35
    The Invitation—'Away to the woodlands, away!' 36
    A Bacchanalian—'What is war and all its joys?' 36
    The Virgin's Choice—'Young Strephon is as fair a swain' 37
    The Happy Pair—'Lucy, since the knot was tied' 38

THE WOMAN OF SPIRIT: A BURLETTA . . 39

POEMS ADDRESSED TO CERTAIN PERSONS :—
  On Mr. Alcock, of Bristol 42
  To Miss Bush, of Bristol 44
  To Miss C., on hearing her play on the harpsichord 45
  To Miss Clarke 45
  Acrostic on Miss Sally Clarke 46
  Song: addressed to Miss C——am, of Bristol 46
  A New Song: to Mr. G. Catcott . . . 48
  Song: Fanny of the Hill 49
  To Mrs. Haywood, the novelist . . . 50
  To Mr. Holland 50
  To the beauteous Miss Hoyland . . . 52
  To Miss Hoyland 53
  To Miss Hoyland 54
  To Miss Hoyland 55
  To Miss Hoyland 56
  To Miss Hoyland 56
  To Miss Hoyland 57
  To Miss Hoyland, with a present . . . 58
  Acrostic on Miss Eleanor Hoyland . . . 58
  Ode to Miss Hoyland 59
  The Complaint: addressed to Miss P—— L——, of Bristol 60
  To Mr. Powel 62
  The Advice: addressed to Miss M[aria] R[umsey], of Bristol 62
  To Horace Walpole 64
  To a friend 65
  To a friend, on his intended marriage . . 65
  Verses to a lady in Bristol 67

SATIRES :—
  The Consuliad 69
  Epistle to the Reverend Mr. Catcott . . 77
  The Exhibition [Extract only] . . . 85
  Fables for the Court: the Shepherds . . 86
  Journal sixth 89

SATIRES—*continued*

Kew Gardens	101
The Whore of Babylon	134
The Prophecy	134
Resignation	138
The Art of Puffing	162
The Defence	163
Happiness	166
Chatterton's Will	170
Fragment: 'Far from the reach of critics and reviews'	172
Fragment: 'Interest, thou universal god of men'	175

ELEGIES:—

February	177
'Haste, haste! ye solemn messengers of night'	179
'Joyless I hail the solemn gloom.' (Written at Stanton Drew)	181
'Joyless I seek the solitary shade'	182
'Why blooms the radiance of the morning sky?'	183
On the death of William Beckford, Esq.	185
To the memory of Mr. Thomas Phillips of Fairford	189
On the death of Mr. Phillips	193
On Thomas Phillips's death	197
On Mr. Wm. Smith	198
On the death of Mr. John Tandey, Sen.	199

MISCELLANEOUS POEMS:—

On the last Epiphany	200
A Hymn for Christmas Day	201
Sly Dick	202
The Churchwarden and the Apparition	204
Apostate Will	205
The Methodist	207
Colin instructed	207
A Burlesque Cantata	208

MISCELLANEOUS POEMS—*continued*

Clifton	209
The Copernican System	213
Translations from Horace:—	
Lib. 1, Carm. v.	214
Lib. 1, Carm. xix.	215
An Epitaph on an Old Maid	216
Sunday: a Fragment	216
Suicide	218
The Resignation	218
On the Immortality of the Soul	219
Enquiry after Happiness	220
Last Verses	221

ACKNOWLEDGED POEMS

THE DEATH OF NICOU

AN AFRICAN ECLOGUE

ON Tiber's banks, Tiber, whose waters glide
In slow meanders down to Gaigra's side;
And circling all the horrid mountain round,
Rushes impetuous to the deep profound;
Rolls o'er the ragged rocks with hideous yell;
Collects its waves beneath the earth's vast shell;
There for a while, in loud confusion hurled,
It crumbles mountains down, and shakes the world,
Till, borne upon the pinions of the air,
Through the rent earth the bursting waves appear;   10
Fiercely propelled the whitened billows rise,
Break from the cavern and ascend the skies:
Then lost and conquered by superior force,
Through hot Arabia holds its rapid course:
On Tiber's banks, where scarlet jasmines bloom,
And purple aloes shed a rich perfume;
Where, when the sun is melting in his heat,
The reeking tigers find a cool retreat,
Bask in the sedges, lose the sultry beam,
And wanton with their shadows in the stream;   20
On Tiber's banks, by sacred priests revered,
Where in the days of old a god appeared;
'Twas in the dead of night, at Chalma's feast,

THE DEATH OF NICOU

The tribe of Alra slept around the priest.
He spoke; as evening-thunders, bursting near,
His horrid accents broke upon the ear;
'Attend, Alraddas, with your sacred priest!
This day the sun is rising in the east;
The sun which shall illumine all the earth
Now, now is rising, in a mortal birth'.   30
He vanished like a vapour of the night,
And sunk away in a faint blaze of light;
Swift from the branches of the holy oak,
Horror, confusion, fear, and torment broke:
And still, when midnight trims her mazy lamp,
They take their way through Tiber's watery swamp.
On Tiber's banks, close ranked, a warring train,
Stretched to the distant edge of Galca's plain:
So, when arrived at Gaigra's highest steep,
We view the wide expansion of the deep,   40
See, in the gilding of her watery robe,
The quick declension of the circling globe,
From the blue sea a chain of mountains rise,
Blended at once with water and with skies,
Beyond our sight in vast extension curled,
The check of waves, the guardians of the world.
Strong were the warriors as the ghost of Cawn,
Who threw the Hill-of-archers to the lawn,
When the soft earth at his appearance fled,
And rising billows played around his head: 50
When a strong tempest, rising from the main,
Dashed the full clouds unbroken on the plain.
Nicou, immortal in the sacred song,
Held the red sword of war, and led the strong.
From his own tribe the sable warriors came,
Well tried in battle, and well known in fame.
Nicou, descended from the god of war
Who lived coeval with the morning star:

THE DEATH OF NICOU

Narada was his name; who cannot tell
How all the world through great Narada fell? 60
Vichon, the god who ruled above the skies,
Looked on Narada, but with envious eyes:
The warrior dared him, ridiculed his might,
Bent his white bow, and summoned him to fight.
Vichon, disdainful, bade his lightnings fly,
And scattered burning arrows in the sky;
Threw down a star, the armour of his feet,
To burn the air with supernatural heat;
Bid a loud tempest roar beneath the ground;
Lifted the sea, and all the earth was drowned. 70
Narada still escaped: a sacred tree
Lifted him up, and bore him through the sea.
The waters still ascending fierce and high,
He towered into the chambers of the sky.
There Vichon sat, his armour on his bed,
He thought Narada with the mighty dead.
Before his seat the heavenly warrior stands,
The lightning quivering in his yellow hands.
The god astonished dropped; hurled from the shore,
He dropped to torments, and to rise no more. 80
Headlong he falls; 'tis his own arms compel,
Condemned in ever-burning fires to dwell.
From this Narada, mighty Nicou sprung;
The mighty Nicou, furious, wild, and young,
Who led the embattled archers to the field,
And bore a thunderbolt upon his shield:
That shield his glorious father died to gain,
When the white warriors fled along the plain;
When the full sails could not provoke the flood,
Till Nicou came and swelled the seas with blood. 90
Slow, at the end of his robust array,
The mighty warrior pensive took his way,
Against the son of Nair, the young Rorest,

Once the companion of his youthful breast.
Strong were the passions of the son of Nair,
Strong, as the tempest of the evening air;
Insatiate in desire; fierce as the boar;
Firm in resolve as Cannie's rocky shore.
Long had the gods endeavoured to destroy
All Nicou's friendship, happiness, and joy.   100
They sought in vain, till Vicat, Vichon's son,
Never in feats of wickedness outdone,
Saw Nica, sister to the mountain king,
Dressed beautiful, with all the flowers of spring.
He saw, and scattered poison in her eyes;
From limb to limb in varied forms he flies;
Dwelt on her crimson lip, and added grace
To every glossy feature of her face.
Rorest was fired with passion at the sight,
Friendship and honour sunk to Vicat's right.   110
He saw, he loved, and, burning with desire,
Bore the soft maid from brother, sister, sire.
Pining with sorrow, Nica faded, died,
Like a fair aloe in its morning pride.
This brought the warrior to the bloody mead,
And sent to young Rorest the threatening reed.
He drew his army forth. Oh! need I tell
That Nicou conquered, and the lover fell?
His breathless army mantled all the plain,
And death sat smiling on the heaps of slain.   120
The battle ended, with his reeking dart
The pensive Nicou pierced his beating heart:
And to his mourning valiant warriors cried,
'I, and my sister's ghost are satisfied.'

C.

Brooke Street, 12*th June*, 1770.

HECCAR AND GAIRA

AN AFRICAN ECLOGUE

3rd January, 1770.

WHERE the rough Caigra rolls the surgy wave,
Urging his thunders through the echoing cave;
Where the sharp rocks, in distant horror seen,
Drive the white currents through the spreading green;
Where the loud tiger, pawing in his rage,
Bids the black archers of the wilds engage;
Stretched on the sand, two panting warriors lay,
In all the burning torments of the day.
Their bloody javelins reeked one living steam,
Their bows were broken at the roaring stream;   10
Heccar, the chief of Jarra's fruitful hill,
Where the dark vapours nightly dews distil,
Saw Gaira, the companion of his soul,
Extended where loud Caigra's billows roll;
Gaira, the king of warring archers, found
Where daily lightnings plough the sandy ground,
Where brooding tempests howl along the sky,
Where rising deserts whirled in circles fly.

HECCAR: Gaira, 'tis useless to attempt the chase,
    Swifter than hunted wolves they urge the race;   20
    Their lessening forms elude the straining eye,
    Upon the plumage of macaws they fly.
    Let us return, and strip the reeking slain,
    Leaving the bodies on the burning plain.

GAIRA: Heccar, my vengeance still exclaims for blood,
    'Twould drink a wider stream than Caigra's flood.

This javelin, oft in nobler quarrels tried,
Put the loud thunder of their arms aside.
Fast as the streaming rain, I poured the dart,
Hurling a whirlwind through the trembling
    heart: 30
But now my lingering feet revenge denies,
O could I throw my javelin from my eyes!

HECCAR : When Gaira the united armies broke,
Death winged the arrow, death impelled the
    stroke.
See, piled in mountains on the sanguine sand,
The blasted of the lightnings of thy hand.
Search the brown desert and the glossy green,
There are the trophies of thy valour seen.
The scattered bones mantled in silver white,
Once animated, dared the foes in fight. 40
The children of the wave, whose pallid race
Views the faint sun display a languid face,
From the red fury of thy justice fled
Swifter than torrents from their rocky bed.
Fear with a sickened silver tinged their hue:
The guilty fear, when vengeance is their due.

GAIRA : Rouse not remembrance from her shadowy cell,
Nor of those bloody sons of mischief tell.
Cawna, O Cawna! decked in sable charms,
What distant region holds thee from my arms? 50
Cawna, the pride of Afric's sultry vales,
Soft as the cooling murmur of the gales;
Majestic as the many-coloured snake,
Trailing his glories through the blossomed brake;
Black as the glossy rocks, where Eascal roars,
Foaming through sandy wastes to Jaghir's shores;
Swift as the arrow, hasting to the breast,
Was Cawna, the companion of my rest.

The sun sat lowering in the western sky,
The swelling tempest spread around the eye ; 60
Upon my Cawna's bosom I reclined,
Catching the breathing whispers of the wind.
Swift from the wood a prowling tiger came,
Dreadful his voice, his eyes a glowing flame ;
I bent the bow, the never-erring dart
Pierced his rough armour, but escaped his heart ;
He fled, though wounded, to a distant waste,
I urged the furious flight with fatal haste ;
He fell, he died—spent in the fiery toil,
I stripped his carcase of the furry spoil, 70
And, as the varied spangles met my eye,
'On this', I cried, 'shall my loved Cawna lie'.
The dusky midnight hung the skies in grey ;
Impelled by love, I winged the airy way ;
In the deep valley and the mossy plain,
I sought my Cawna, but I sought in vain.
The pallid shadows of the azure waves
Had made my Cawna, and my children, slaves.
Reflection maddens to recal the hour ;
The gods had given me to the demon's power. 80
The dusk slow vanished from the hated lawn,
I gained a mountain glaring with the dawn.
There the full sails, expanded to the wind,
Struck horror and distraction in my mind ;
There Cawna, mingled with a worthless train,
In common slavery drags the hated chain.
Now judge, my Heccar, have I cause for rage ?
Should aught the thunder of my arm assuage ?
In ever-reeking blood this javelin dyed
With vengeance shall be never satisfied ; 90
I'll strew the beaches with the mighty dead,
And tinge the lily of their features red.

HECCAR : When the loud shriekings of the hostile cry
　　Roughly salute my ear, enraged I'll fly ;
　　Send the sharp arrow quivering through the heart,
　　Chill the hot vitals with the venomed dart ;
　　Nor heed the shining steel or noisy smoke,
　　Gaira and vengeance shall inspire the stroke.

NARVA AND MORED

AN AFRICAN ECLOGUE

' RECITE the loves of Narva and Mored ',
The priest of Chalma's triple idol said.
High from the ground the youthful warriors sprung,
Loud on the concave shell the lances rung.
In all the mystic mazes of the dance,
The youths of Banny's burning sands advance,
Whilst the soft virgin panting looks behind,
And rides upon the pinions of the wind,
Ascends the mountain's brow, and measures round
The steepy cliffs of Chalma's sacred ground :　　10
Chalma, the god whose noisy thunders fly
Through the dark covering of the midnight sky,
Whose arm directs the close-embattled host,
And sinks the labouring vessels on the coast ;
Chalma, whose excellence is known from far,
From Lupa's rocky hill to Calabar :
The guardian god of Afric and the isles,
Where nature in her strongest vigour smiles ;
Where the blue blossom of the forky thorn
Bends with the nectar of the opening morn ;　　20
Where ginger's aromatic, matted root,
　Creep through the mead, and up the mountains shoot.

Three times the virgin, swimming on the breeze,
Danced in the shadow of the mystic trees;
When, like a dark cloud spreading to the view,
The first-born sons of war and blood pursue;
Swift as the elk they pour along the plain;
Swift as the flying clouds distilling rain;
Swift as the boundings of the youthful roe,
They course around, and lengthen as they go.   30
Like the long chain of rocks, whose summits rise
Far in the sacred regions of the skies,
Upon whose top the blackening tempest lowers,
Whilst down its side the gushing torrent pours;
Like the long cliffy mountains which extend
From Lorbar's cave, to where the nations end,
Which sink in darkness, thickening and obscure,
Impenetrable, mystic, and impure;
The flying terrors of the war advance,
And round the sacred oak repeat the dance.   40
Furious they twist around the gloomy trees,
Like leaves in autumn twirling with the breeze.
So, when the splendour of the dying day
Darts the red lustre of the watery way,
Sudden beneath Toddida's whistling brink
The circling billows in wild eddies sink,
Whirl furious round, and the loud bursting wave
Sinks down to Chalma's sacerdotal cave,
Explores the palaces on Zira's coast,
Where howls the war-song of the chieftain's ghost;   50
Where the artificer, in realms below,
Gilds the rich lance or beautifies the bow;
From the young palm tree spins the useful twine,
Or makes the teeth of elephants divine;
Where the pale children of the feeble sun,
In search of gold, through every climate run:
From burning heat to freezing torments go,
And live in all vicissitudes of woe.

Like the loud eddies of Toddida's sea,
The warriors circle the mysterious tree, 60
Till, spent with exercise, they spread around
Upon the opening blossoms of the ground.
The priestess, rising, sings the sacred tale,
And the loud chorus echoes through the dale.

PRIESTESS : Far from the burning sands of Calabar ;
    Far from the lustre of the morning star ;
    Far from the pleasure of the holy morn ;
    Far from the blessedness of Chalma's horn,
    Now rest the souls of Narva and Mored,
    Laid in the dust, and numbered with the dead. 70
    Dear are their memories to us, and long,
    Long shall their attributes be known in song.
    Their lives were transient as the meadow flower,
    Ripened in ages, withered in an hour.
    Chalma reward them in his gloomy cave,
    And open all the prisons of the grave !
    Bred to the service of the godhead's throne,
    And living but to serve his god alone,
    Narva was beauteous as the opening day,
    When on the spangling waves the sunbeams play, 80
    When the macaw, ascending to the sky,
    Views the bright splendour with a steady eye :
    Tall, as the house of Chalma's dark retreat,
    Compact and firm, as Rhadal Ynca's fleet,
    Completely beauteous as a summer's sun,
    Was Narva, by his excellence undone.
    Where the soft Togla creeps along the meads,
    Through scented calamus and fragrant reeds ;
    Where the sweet Zinsa spreads its matted bed,
    Lived the still sweeter flower, the young Mored. 90
    Black was her face, as Togla's hidden cell ;
    Soft, as the moss where hooting adders dwell.
    As to the sacred court she brought a fawn,

The sportive tenant of the spicy lawn,
She saw and loved ! and Narva too forgot
His sacred vestment and his mystic lot.
Long had the mutual sigh, the mutual tear,
Burst from the breast and scorned confinement
　　there.
Existence was a torment ! O my breast !
Can I find accents to unfold the rest ?　　　100
Locked in each other's arms, from Hyga's cave
They plunged relentless to a watery grave ;
And, falling, murmured to the powers above,
' Gods ! take our lives, unless we live to love '.
　　　　　　　　　　　　　　　　　C.
Shoreditch, *2nd May*, 1770.

THE REVENGE

A BURLETTA

DRAMATIS PERSONÆ

Jupiter	MR REINHOLD
Bacchus	MR BANNISTER
Cupid	MASTER CHENEY
Juno	[MRS THOMPSON]

ACT I, SCENE I

Recitative

JUPITER : I swear by Styx, this usage is past bearing;
My lady Juno ranting, tearing, swearing !
Why, what the devil will my godship do,
If blows and thunder cannot tame a shrew ?

Air

Though the loud thunder rumbles,
　Though storms rend the sky ;
Yet louder she grumbles,
　And swells the sharp cry.

Her jealousy teasing,
  Disguesting her form :   10
Her music as pleasing
  As pigs in a storm.

I fly her embraces,
  To wenches more fair ;
And leave her wry faces,
  Cold sighs, and despair.

Recitative

And oh ! ye tedious minutes, steal away ;
Come evening, close the folding doors of day ;
Night, spread thy sable petticoat around,
And sow thy poppies on the slumbering ground ;   20
Then raving into love, and drunk with charms,
I'll lose my Juno's tongue in Maia's arms.

Air

Sighing,
Dying,
Lying,
Frying,
In the furnace of desire ;
Creeping,
Sleeping,
Oh ! how slow the hours retire !   30

When the busy heart is beating,
  When the bosom's all on fire,
Oh ! how welcome is the meeting !
  Oh ! how slow the hours retire !

Recitative

But see—my Fury comes ; by Styx, I tremble :
I'll creep aside—'tis folly to dissemble.

THE REVENGE 13

Scene II

Juno, Jupiter

Recitative

JUNO : See, see, my good man steals aside !
    In spite of his thunder,
    I make him knock under,
  And own the superior right of a bride.   40

Air

    How happy the life
    Of a governing wife,
How charming, how easy, the swift minutes pass ;
      Let her do what she will,
      The husband is still,
And but for his horns you would think him an ass.
      How happy the spouse
      In his dignified brows ;
How worthy with heroes and monarchs to class:
      Both above and below,   50
      Experience will shew,
But take off the horns and each husband's an ass.

Recitative   [*Aside*

JUPITER : Zounds, I'll take heart of grace, and brave her clapper :
And, if my courage holds, egad, I'll strap her :
Through all Olympus shall the thunders roll,
And earth shall echo to the mustard bowl ;
Should she prove sturdy, by the Lord, I'll heave hence,
Down to some brandy shop, this noisy grievance.

Air

What means this horrid rattle?
  And must that tongue of riot   60
Wage one eternal battle
  With happiness and quiet?

Air continued

JUNO: What means your saucy question?
  D'ye think I mind your bluster?
Your godship's always best in
  Words, thunder, noise, and fluster.

Recitative

JUPITER: Hence, thou eternal tempest, from our regions,
  And yell in concert with infernal legions:
Hence, or be calm—our will is fate—away hence,
  Or on the lightning's wings you'll find conveyance.   70

Recitative

JUNO: I brave your vengeance—
JUPITER: Oh! 'tis most provoking!
JUNO: Should not my spirit better my condition,
  I've one way left—remonstrance and petition
  To all the gods in senate: 'tis no joking—

Air

I will never tamely bear
  All my wrongs and slights, sir;
Heaven and all the gods shall hear
  How you spend your nights, sir.
    Drinking, swearing,   80
    Roaring, tearing,
Wenching, roving everywhere;

        Whilst poor I
        At home must lie,
        Wishing, scheming,
        Sighing, dreaming,
    Grasping nothing but the air.

              Recitative

PITER : O how shall I escape the swelling clatter—
    I'll slit her tongue, and make short work o' th'
    matter.

                 Air

             Fury, cease,   90
             Give me peace,
             Still your racket,
             Or your jacket
             I'll be drubbing,
             For your snubbing;
    By the gods, you shall knock under.
             Must you ever
             Thus endeavour,
             Rumbling,
             Grumbling,   100
             Rowling,
             Growling,
    To outsound the noisy thunder?

              Recitative   [*Aside*

VO : Ah! I'm quite out here—plaguily mistaken—
    The man's in earnest—I must save my bacon;
        Since scolding but provokes him,
            A method I'll pursue.
        I'll soothe him, tickle, coax him,
            Then I shall have my due.

Air

Ah, cruel, cruel Jove, 110
And is it thus a love,
So pure, so chaste, so strong as mine,
Is slighted, disrespected,
Unnoticed and neglected,
Returned with such a love as thine?

Air

JUPITER : Did the foolish passion tease ye,
Would you have a husband please ye,
Suppliant, pliant, amorous, easy?
Never rate him like a fury;
By experience I'll assure ye, 120
Kindness, and not rage, must cure ye.

Recitative [*Aside*

JUNO : He's in the right on't—hits it to a tittle—
But Juno must display her tongue a little.

Air

I own my error, I repent
Let thy sparkling eyes behold me,
Let thy lovely arms enfold me;
Let thy stubborn heart relent.

Recitative

JUPITER : Egad, why this is more than I desire,
'Tis from the frying-pan to meet the fire,
Zounds, I've no stomach to the marriage bed; 130
But something must be either sung or said.

THE REVENGE

Air

What is love? the wise despise it;
'Tis a bubble blown for boys:
Gods and heroes should not prize it,
Jove aspires to greater joys.

Air continued

JUNO: What is love? 'tis nature's treasure,
'Tis the storehouse of her joys;
'Tis the highest heaven of pleasure,
'Tis a bliss which never cloys.

Air continued

JUPITER: What is love? an air-blown bubble, 140
Only silly fools receive it;
'Tis a magazine of trouble;
'Tis but folly—thus I leave it.

[Jupiter runs off

SCENE III

Recitative

JUNO: Gods, he is gone and I must curse my fate,
That linked my gentle love to such a mate;
He neither fills my freezing bed, my heart, nor
My vainly-folding arms: oh! such a partner!

Air

When a woman's tied down
To a spiritless log,
Let her fondle or frown, 150
Yet still he's a clog.

Let her please her own mind,
Abroad let her roam;
Abroad she may find
What she can't find at home.

Scene IV

Juno, Cupid

Recitative

CUPID: Ho! mistress Juno—here's a storm a-brewing—
  Your devil of a spouse is always doing—
  Pray step aside—this evening, I protest,
  Jove and Miss Maia—you may guess the rest—

JUNO: How! what? when? where?—nay, prithee now, unfold it. 160

CUPID: 'Gad—so I will; for, faith, I cannot hold it.
  His mighty godship in a fiery flurry
  Met me just now—confusion to his hurry!
  I stopped his way, forsooth, and, with a thwack,
  He laid a thunderbolt across my back:
  Bless me! I feel it now—my short ribs ache yet—
  I vowed revenge, and now, by Styx, I'll take it.
  Miss Maia, in her chamber, after nine,
  Receives the thunderer, in his robes divine.
  I undermined it all; see, here's the letter— 170
  Could dukes spell worse, whose tutors spelt no better?
  You know false spelling now is much the fashion—

JUNO: Lend me your drops—oh! I shall swoon with passion!
  I'll tear her eyes out! oh! I'll stab—I'll strangle!
  And worse than lover's English, her I'll mangle!

CUPID: Nay, pray be calm; I've hit off an expedient
  To do you right—

THE REVENGE

JUNO :   Sweet Cupid, your obedient—

CUPID : Tie Maia by the leg ; steal in her stead
   Into the smuggled raptures of her bed ;   180
   When the god enters let him take possession.

JUNO : O heavenly scheme ! O joy beyond expression !

CUPID : Nay, never stay ; delaying may confute it.

JUNO : O happy thought ! I fly to execute it.
                              [*Exit Juno.*

Scene V

Recitative

CUPID : See how she flies, whilst warring passions shake her,
   Nor thought nor lightning now can overtake her.

Air

   How often in the married state
   The wise, the sensible, the great,
      Find misery and woe ;
   Though, should we dive in nature's laws   190
   To trace the first primæval cause,
      The wretch is self-made so.

Air changes

   Love's a pleasure, solid, real,
   Nothing fanciful, ideal,
      'Tis the bliss of human kind ;
   All the other passions move
   In subjection under love,
      'Tis the tyrant of the mind.

THE REVENGE

Scene VI

Cupid, Bacchus *with a bowl*

Recitative

BACCHUS : 'Odsniggers, t'other draught, 'tis devilish heady,
Olympus turns about ; (*staggers*) steady, boys, steady !   200

Air

If Jove should pretend that he governs the skies,
I swear by this nectar his thundership lies :
A slave to his bottle, he governs by wine,
And all must confess he's a servant of mine.

Air changes

Rosy, sparkling, powerful wine,
Heaven and earth and all is thine !
Search the drinking world around,
Bacchus everywhere sits crowned :
Whilst we lift the flowing bowl,
Unregarded thunders roll.   210

Air changes

Since man, as says each bearded sage,
  Is but a piece of clay,
Whose mystic moisture lost by age,
  To dust it falls away.

'Tis orthodox beyond a doubt,
  That drought will only fret it ;
To make the brittle stuff hold out,
  Is thus to drink and wet it.

Recitative

Ah ! Master Cupid, 'slife, I did not see ye,
'Tis excellent champagne, and so here's to ye :   220

THE REVENGE

I bought it in these gardens as imported,
'Tis bloody strong—you need not twice be courted.
Come drink, my boy—

Recitative

CUPID : Hence, monster, hence,
        I scorn thy ivy branch,
        Thy full flowing bowl
        Degenerates the soul ;
        It puts our judgments down
        And prostitutes our sense.

Recitative

BACCHUS : Gadso, methinks the youngster's woundy moral ! 230
    He plays with ethics like a bell and coral.

Air

'Tis madness to think
To judge ere you drink,—
The bottom all wisdom contains :
Then let you and I
Now drink the bowl dry,
We both shall grow wise for our pains.

Recitative

CUPID : Hence, keep your distance, beast, and cease your bawling,
    Or with this dart I'll send you catterwauling.

Air

The charms of wine cannot compare 240
With the soft raptures of the fair :
Can drunken pleasures ever find
A place with love and womankind?

Can the full bowl pretend to vie
With the soft languish of the eye?
Can the mad roar our passions move
Like gentle breathing sighs of love?

Air

BACCHUS: Go whine and complain
  To the girls of the plain,
And sigh out your soul ere she come to the mind: 250
  My mistress is here,
  And, faith, I don't fear,
I always am happy, she always is kind.

Air changes

A pox o' your lasses!
A shot of my glasses
Your arrow surpasses;
For nothing but asses
 Will draw in your team;
Whilst thus I am drinking,
My misery sinking, 260
The cannikin clinking,
I'm lost to all thinking,
 And care is a dream.

Recitative

CUPID: Provoking insolence!

BACCHUS: What words it utters,
 Alas! poor little creature, how it sputters!

CUPID: Away, you drunkard wild—

BACCHUS: Away, you silly child—

CUPID: Fly, or else I'll wound thy soul.

BACCHUS: Zounds, I'll drown thee in the bowl! 270

THE REVENGE

CUPID: You rascally broacher,
    You hogshead of liquor—

BACCHUS: You shadow, you poacher!
    Ahoy!—bring me a stick here,
    I'll give you a trimmer,
    You bladder of air—

CUPID: You soul of a brimmer—

BACCHUS: You tool of the fair—

CUPID: You moveable tun,
    You tippler, you sot—   280

BACCHUS: Nay, then the work's done,
    My arrow is shot. [*Throws the contents of the bowl in Cupid's face, and runs off*

SCENE VII

Recitative

CUPID: Kind usage this, it sorely shall befall him,
    Here's my best arrow, and, by heaven, I'll maul him.
    Revenge! revenge! Oh, how I long to wound him;
    Now all the pangs of slighted love confound him!

Air

    No more in the bowl
    His brutalized soul
Shall find a retreat from the lass:
    I'll pay him,   290
    And slay him,
His love shall be dry as his glass.   [*Exit*

END OF ACT I

Act II, Scene I

BACCHUS, *with his bowl on his head*

Air

ALAS, alas! how fast
   I feel my spirits sinking;
The joys of life are past,
   I've lost the power of drinking.
'Egad, I find at last
   The heavenly charms of tinking,
And in the sound I cast
   The miseries of thinking.   300

Recitative

I'm plaguy ill—in devilish bad condition—
What shall I do?—I'll send for a physician:
But then the horrid fees—aye, there's the question—
'Tis losing all a man's estate in jesting,
Whilst nurses and apothecaries partake—
Zounds, this will never do, 'twill make my heart ache.
Come then, ye fiddlers, play up t'other bout,
I've a new nostrum, and I'll sing it out.

Air

Scrape, ye fiddlers, tinkle, tinkle,
Music makes my twinklers twinkle;   310
    Humming,
    Thrumming,
    Groaning,
    Toning,
    Squeaking,
    Shrieking,
    Bawling,
    Squalling,
O the sweet charms of tinkle, tinkle!

Recitative

But this is trifling with the hot disease,   320
Nor wine nor brandy now can give me ease.

Air

When a jolly toper ails,
And his nectar-bottle fails,
He's in a most heavenly condition :
Unless he can drink,
To the grave he must sink,
And death be his only physician.

Recitative

Zounds, can't I guess the cause—hum—could I say a
Short prayer or two, with pretty Mistress Maia?
Ah! there it is! why, I was woundy stupid—   330
Faith, this is all the handy-work of Cupid.
Since I'm in love then, over ears and head in,
'Tis time to look about for bed and bedding;
But first uncovering, in this magic helmet,
I'll shew the god that love and wine are well met.

Air

Fill the bowl, and fill it high,
Vast as the extended sky!
Since the dire disease is found,
Wine's a balm to cure the wound.
O the rapturous delights,   340
When with women wine unites!

Recitative

O here, my satyrs, fill the mighty cup,
Haste, fly, begone! I'm dying for a sup.

Air

I'll fly to her arms,
And rifle her charms,

> In kisses and compliments lavish:
> When heated by wine,
> If she should not incline,
> I'll try all my courage, and ravish.

Scene II : *A dark Room*

Recitative

JUNO : Now, Master Jupiter, I'll catch you napping— 350
'Gad, you'll be finely hampered your own trap in.
Would every husband follow your example,
And take upon himself his own adorning,
No more would wives upon their trammels trample,
No more would stand the ancient trade of horning.

Air

> What wife but, like me,
> Her husband would see
A rakehelly fellow, a ranter, a rover;
> If, mistaking her charms,
> He should die in her arms, 360
And lose the cold spouse in the warmth of the lover?

Recitative

Impatiently I wait—

Air

> Hark, hark! the god approaches,
> He longs to ease his pain;
> Oh, how this love encroaches
> Through every trembling vein.

> Oh, how my passion's rising,
> And thumping in my breast!
> 'Tis something most surprising,
> I must be doubly blest. 370

Recitative

He's here : now prosper, Love, my undertaking.
I'll steal aside, I'm in a piteous quaking.

Scene III

Juno *and* Bacchus

Recitative

BACCHUS : Now, pretty Mistress Maia, I'm your humble—
But, faith, I'd better look before I tumble :
For should the little gipsy make resistance,
And call in witnesses to her assistance,
Then, Bacchus, should your friends or sister fail ye,
You'll look confounded queer at the Old Bailey.

Air

The man that has no friend at court,
Must make the laws confine his sport ;   380
But he that has, by dint of flaws,
May make his sport confine the laws.

Recitative

Zounds ! I've a project, and a fine one too—
What will not passion and invention do?
I'll imitate the voice and sound of Jove,
The girl's ambition won't withstand his love.
But should she squall, and cry a rape, and scream on't,
Presto, I'm gone, and Jove will bear the blame on't.
The farce begins, the prologue's wonderous teasing,
Pray Cupid, the catastrophe be pleasing !   390

Air

Oh ! where is my Maia ? O say
  What shadow conceals the fair maid ?
Bring hither the lantern of day,
  And shew me where Maia is laid.

Envious vapours, fly away;
  Come, ye streaming lights, discover,
  To an ardent, dying lover,
Maia and the charms of day.

Recitative   [*Aside*

JUNO: I have you fast, by all my wrongs, I'll fit ye,
  Wise as you are, perhaps I may outwit ye.   400

Air

Here thy longing Maia lies,
Passion flaming in her eyes;
Whilst her heart
Is thumping, beating,
All in a heat, in
Every part:
Like the ocean,
All commotion,
Through her veins the billows roll,
And the soft tempest ruffles all her soul.   410

Recitative   [*Aside*

BACCHUS: Gods! I have struck upon the very minute:
I shall be happy, or the devil's in it:
It seems some assignation was intended,
I'd pump it—but least said is soonest mended.

Air

Happy, happy, happy hour!
Cupid now exalts his power;
In my breast the passion raging,
All my trembling frame engaging,
Sets my every sense on fire;
Let us, Maia, now retire.   420

THE REVENGE

Recitative

JUNO : But, say, should I resign my virgin charms,
Would you be ever constant to my arms?
Would not your Juno rob me of your kindness?
Must you not truckle to her royal highness?

BACCHUS : No! by the dirty waves of Styx I swear it,
My love is yours, my wife shall never share it.

JUNO: 'Tis a sad compliment, but I must bear it. [*Aside*

Air

BACCHUS : Then let's away,
    And never delay,
    'Tis folly to stay   430
      From rapture and love :
    I sicken, I die ;
    O come, let us fly,
    From the blue vaulted sky
      To the Paphian Grove.

Air

JUNO : Then away!
    I obey
      Love and nature.

Air continued

BACCHUS : Since 'tis so,
    Let us go,   440
      Dearest creature !

Scene IV

JUNO, BACCHUS, JUPITER

Recitative

JUPITER : I heard a voice within, or else I'm tipsy—
Maia, where are you ? Come, you little gipsy.

BACCHUS: Maia's with me, sir; who the devil are ye?
Sirrah, be gone; I'll trim you if you tarry.

JUPITER: Fine lingo this to Jupiter!—why truly I'm Jove the thunderer—

JUNO: Out, you rascal, you lie—

BACCHUS: 'Tis I am Jupiter, I wield the thunder!
Zounds, I'll sneak off before they find the blunder. 450
[*Aside*

JUPITER: Breaking from above, below,
Flow, ye gleams of morning, flow;
Rise, ye glories of the day,
Rise at once with strengthened ray!
[*Sudden light; all astonished*

BACCHUS: Zounds! what can this mean?

JUNO: I am all confusion!

JUPITER: Your pardon, Juno, for this rude intrusion.
Insatiate monster! I may now be jealous;
If I've my mistresses, you have your fellows:
I'm now a very husband without doubt, 460
I feel the honours of my forehead sprout.

Air

Was it for this, from morning to night,
 Tempests and hurricanes dwelt on your tongue;
Ever complaining of coldness and slight,
 And the same peal was eternally wrung?
Was it for this I was stinted of joy,
 Pleasure and happiness banished my breast,
Poisoned with fondness which ever must cloy,
 Pinned to your sleeve, and denied to be blest?

THE REVENGE

Recitative

I swear by Styx, and that's a horrid oath,   470
I'll have revenge, and that upon you both.

JUNO: Nay, hear me, Jove, by all that's serious, too,
I swear I took the drunken dog for you.

BACCHUS: And with as safe a conscience, I can say, as
I now stand here, I thought the chamber Maia's.

JUPITER: It cannot be—

Air

       I'll not be cheated,
       Nor be treated
Like the plaything of your will.
JUNO: I'll not be slighted,   480
       I'll be righted,
And I'll keep my spirits still.

JUPITER: You pitiful cully—   [*To Bacchus*

JUNO AND BACCHUS: You rakehelly bully, [*To Jupiter*
       Your blustering,
       Clattering,
       Flustering,
       Spattering,
       Thundering,
       Blundering,   490
       I defy.

JUPITER: Go mind your toping,
       Never come groping
         Into my quarters, I desire, sir:
       Here you come horning,
       And adorning—

THE REVENGE

JUNO: You are a liar, sir.
BACCHUS: You lie, sir, you lie.

SCENE V

JUNO, BACCHUS, JUPITER, CUPID

Recitative

CUPID: Here are the lovers all at clapper-clawing;
A very pretty scene for Collett's drawing.   500
Oh! ho! immortals, why this catterwauling?
Through all Olympus I have heard you bawling.

JUNO: Ah! Cupid, your fine plotting, with a pox,
Has set all in the wrong box.
Unravel quickly, for the thunderer swears
To pull creation down about our ears.

Air

CUPID: Attend! attend! attend!
God, demi-god, and fiend,
Mortals and immortals see;
Hither turn your wondering eyes,   510
See the rulers of the skies
Conquered all, and slaves to me!

Recitative

JUPITER: Pox 'o your brawling! haste, unriddle quickly,
Or, by the thunder of my power, I'll tickle ye!

CUPID: You, Jove, as punctual to your assignation,
Came here, with Maia to be very happy;
But Juno, out of a fond inclination,
Stepped in her room, of all your love to trap ye.
Struck by my power, which the slave dared despise,
Bacchus was wounded too by Maia's eyes,
And hither stealing to appease his love,

Thought Juno Maia: she thought Bacchus Jove.
Here rests the matter,—are you all contented?

JUNO: No, no! not I—

BACCHUS: I'm glad I was prevented. [*Aside*

JUPITER: A lucky disappointment, on my life,
All love is thrown away upon a wife:
How sad! my interruption could not please her.
She moves my pity—

CUPID: Soften, Jove, and ease her. 530

JUPITER: Juno, thy hand, the girls no more I'll drive at,
I will be ever thine—or wench more private.
[*Aside*

Air

Smoothe the furrows of thy brow,
Jove is all the lover now:
Others he'll no more pursue,
But be ever fixed to you.

JUNO: Then contented I resign
My prerogative of scolding;
Quiet when thy love is mine,
When my arms with thine are folding. 540

CUPID: Then, jolly Bacchus, why should we stand out?
If we have quarrelled, zounds! we'll drink about.

Air

Love and wine uniting,
Rule without control,
'Tis to the sense delighting,
And captivate the soul.

THE REVENGE

    Love and wine uniting
        Are everywhere adored;
    Its pleasures are inviting,
        All heaven it can afford.   540

BACCHUS: Zounds, I agree, 'tis folly to oppose it:
Let's pay our duty here, and then we'll close it.

Air   [*To the audience*

    To you, ye brave, ye fair, ye gay,
    Permit me from myself to say:
    The juicy grape for you shall rise
    In all the colours of the skies;
    For you the vine's delicious fruit
    Shall on the lofty mountains shoot;
    And every wine to Bacchus dear
    Shall sparkle in perfection here.   550

Air

CUPID: For you, ye fair, whose heavenly charms
    Make all my arrows useless arms,
    For you shall Handel's lofty flight
    Clash on the listening ear of night,
    And the soft, melting, sinking lay
    In gentle accents die away.
    And not a whisper shall appear
    Which modesty would blush to hear-

Air

JUNO: Ye brave, the pillars of the state,
    In valour and in conduct great,   560
    For you the rushing clang of arms,
    The yell of battle and alarms,
    Shall from the martial trumpets fly,
    And echo through the mantling sky.

SONGS IN 'THE REVENGE'

Air

JUPITER : From you, ye glories of mankind,
    We hope a firm support to find ;
    All that our humble powers can do
    Shall be displayed to pleasure you.
    On you we build a wished success,
    'Tis yours, like deities, to bless ;   570
    Your smiles will better every scene,
    And clothe our barren waste in green.

CHORUS : So, when along the eastern skies
    The glories of the morning rise,
    The humble flower which slept the night,
    Expands its beauties to the light,
    Glows in its glossy new array,
    And shines amidst the shining day.

SONGS

(To be sung in 'The Revenge')

A BACCHANALIAN

SUNG BY MR REINHOLD

BACCHUS, ever smiling power,
Patron of the festive hour !
Here thy genuine nectar roll
To the wide capacious bowl,
While gentility and glee
Make these gardens worthy thee.

Bacchus, ever mirth and joy,
Laughing, wanton, happy boy !

Here advance thy clustered crown,
Send thy purple blessings down ;
With the nine to please conspire,
Wreathe the ivy round the lyre.

THE INVITATION

TO BE SUNG BY MRS BARTHELEMON AND BY MASTER CHENEY

Away to the woodlands, away!
  The shepherds are forming a ring,
To dance to the honour of May,
  And welcome the pleasures of spring.
The shepherdess labours a grace,
  And shines in her Sunday's array,
And bears in the bloom of her face
  The charms and the beauties of May.
    Away to the woodlands away!
    The shepherds are forming a ring, etc.

Away to the woodlands, away!
  And join with the amorous train:
'Tis treason to labour to-day,
  Now Bacchus and Cupid must reign.
With garlands of primroses made,
  And crowned with the sweet blooming spray,
Through woodland, and meadow, and shade,
  We'll dance to the honour of May.
    Away to the, etc.

A BACCHANALIAN

What is war and all its joys?
Useless mischief, empty noise.

What are arms and trophies won?
Spangles glittering in the sun.
Rosy Bacchus, give me wine,
Happiness is only thine!

What is love without the bowl?
'Tis a languor of the soul:
Crowned with ivy, Venus charms;
Ivy courts me to her arms.   10
Bacchus, give me love and wine,
Happiness is only thine!

THE VIRGIN'S CHOICE

YOUNG Strephon is as fair a swain
As e'er a shepherd of the plain
   In all the hundred round;
But Ralph has tempting shoulders true,
And will as quickly buckle to
   As any to be found.

Young Colin has a comely face,
And cudgels with an active grace,
   In everything complete!
But Hobbinol can dance divine,   10
Gods! how his manly beauties shine,
   When jigging with his feet!

Roger is very stout and strong,
And Thyrsis sings a heavenly song,
   Soft Giles is brisk and small.
Who shall I choose? who shall I shun?
Why must I be confined to one?
   Why can't I have them all?

THE HAPPY PAIR

STREPHON : Lucy, since the knot was tied,
    Which confirmed thee Strephon's bride
    All is pleasure, all is joy,
    Married love can never cloy;
    Learn, ye rovers, learn from this,
    Marriage is the road to bliss.

LUCY : Whilst thy kindness every hour
    Gathers pleasure with its power,
    Love and tenderness in thee
    Must be happiness to me.   10
    Learn, ye rovers, learn from this,
    Marriage is substantial bliss.

BOTH : Godlike Hymen, ever reign,
    Ruler of the happy train,
    Lift thy flaming torch above
    All the flights of wanton love :
    Peaceful, solid, blest, serene,
    Triumph in the married scene.

STREPHON : Blest with thee, the sultry day
    Flies on wings of down away.   20
    Labouring o'er the yellow plain
    Open to the sun and rain,
    All my painful labours fly,
    When I think my Lucy's nigh.

LUCY : O my Strephon, could my heart
    Happiness to thee impart,
    Joy should sing away the hour,
    Love should every pleasure shower :

Search my faithful breast, and see,
  I am blest in loving thee.

BOTH: God like Hymen, ever reign,
  Ruler of the happy train,
  Lift thy flaming torch above
  All the flights of wanton love;
  Peaceful, solid, blest, serene,
  Triumph in the married scene.

THE WOMAN OF SPIRIT

A BURLETTA

DRAMATIS PERSONÆ

Distort . . .	MR BANNISTER
Counsellor Latitat .	MR REINHOLD
Endorse . .	MASTER CHENEY
Lady Tempest .	MRS THOMPSON

ACT I, SCENE I

LADY TEMPEST AND LATITAT

LATITAT: I tell you, Lady Tempest—

LADY TEMPEST: And I tell you, Mr Latitat, it shall not be.—I'll have no Society of Antiquaries meet here. None but the honourable Members of the Coterie shall assemble here, you shall know.

LATITAT: Suspend your rage, Lady Tempest, and let me open my brief. Have you not this day, moved by the instigation of the devil,

and not having the fear of God before your
eyes, wilfully and wittingly and maliciously,
driven all my friends out of my house? Was
it done like a woman of quality?

LADY TEMPEST: It was done like a woman
of spirit: a character, it shall ever be my
task to maintain.

Air

Away with your maxims, and dull formal rules,
The shackels of pleasure, and trammels of fools;
For wisdom and prudence I care not a straw,
I'll act as I please, for my will is my law.

LATITAT: But upon my soul, Madam, I have
one more consideration which should especially
move you to bridle your passion, for it
spoils your face. When you knocked down
Lord Rust with the bust of Marcus Aurelius,
you looked the very picture of the Alecto last
taken out of the Herculaneum.

Air

Passion worse than age will plough
Furrows on the frowning brow;
Rage and passion will disgrace
Every beauty of the face;
Whilst good-nature will supply
Beauties, which can never die.

LADY TEMPEST: Mr Latitat, I won't be abused
—Did I for this condescend to forget my
quality and marry such a tautology of
nothing?—I will not be abused.

Scene II

Distort, Latitat, Lady Tempest

DISTORT: Pray, Madam, what has enraged you? May I have the honour of knowing?

LATITAT: Mr Distort shall be our referee.

LADY TEMPEST: That is, if I please, sir.

LATITAT: Pray, my lady, let me state the case, and you may afterwards make a reply. You must know, sir—

LADY TEMPEST: Yes, sir, you must know, this morning Mr Latitat had invited all his antiquated friends, Lord Rust, Horatio Trefoil, Col. Tragedus, Professor Vase, and Counterfeit the Jew, to sit upon a brass half-penny, which being a little worn, they agreed, *nem. con.*, to be an Otho.

LATITAT: And it is further necessary to be known, that, while we were all warm in debate upon the premises, my lady made a forcible entry into the parlour, and seizing an antique bust of Marcus Aurelius, of malice propense and aforethought, did, with three blows of the said bust, knock down Anthony, Viscount Rust, and—

LADY TEMPEST: And drove them all out of the house.

LATITAT: And furthermore—

LADY TEMPEST: Silence Mr Latitat, I insist on the privilege of English wife.

LATITAT: And moreover—

DISTORT: Nay, Counsellor, as I am your referee, I command silence. Pray what do you lay your damages at?

LATITAT: My lady has in her cabinet a Jupiter Tonans, which, in spite of all my endeavours 70
to open her eyes, she persists in calling an Indian Pagod, and upon condition of my receiving that, I drop the prosecution.

DISTORT: 'Tis a trifle, Madam, let him have it, it may turn to account. [*Aside to Lady*

LADY TEMPEST: A very toy: he shall have it instantly, on condition I have the use of my tongue.

Air

What are all your favourite joys?
What are [all] our pleasures?   So
* * * * * *

ON MR ALCOCK, OF BRISTOL

AN EXCELLENT MINIATURE PAINTER

YE nine, awake the chorded shell,
Whilst I the praise of Alcock tell
   In truth-dictated lays:
On wings of genius take thy flight,
O muse! above the Olympic height,
   Make echo sing his praise.

ON MR ALCOCK, OF BRISTOL

Nature, in all her glory drest,
Her flowery crown, her verdant vest,
   Her zone ethereal blue,
Receives new charms from Alcock's hand;
The eye surveys, at his command,
   Whole kingdoms at a view.

His beauties seem to roll the eye,
And bid the real arrows fly,
   To wound the gazer's mind;
So taking are his men displayed,
That oft the unguarded wounded maid
   Hath wished the painter blind.

His pictures like to nature shew,
The silver fountains seem to flow,
   The hoary woods to nod;
The curling hair the flowing dress,
The speaking attitude, confess
   The fancy-forming god.

Ye classic Roman-loving fools,
Say, could the painters of the schools
   With Alcock's pencil vie?
He paints the passions of mankind,
And in the face displays the mind,
   Charming the heart and eye.

Thrice happy artist, rouse thy powers,
And send, in wonder-giving showers,
   Thy beauteous works to view:
Envy shall sicken at thy name,
Italians leave the chair of fame,
   And own the seat thy due.

                        ASAPHIDES

Bristol, *29th Jan.* 1769.

TO MISS BUSH, OF BRISTOL

BEFORE I seek the dreary shore
Where Gambia's rapid billows roar,
    And foaming pour along,
To you I urge the plaintive strain,
And though a lover sings in vain,
    Yet you shall hear the song.

Ungrateful, cruel, lovely maid,
Since all my torments were repaid
    With frowns or languid sneers:
With assiduities no more   10
Your captive will your health implore,
    Or tease you with his tears.

Now to the regions where the sun
Does his hot course of glory run,
    And parches up the ground;
Where o'er the burning cleaving plains,
A long eternal dog-star reigns,
    And splendour flames around:

There will I go, yet not to find
A fire intenser than my mind,   20
    Which burns a constant flame:
There will I lose thy heavenly form,
Nor shall remembrance, raptured, warm,
    Draw shadows of thy frame.

In the rough element, the sea,
I'll drown the softer subject, thee,
    And sink each lovely charm:
No more my bosom shall be torn,
No more, by wild ideas borne,
    I'll cherish the alarm.   30

Yet, Polly, could thy heart be kind,
Soon would my feeble purpose find
    Thy sway within my breast:
But hence, soft scenes of painted woe,
Spite of the dear delight I'll go,
    Forget her, and be blest.

CELORIMON

TO MISS C.

ON HEARING HER PLAY ON THE HARPSICHORD

HAD Israel's monarch, when misfortune's dart
  Pierced to its deepest core his heaving breast,
Heard but thy dulcet tones, his sorrowing heart,
  At such soft tones, had soothed itself to rest.

Yes, sweeter far than Jesse's son's thy strains,
  Yet what avail if sorrow they disarm?
Love's sharper sting within the soul remains,
  The melting movements wound us as they charm.

TO MISS CLARKE

To sing of Clarke my muse aspires,
  A theme by charms made quite divine.
Ye tuneful virgins, sound your lyres,
  Apollo aid the feeble line.

If truth and virtue, wit and charms,
  May for a fixed attention call,
The darts of love and wounding arms—
  The beauteous Clarke shall hold o'er all.

'Tis not the tincture of a skin,
 The rosy lip, the charming eye ;   10
No, 'tis a greater power within,
 That bids the passion never die.

These Clarke possesses, and much more.
 All beauty in her glances sport ;
She is the goddess all adore
 In country, city, and at court.

ACROSTIC ON MISS SALLY CLARKE

Seraphic virgins of the tuneful choir,
Assist me to prepare the sounding lyre.
Like her I sing, soft, sensible, and fair,
Let the smooth numbers warble in the air.
Ye prudes, coquettes, and all the misled throng,
Can beauty, virtue, sense, demand the song?
Look then on Clarke, and see them all unite :
A beauteous pattern to the always-right.
Rest here, my muse, nor soar above thy sphere—
Kings might pay adoration to the fair,   10
Enchanting, full of joy, peerless in face and air.

A SONG

ADDRESSED TO MISS C—AM, OF BRISTOL

As spring now approaches with all his gay train,
And scatters his beauties around the green plain,
Come then, my dear charmer, all scruples remove,
Accept of my passion, allow me to love.

A SONG

Without the soft transports which love must inspire,
Without the sweet torment of fear and desire,
Our thoughts and ideas are never refined,
And nothing but winter can reign in the mind.

But love is the blossom, the spring of the soul,
The frosts of our judgments may check, not control ; 10
In spite of each hindrance, the spring will return,
And nature with transports refining will burn.

This passion celestial by heaven was designed
The only fixed means of improving the mind ;
When it beams on the senses, they quickly display
How great and prolific, how pleasing the ray.

Then come, my dear charmer, since love is a flame
Which polishes nature, and angels your frame,
Permit the soft passion to rise in your breast,
I leave your good nature to grant me the rest.   20

Shall the beautiful flowerets all blossom around,
Shall Flora's gay mantle enamel the ground,
Shall the red-blushing blossom be seen on the tree,
Without the least pleasure or rapture for me?

And yet, if my charmer should frown when I sing,
Ah ! what are the beauties, the glories of spring?
The flowers will be faded, all happiness fly,
And clouds veil the azure of every bright sky.

C.

London, 4th May, 1770.

A NEW SONG

TO MR G. CATCOTT

Ah blame me not, Catcott, if from the right way
    My notions and actions run far;
How can my ideas do other but stray,
    Deprived of their ruling north-star?

Ah blame me not, Broderip, if, mounted aloft,
    I chatter, and spoil the dull air;
How can I imagine thy foppery soft,
    When discord's the voice of my fair?

If Turner remitted my bluster and rhymes,
    If Harding was girlish and cold,   10
If never an ogle was got from Miss Grimes,
    If Flavia was blasted and old;

I chose without liking, and left without pain,
    Nor welcomed the frown with a sigh;
I scorned like a monkey to dangle my chain,
    And paint them new charms with a lie.

Once Cotton was handsome; I flamed and I burned,
    I died to obtain the bright queen:
But when I beheld my epistle returned,
    By Jesu, it altered the scene.   20

'She's damnable ugly,' my vanity cried,
    'You lie,' says my conscience, ' you lie.'
Resolving to follow the dictates of pride,
    I'd view her a hag to my eye.

But would she regain her bright lustre again,
   And shine in her natural charms,
'Tis but to accept of the works of my pen,
   And permit me to use my own arms.

SONG

FANNY OF THE HILL

If gentle love's immortal fire
   Could animate the quill,
Soon should the rapture-speaking lyre
   Sing Fanny of the Hill.

My panting heart incessant moves,
   No interval 'tis still;
And all my ravished nature loves
   Sweet Fanny of the Hill.

Her dying soft expressive eye,
   Her elegance must kill;   10
Ye gods! how many thousands die
   For Fanny of the Hill.

A love-taught tongue, angelic air,
   A sentiment, a skill
In all the graces of the fair,
   Mark Fanny of the Hill.

Thou mighty power, eternal fate,
   My happiness to fill,
O! bless a wretched lover's state
   With Fanny of the Hill.   20

TO MRS HAYWOOD, THE NOVELIST

Let Sappho's name be heard no more,
  Or Dido's fate by bards be sung,
When on the billow-beaten shore
  The echo of Æneas rung.

Love, the great ruler of the breast,
  Proud and impatient to control,
In every novel stands confessed
  Waking to nature's scenes the soul.

Haywood! thy genius was divine;
  The softer passions owned thy sway;
Thy easy prose, the flowing line,
  Accomplishments supreme display.

Pope, son of envy and of fame,
  Penned the invidious line in vain;
To blast thy literary name
  Exceeds the power of human strain.

Ye gay, ye sensible, ye fair,
  To what her genius wrote, attend;
You'll find engaging morals there
  To help the lover and the friend.

TO MR HOLLAND

What numbers, Holland, can the muses find,
  To sing thy merit in each varied part,
When action, eloquence, and ease combined,
  Make nature but a copy of thy art?

TO MR HOLLAND

Majestic as the eagle on the wing,
    Or the young sky-helmed, mountain-rooted tree;
Pleasing as meadows blushing with the spring,
    Loud as the surges of the Severn sea.

In terror's strain, as clanging armies drear;
    In love, as Jove, too great for mortal praise;   10
In pity, gentle as the falling tear;
    In all, superior to my feeble lays.

Black anger's sudden rise, ecstatic pain;
    Tormenting jealousy's self-cankering sting;
Consuming envy, with her yelling train;
    Fraud, closely shrouded with the turtle's wing:

Whatever passions gall the human breast,
    Play in thy features, and await thy nod.
In thee, by art, the demon stands confessed
    But nature on thy soul has stamped the god.   20

So just thy action with thy part agrees,
    Each feature does the office of a tongue;
Such is thy native elegance and ease,
    By thee the harsh line smoothly glides along.

At thy feigned woe, we're rëally distressed,
    At thy feigned tears, we let the rëal fall;
By every judge of nature 'tis confessed,
    No single part is thine, thou'rt all in all.

                                                D. B.
    Bristol, 21*st July* [1769].

TO THE BEAUTEOUS MISS HOYLAND

FAR distant from Britannia's lofty isle,
What shall I find to make the genius smile?
The bubbling fountains lose the power to please,
The rocky cataracts, the shady trees,
The juicy fruitage of enchanting hue,
Whose luscious virtues England never knew;
The variegated daughters of the land,
Whose numbers Flora strews with bounteous hand;
The verdant vesture of the smiling fields,
All the rich pleasures nature's store-house yields, 10
Have all their powers to wake the chorded string:
But still they're subjects that the muse can sing.
Hoyland, more beauteous than the god of day,
Her name can quicken and awake the lay;
Rouse the soft muse from indolence and ease,
To live, to love, and rouse her powers to please.
In vain would Phœbus, did not Hoyland, rise:
'Tis her bright eyes that gilds the eastern skies;
'Tis she alone deprives us of the light;
And when she slumbers, then indeed 'tis night. 20
To tell the separate beauties of her face
Would stretch eternity's remotest space,
And want a more than man to pen the line;
I rest—let this suffice, dear Hoyland's all divine.

TO MISS HOYLAND

Once more the muse to beauteous Hoyland sings;
Her grateful tribute of harsh numbers brings
To Hoyland! Nature's richest, sweetest store,
She made an Hoyland, and can make no more.
Nor all the beauties of the world's vast round
United, will as sweet as her be found.
Description sickens to rehearse her praise,
Her worth alone will deify my days.
Enchanting creature! Charms so great as thine
May all the beauties of the day outshine.   10
Thy eyes to every gazer send a dart,
Thy taking graces captivate the heart.
O for a muse that shall ascend the skies,
And like the subject of the epode rise;
To sing the sparkling eye, the portly grace,
The thousand beauties that adorn the face
Of my seraphic maid, whose beauteous charms
Might court the world to rush at once to arms;
Whilst the fair goddess, native of the skies,
Shall sit above, and be the victor's prize.   20
O now, whilst yet I sound the tuneful lyre,
I feel the thrilling joy her hands inspire;
When the soft tender touch awakes my blood,
And rolls my passions with the purple flood.
My pulse beats high; my throbbing breast's on fire
In sad variety of wild desire.
O Hoyland! heavenly goddess! angel! saint!
Words are too weak thy mighty worth to paint;
Thou best, completest work that nature made,
Thou art my substance, and I am thy shade.   30

Possessed of thee, I joyfully would go
Through the loud tempest, and the depth of woe.
From thee alone my being I derive,
One beauteous smile from thee makes all my hopes alive.

TO MISS HOYLAND

SINCE short the busy scene of life will prove,
Let us, my Hoyland, learn to live and love :
To love with passions pure as morning light,
Whose saffron beams, unsullied by the night,
With rosy mantles do the heavens streak,
Faint imitators of my Hoyland's cheek.
The joys of nature in her ruined state
Have little pleasure, though the pains are great.
Virtue and love, when sacred bands unite,
'Tis then that nature leads to true delight.　　　10
Oft as I wander through the myrtle grove,
Bearing the beauteous burden of my love,
A secret terror, lest I should offend
The charming maid on whom my joys depend,
Informs my soul, that virtuous minds alone
Can give a pleasure, to the vile unknown.
But when the body charming, and the mind
To every virtuous christian act inclined,
Meet in one person, maid and angel join,
Who must it be, but Hoyland the divine?　　　20
What worth intrinsic will that man possess,
Whom the dear charmer condescends to bless?
Swift will the minutes roll, the flying hours,
And blessings overtake the pair by showers :
Each moment will improve upon the past,
And every day be better than the last:

Love means an unadulterated flame,
Though lust too oft usurps the sacred name;
Such passion as in Hoyland's breast can move,
'Tis that alone deserves the name of love.   30
Oh, were my merit great enough to find
A favoured station in my Hoyland's mind,
Then would my happiness be quite complete,
And all revolving joys as in a centre meet.

TO MISS HOYLAND

TELL me, god of soft desires,
   Little Cupid, wanton boy,
How thou kindlest up thy fires,
   Giving pleasing pain and joy?

Hoyland's beauty is thy bow,
   Striking glances are thy darts:
Making conquests never slow,
   Ever gaining conquered hearts.

Heaven is seated in her smile,
   Juno's in her portly air;   10
Not Britannia's favourite isle
   Can produce a nymph so fair.

In a desert vast and drear,
   Where disorder springs around,
If the lovely fair is there,
   'Tis a pleasure-giving ground.

Oh my Hoyland! blest with thee,
   I'd the raging storm defy,
In thy smiles I live, am free;
   When thou frownest, I must die.   20

TO MISS HOYLAND

Count all the flowers that deck the meadow's side,
When Flora flourishes in new-born pride;
Count all the sparkling orbits in the sky;
Count all the birds that through the ether fly;
Count all the foliage of the lofty trees,
That fly before the bleak autumnal breeze;
Count all the dewy blades of verdant grass;
Count all the drops of rain that softly pass
Through the blue ether, or tempestuous roar;
Count all the sands upon the breaking shore; 10
Count all the minutes since the world began;
Count all the troubles of the life of man;
Count all the torments of the damned in hell;
More are the beauteous charms that make my nymph excel.

TO MISS HOYLAND

Sweet are thy charming smiles, my lovely maid,
Sweet as the flowers in bloom of spring arrayed;
Those charming smiles thy beauteous face adorn,
As May's white blossoms gaily deck the thorn.
Then why, when mild good nature basking lies
'Midst the soft radiance of thy melting eyes;
When my fond tongue would strive thy heart to move,
And tune its tones to every note of love;
Why do those smiles their native soil disown,
And (changed their movements) kill me in a frown? 10

   Yet is it true, or is it dark despair
That fears your cruel whilst it owns you fair?

O speak, dear Hoyland! speak my certain fate,
Thy love enrapturing, or thy constant hate.
If death's dire sentence hangs upon thy tongue,
Ev'n death were better than suspense so long.

TO MISS HOYLAND

Go, gentle muse, and to my fair one say,
My ardent passion mocks the feeble lay;
That love's pure flame my panting breast inspires,
And friendship warms me with her chaster fires.
Yes, more my fond esteem, my matchless love,
Than the soft turtle's, cooing in the grove;
More than the lark delights to mount the sky,
Then, sinking on the greensward, soft to lie;
More than the bird of eve, at close of day,
To pour in solemn solitude her lay;   10
More than grave Camplin with his deep-toned note,
To mouth the sacred service got by rote;
More than sage Catcott does his storm of rain,
Sprung from the abyss of his eccentric brain;
Or than his wild-antique and sputtering brother
Loves in his ale-house chair to drink and pother;
More than soft Lewis, that sweet pretty thing,
Loves in the pulpit to display his ring;
More than frail mortals love a brother sinner,
And more than Bristol aldermen their dinner.   20
(When full four pounds of the well-fattened haunch
In twenty mouthfuls fill the greedy paunch.)

   If these true strains can thy dear bosom move,
Let thy soft blushes speak a mutual love:
But if thy purpose settles in disdain,
Speak my dread fate, and bless thy favourite swain.
                                         D. B.

TO MISS HOYLAND

WITH A PRESENT

ACCEPT, fair nymph this token of my love,
    Nor look disdainful on the prostrate swain :
By every sacred oath, I'll constant prove,
    And act as worthy for to wear your chain.

Not with more constant ardour shall the sun
    Chase the faint shadows of the night away ;
Nor shall he on his course more constant run,
    And cheer the universe with coming day,

Than I in pleasing chains of conquest bound,
    Adore the charming author of my smart ;   10
For ever will I thy sweet charms resound,
    And paint the fair possessor of my heart.

ACROSTIC ON MISS ELEANOR HOYLAND

ENCHANTING is the mighty power of love ;
Life stripped of amorous joys would irksome prove :
E'en heaven's great thunderer wore the easy chain,
And over all the world love keeps his reign.
No human heart can bear the piercing blade,
Or I than others am more tender made.
Right through my heart a burning arrow drove,
Hoyland's bright eyes were made the bows of love.
Oh ! torture inexpressibly severe !
You are the pleasing author of my care.   10

Look down, fair angel, on a swain distressed
A gracious smile from you would make me blest
Nothing but that blest favour stills my grief,
Death, that denied, will quickly give relief.

ODE TO MISS HOYLAND

AMIDST the wild and dreary dells,
The distant echo-giving bells,
   The bending mountain's head ;
Whilst evening, moving through the sky,
Over the object and the eye,
   Her pitchy robes doth spread ;

There, gently moving through the vale,
Bending before the blustering gale,
   Fell apparitions glide ;
Whilst roaring rivers echo round,   10
The drear reverberating sound
   Runs through the mountain side ;

Then steal I softly to the grove,
And, singing of the nymph I love,
   Sigh out my sad complaint ;
To paint the tortures of my mind,
Where can the muses numbers find?
   Ah ! numbers are too faint !

Ah ! Hoyland, empress of my heart,
When will thy breast admit the dart,   20
   And own a mutual flame?
When, wandering in the myrtle groves,
Shall mutual pleasures seal our loves,
   Pleasures without a name?

Thou greatest beauty of the sex,
When will the little god perplex
  The mansions of thy breast?
When wilt thou own a flame as pure
As that seraphic souls endure,
  And make thy Baker blest?   30

O! haste to give my passion ease,
And bid the perturbation cease
  That harrows up my soul!
The joy such happiness to find
Would make the functions of my mind
  In peace and love to roll.

THE COMPLAINT

ADDRESSED TO MISS P—L—, OF BRISTOL

Love, lawless tyrant of my breast,
When will my passions be at rest,
  And in soft murmurs roll—
When will the dove-eyed goddess, Peace,
Bid black despair and torment cease,
  And wake to joy my soul?

Adieu! ye flower-bespangled hills;
Adieu! ye softly-purling rills,
  That through the meadows play;
Adieu! the cool refreshing shade,   10
By hoary oaks and woodbines made,
  Where oft with joy I lay.

THE COMPLAINT

No more beneath your boughs I hear,
With pleasure unallayed by fear,
   The distant Severn roar—
Adieu! the forest's mossy side
Decked out in Flora's richest pride:
   Ye can delight no more.

Oft at the solitary hour
When melancholy's silent power   20
   Is gliding through the shade;
With raging madness by her side,
Whose hands, in blood and murder dyed,
   Display the reeking blade,

I catch the echo of their feet,
And follow to their drear retreat
   Of deadliest nightshade wove:
There, stretched upon the dewy ground,
Whilst noxious vapours rise around,
   I sigh my tale of love.   30

Oft has the solemn bird of night,
When rising to his gloomy flight,
   Unseen against me fled;
Whilst snakes in curling orbs uprolled,
Bedropped with azure, flame, and gold,
   Hurled poison at my head.

O say! thou best of womankind,
Thou miracle, in whom we find
   Wit, charms, and sense unite,
Can plagues like these be always borne?   40
No; if I still must meet your scorn,
   I'll seek the realms of night.
                    C.

TO MR POWEL

WHAT language, Powel! can thy merits tell,
By nature formed in every path t' excel,
To strike the feeling soul with magic skill,
When every passion bends beneath thy will?
Loud as the howlings of the northern wind,
Thy scenes of anger harrow up the mind;
But most thy softer tones our bosoms move,
When Juliet listens to her Romeo's love.
How sweet thy gentle movements then to see—
Each melting heart must sympathise with thee. 10

   Yet, though designed in every walk to shine,
Thine is the furious, and the tender thine;
Though thy strong feelings and thy native fire
Still force the willing gazers to admire,
Though great thy praises for thy scenic art,
We love thee for the virtues of thy heart.

THE ADVICE

ADDRESSED TO MISS M[ARIA] R[UMSEY], OF BRISTOL

REVOLVING in their destined sphere,
The hours begin another year,
   As rapidly to fly;
Ah! think, Maria, (ere in grey
Those auburn tresses fade away),
   So youth and beauty die.

THE ADVICE

Though now the captivated throng
Adore with flattery and song,
    And all before you bow;
Whilst, unattentive to the strain,
You hear the humble muse complain,
    Or wreath your frowning brow:

Though poor Pitholeon's feeble line,
In opposition to the nine,
    Still violates your name:
Though tales of passion, meanly told,
As dull as Cumberland, as cold,
    Strive to confess a flame:

Yet, when that bloom and dancing fire
In silvered reverence shall expire,
    Aged, wrinkled, and defaced;
To keep one lover's flame alive
Requires the genius of a Clive,
    With Walpole's mental taste.

Though rapture wantons in your air,
Though beyond simile you're fair,
    Free, affable, serene;
Yet still one attribute divine
Should in your composition shine,
    Sincerity, I mean.

Though numerous swains before you fall,
'Tis empty admiration all,
    'Tis all that you require;
How momentary are their chains!
Like you, how insincere the strains
    Of those who but admire!

TO HORACE WALPOLE

    Accept, for once, advice from me,
    And let the eye of censure see
        Maria can be true :
    No more, for fools or empty beaux   40
    Heaven's representatives disclose,
        Or butterflies pursue ;

    Fly to your worthiest lover's arms,
    To him resign your swelling charms
        And meet his generous breast
    Or, if Pitholeon suits your taste,
    His muse, with tattered fragments graced,
        Shall read your cares to rest.
                          D. B.
1st January 1770.

TO HORACE WALPOLE

WALPOLE, I thought not I should ever see
So mean a heart as thine has proved to be.
Thou who, in luxury nursed, behold'st with scorn
The boy, who, friendless, fatherless, forlorn,
Asks thy high favour—thou mayest call me cheat.
Say, didst thou never practise such deceit?
Who wrote Otranto? but I will not chide :
Scorn I'll repay with scorn, and pride with pride.
Still, Walpole, still thy prosy chapters write,
And twaddling letters to some fair indite ;   10
Laud all above thee, fawn and cringe to those
Who, for thy fame, were better friends than foes ;
Still spurn th' incautious fool who dares—
    *   *   *   *   *   *
Had I the gifts of wealth and luxury shared,
Not poor and mean, Walpole ! thou hadst not dared
Thus to insult. But I shall live and stand
By Rowley's side, when thou art dead and damned.
                                  T. C.

TO A FRIEND

6th March 1768

Dear Friend.—I have received both your favours—
The muse alone must tell my joy.

O'ERWHELMED with pleasure at the joyful news,
I strung the chorded shell, and woke the muse.
Begin, O servant of the sacred nine!
And echo joy through every nervous line;
Bring down the ethereal choir to aid the song;
Let boundless raptures smoothly glide along.
My Baker's well! Oh words of sweet delight!
Now! now! my muse, soar up the Olympic height.
What wondrous numbers can the goddess find
To paint the ecstatic raptures of my mind?   10
I leave it to a goddess more divine,
The beauteous Hoyland shall employ my line.

TO A FRIEND

ON HIS INTENDED MARRIAGE

MARRIAGE, dear M[ason], is a serious thing;
  'Tis proper every man should think it so;
'Twill either every human blessing bring,
  Or load thee with a settlement of woe.

Sometimes indeed it is a middle state,
  Neither supremely blest, nor deeply cursed;
A stagnant pool of life, a dream of fate:
  In my opinion, of all states the worst.

Observe the partner of thy future state :
   If no strong vice is stamped upon her mind,   10
Take her ; and let her ease thy amorous pain :
   A little error proves her human-kind.

What we call vices are not always such ;
   Some virtues scarce deserve the sacred name ;
Thy wife may love, as well as pray too much,
   And to another stretch her rising flame.

Choose no religionist ; whose every day
   Is lost to thee and thine, to none a friend :
Know too, when pleasure calls the heart astray,
   The warmest zealot is the blackest fiend.   20

Let not the fortune first engross thy care,
   Let it a second estimation hold ;
A Smithfield-marriage is of pleasures bare,
   And love, without the purse, will soon grow cold.

Marry no lettered damsel, whose wise head
   May prove it just to graft the horns on thine :
Marry no idiot, keep her from thy bed ;
   What the brains want will often elsewhere shine.

A disposition good, a judgment sound,
   Will bring substantial pleasures in a wife :   30
Whilst love and tenderness in thee are found,
   Happy and calm will be the married life.

      THOMAS CHATTERTON

VERSES

TO A LADY IN BRISTOL

To use a worn-out simile,
From flower to flower the busy bee
   With anxious labour flies,
Alike from scents which give distaste,
By fancy as disgusting placed,
   Repletes his useful thighs.

Nor does his vicious taste prefer
The fopling of some gay parterre,
   The mimicry of art,
But round the meadow-violet dwells;   10
Nature, replenishing his cells,
   Does ampler stores impart.

So I, a humble dumble drone,
Anxious and restless when alone,
   Seek comfort in the fair;
And featured up in tenfold brass,
A rhyming, staring, amorous ass,
   To you address my prayer.

But ever in my love-lorn flights
Nature untouched by art delights—   20
   Art ever gives disgust.
'Why?' says some priest of mystic thought;
The bard alone, by nature taught,
   Is to that nature just.

But ask your orthodox divine,
If ye perchance should read this line
   Which fancy now inspires:

Will all his sermons, preaching, prayers,
His hell, his heaven, his solemn airs,
   Quench nature's rising fires?

In natural religion free,
I to no other bow the knee,
   Nature's the god I own :
Let priests of future torments tell,
Your anger is the only hell,
   No other hell is known.

I, steeled by destiny, was born
Well fenced against a woman's scorn,
   Regardless of that hell ;
I, fired by burning planets, came
From flaming hearts to catch a flame,
   And bid the bosom swell.

Then catch the shadow of a heart,
I will not with the substance part,
   Although that substance burn,
Till as a hostage you remit
Your heart, your sentiment, your wit,
   To make a safe return.

A reverend cully mully puff
May call this letter odious stuff,
   With no Greek motto graced ;
Whilst you, despising the poor strain,
' The dog's insufferably vain
   To think to please my taste !'

This vanity, this impudence
Is all the merit, all the sense
   Through which to fame I trod ;

These (by the Trinity 'tis true)
Procure me friends and notice too,
    And shall gain you, by God.   60

THE CONSULIAD

AN HEROIC POEM

OF warring senators, and battles dire,
Of quails uneaten, muse, awake the lyre !
Where Campbell's chimneys overlook the square,
And Newton's future prospects hang in air ;
Where counsellors dispute, and cockers match,
And Caledonian earls in concert scratch ;
A group of heroes occupied the round,
Long in the rolls of infamy renowned.
Circling the table all in silence sat,
Now tearing bloody lean, now champing fat ;   10
Now picking ortolans and chicken slain
To form the whimsies of an *à-la-reine* ;
Now storming castles of the newest taste,
And granting articles to forts of paste ;
Now swallowing bitter draughts of Prussian beer ;
Now sucking tallow of salubrious deer.
The god of cabinets and senates saw
His sons, like asses, to one centre draw.

    Inflated discord heard, and left her cell,
With all the horrors of her native hell ;   20
She on the soaring wings of genius fled,
And waved the pen of Junius round her head.
Beneath the table, veiled from sight, she sprung,
And sat astride on noisy Twitcher's tongue :

Twitcher, superior to the venal pack
Of Bloomsbury's notorious monarch, Jack ;
Twitcher, a rotten branch of mighty stock,
Whose interest winds his conscience as his clock ;
Whose attributes detestable have long
Been evident and infamous in song. 30
A toast's demanded : Madoc swift arose,
Pactolian gravy trickling down his clothes :
His sanguine fork a murdered pigeon pressed,
His knife with deep incision sought the breast ;
Upon his lips the quivering accents hung,
And too much expedition chained his tongue ;
When thus he sputtered : 'All the glasses fill,
And toast the great Pendragon of the hill,
Mab-Uther Owein, a long train of kings,
From whom the royal blood of Madoc springs : 40
Madoc, undoubtedly of Arthur's race,
You see the mighty monarch in his face :
Madoc, in bagnios and in courts adored,
Demands this proper homage of the board'.

'Monarchs !' said Twitcher, setting down his beer,
His muscles wreathing a contemptuous sneer ;
'Monarchs—of mole-hills, oyster-beds, a rock—
These are the grafters of your royal stock :
My pony Scrub can sires more valiant trace—'
The mangled pigeon thunders on his face ; 50
His opening mouth the melted butter fills,
And dropping from his nose and chin distils.
Furious he started, rage his bosom warms ;
Loud as his lordship's morning dun he storms.
'Thou vulgar imitator of the great,
Grown wanton with the excrements of state,
This to thy head notorious Twitcher sends—'
His shadow body to the table bends,

THE CONSULIAD

His straining arm uprears a loin of veal,
In these degenerate days for three a meal;
In ancient times, as various writers say,
An alderman or priest eat three a day.
With godlike strength the grinning Twitcher plies
His stretching muscles, and the mountain flies.
Swift as a cloud that shadows o'er the plain
It flew, and scattered drops of oily rain.
In opposition to extended knives,
On royal Madoc's spreading chest it drives;
Senseless he falls upon the sandy ground,
Pressed with the steamy load that oozed around.
And now confusion spread her ghastly plume,
And faction separates the noisy room.
Balluntun, exercised in every vice
That opens to a courtier's paradise,
With Dyson trammelled, scruples not to draw
Injustice up the rocky hill of law:
From whose humanity the laurels sprung,
Which will in George's-Fields be ever young—
The vile Balluntun, starting from his chair,
To fortune thus addressed his private prayer:
'Goddess of fate's rotundity, assist
With thought-winged victory my untried fist:
If I the grinning Twitcher overturn,
Six Russian frigates at thy shrine shall burn;
Nine rioters shall bleed beneath thy feet;
And hanging cutters decorate each street'.
The goddess smiled, or rather smoothed her frown,
And shook the triple feathers of her crown;
Instilled a private pension in his soul.
With rage inspired, he seized a Gallic roll;
His bursting arm the missive weapon threw,
High o'er his rival's head it whistling flew;

Curraras, for his Jewish soul renowned,
Received it on his ear, and kissed the ground :
Curraras, versed in every little art,
To play the minister's or felon's part ;
Grown hoary in the villanies of state,
A title made him infamously great ;
A slave to venal slaves, a tool to tools,
The representative to knaves and fools.　　　100
But see commercial Bristol's genius sit,
Her shield a turtle-shell, her lance a spit :
See, whilst her nodding aldermen are spread,
In all the branching honours of the head ;
Curraras, ever faithful to the cause,
With beef and venison their attention draws :
They drink, they eat, then sign the mean address ;
Say, could their humble gratitude do less?
By disappointment vexed, Balluntun flies,
Red lightnings flashing in his dancing eyes.　　　110
Firm as his virtue, mighty Twitcher stands,
And elevates for furious fight his hands :
One pointed fist his shadowed corpse defends,
The other on Balluntun's eyes descends :
A darkling, shaking light his optics view,
Circled with livid tinges red and blue.
Now fired with anguish and inflamed by pride,
He thunders on his adversary's side :
With pattering blows prolongs the unequal fight ;
Twitcher retreats before the man of might.　　　120
But fortune, (or some higher power or god),
Oblique extended forth a sable rod :
As Twitcher retrograde maintained the fray,
The hardened serpent intercepts his way :
He fell, and falling with a lordly air,
Crushed into atoms the judicial chair.

Curraras, for his Jewish soul renowned,
Arose, but deafened with a singing sound.
A cloud of discontent o'erspread his brows;
Revenge in every bloody feature glows.   130
Around his head a roasted gander whirls,
Dropping Manilla sauces on his curls;
Swift to the vile Balluntun's face it flies,
The burning pepper sparkles in his eyes:
His India waistcoat, reeking with the oil,
Glows brighter red, the glory of the spoil.

The fight is general; fowl repulses fowl;
The victors thunder, and the vanquished howl.
Stars, garters, all the implements of show,
That decked the powers above, disgraced below.   140
Nor swords, nor mightier weapons did they draw,
For all were well acquainted with the law.
Let Draper to improve his diction fight;
Our heroes, like Lord George, could scold and write.
Gogmagog, early of the jockey club,
Empty as C—br—ke's oratorical tub,
A rusty link of ministerial chain,
A living glory of the present reign,
Versed in the arts of ammunition-bread,
He waved a red-wheat manchet round his head.   150
David-ap-Howel, furious, wild, and young,
From the same line as royal Madoc sprung,
Occurred, the object of his bursting ire,
And on his nose received the weapon dire:
A double river of congealing blood
O'erflows his garter with a purple flood.
Mad as a bull by daring mastiffs tore,
When ladies scream and greasy butchers roar;
Mad as B—rg—e when, groping through the park,
He kissed his own dear lady in the dark;   160

The lineal representative of kings
A carving weapon seized, and up he springs:
A weapon long in cruel murders stained,
For mangling captive carcases ordained.
But fortune, providence, or what you will,
To lay the rising scenes of horror still,
In Fero's person seized a shining pot,
Where bubbled scrips and contracts, flaming hot,
In the fierce Cambrian's breeches drains it dry:
The chapel totters with the shrieking cry,   170
Loud as the mob's reiterated yell,
When Sawny rose, and mighty Chatham fell.

Flaccus, the glory of a masquerade,
Whose every action is of trifles made,
At Grafton's well-stored table ever found ;
Like Grafton too for every vice renowned :
Grafton, to whose immortal sense we owe
The blood which will from civil discord flow ;
Who swells each grievance, lengthens every tax,
Blind to the ripening vengeance of the axe :   180
Flaccus, the youthful, *degagé*, and gay,
With eye of pity saw the dreary fray :
Amidst the greasy horrors of the fight,
He trembled for his suit of virgin white.
Fond of his eloquence and easy flow
Of talk verbose, whose meaning none can know,
He mounts the table, but through eager haste
His foot upon a smoking court-pie placed :
The burning liquid penetrates his shoe,
Swift from the rostrum the declaimer flew ;   190
But, learnedly heroic, he disdains
To spoil his pretty countenance with strains.
Remounted on the table now he stands,
Waves his high-powdered head and ruffled hands.

' Friends ! Let this clang of hostile fury cease,
Ill it becomes the plenipos of peace ;
Shall olios, from internal battle dressed,
Like bullets outward perforate the breast ?
Shall javelin bottles blood ethereal spill ?
Shall luscious turtle without surfeit kill ? '   200
More had he said : when, from Doglostock flung,
A custard pudding trembled on his tongue :
And, ah ! misfortunes seldom come alone,
Great Twitcher rising seized a polished bone ;
Upon his breast the oily weapon clangs ;
Headlong he falls, propelled by thickening bangs.
The prince of trimmers, for his magic famed,
Quarlendorgongos by infernals named,
By mortals Alavat in common styled—
Nursed in a furnace, Nox and Neptune's child—   210
Bursting with rage, a weighty bottle caught,
With crimson blood and vital spirits fraught ;
To Doxo's head the gurgling woe he sends :
Doxo, made mighty in his mighty friends.
Upon his front the stubborn vessel sounds,
Back from his harder front the bottle bounds :
He fell. The royal Madoc rising up,
Reposed him weary on his painful crup :
The head of Doxo, first projecting down,
Thunders upon the kingly Cambrian's crown :   220
The sanguine tumour swells ; again he falls ;
On his broad chest the bulky Doxo sprawls.
Tyro the sage, the sensible, the strong,
As yet unnoticed in the muse-taught song :
Tyro, for necromancy far renowned,
A greater adept than Agrippa found ;
Oft as his phantom-reasons intervened,
De Vir is pensioned, the defaulter screened ;

Another Carteret remains in Clare ;
In Fletcher, fifty Jefferies appear ; 230
Tyro stood neuter, till the champions, tired,
In languid attitudes a truce desired.
Long was the bloody fight ; confusion dire
Has hid some circumstances from the lyre :
Suffice it, that each hero kissed the ground,
Tyro excepted, for old laws renowned ;
Who stretching his authoritative hand,
Loudly thus issued forth his dread command.
' Peace, wrangling senators, and placemen, peace,
In the king's name, let hostile vengeance cease !' 240
Aghast the champions hear the furious sound,
The fallen unmolested leave the ground.
'What fury, nobles, occupies your breast ?
What, patriot spirits, has your minds possessed ?
Nor honorary gifts nor pensions please,
Say, are you Covent-Garden patentees ?
How, wist you not what ancient sages said ?
"The council quarrels, and the poor have bread"
See this court-pie with twenty-thousand dressed ;
Be every thought of enmity at rest : 250
Divide it, and be friends again ', he said :
The council-god returned ; and discord fled.

C.

Bristol, 4*th January* 1770

EPISTLE

TO THE REVEREND MR CATCOTT

6th December 1769

WHAT strange infatuations rule mankind!
How narrow are our prospects, how confined!
With universal vanity possessed,
We fondly think our own ideas best;
Our tottering arguments are ever strong;
We're always self-sufficient in the wrong.

   What philosophic sage of pride austere
Can lend conviction an attentive ear?
What pattern of humility and truth
Can bear the jeering ridicule of youth?   10
What blushing author ever ranked his muse
With Fowler's, poet-laureate of the stews?
Dull Penny, nodding o'er his wooden lyre,
Conceits the vapours of Geneva fire.
All in the language of apostles cry,
If angels contradict me, angels lie.
As all have intervals of ease and pain,
So all have intervals of being vain:
But some of folly never shift the scene,
Or let one lucid moment intervene;   20
Dull single acts of many-footed prose
Their tragi-comedies of life compose;
Incessant madding for a system toy,
The greatest of creation's blessings cloy;
Their senses dozing a continual dream,
They hang enraptured o'er the hideous scheme:

So virgins, tottering into ripe three-score,
Their greatest likeness in baboons adore.

When you advance new systems, first unfold
The various imperfections of the old ; 30
Prove nature hitherto a gloomy night,
You the first focus of primæval light.
'Tis not enough you think your system true,
The busy world would have you prove it too :
Then, rising on the ruins of the rest,
Plainly demonstrate your ideas best.
Many are best ; one only can be right,
Though all had inspiration to indite.

Some this unwelcome truth perhaps would tell,
Where Clogher stumbled, Catcott fairly fell. 40
Writers on rolls of science long renowned
In one fell page are tumbled to the ground.
We see their systems unconfuted still ;
But Catcott can confute them—if he will.
Would you the honour of a priest mistrust,
An excommunication proves him just.

Could Catcott from his better sense be drawn
To bow the knee to Baal's sacred lawn?
A mitred rascal to his long-eared flocks
Gives ill example, to his whores, the pox. 50
Yet we must reverence sacerdotal black,
And saddle all his faults on nature's back ;
But hold, there's solid reason to revere :
His lordship has six thousand pounds a year.
In gaming solitude he spends the nights,
He fasts at Arthur's, and he prays at White's ;
Rolls o'er the pavement with his Swiss-tailed six,
At White's, the Athanasian creed for tricks ;
Whilst the poor curate in his rusty gown
Trudges unnoticed through the dirty town. 60

EPISTLE

If God made order, order never made
These nice distinctions in the preaching trade.
The servants of the devil are revered,
And bishops pull the fathers by the beard.
Yet in these horrid forms salvation lives,
These are religion's representatives;
Yet to these idols must we bow the knee—
Excuse me, Broughton, when I bow to thee.
But sure religion can produce at least
One minister of God—one honest priest. 70

Search nature o'er, procure me if you can
The fancied character, an honest man;
(A man of sense, not honest by constraint,
For fools are canvas, living but in paint).
To mammon or to superstition slaves,
All orders of mankind are fools, or knaves;
In the first attribute by none surpassed,
Taylor endeavours to obtain the last.

Imagination may be too confined;
Few see too far; how many are half blind? 80
How are your feeble arguments perplexed
To find out meaning in a senseless text?
You rack each metaphor upon the wheel,
And words can philosophic truths conceal.
What Paracelsus humoured as a jest,
You realise, to prove your system best.
Might we not, Catcott, then infer from hence,
Your zeal for scripture hath devoured your sense?
Apply the glass of reason to your sight,
See nature marshal oozy atoms right; 90
Think for yourself, for all mankind are free;
We need not inspiration how to see.
If scripture contradictory you find,
Be orthodox, and own your senses blind.

How blinded are their optics who aver
What inspiration dictates cannot err.
Whence is this boasted inspiration sent,
Which makes us utter truths we never meant?
Which couches systems in a single word,
At once depraved, abstruse, sublime, absurd?   100

What Moses tells us might perhaps be true,
As he was learned in all the Egyptians knew.

But to assert that inspiration's given,
The copy of philosophy in heaven,
Strikes at religion's root, and fairly fells
The awful terrors of ten thousand hells.
Attentive search the scriptures, and you'll find
What vulgar errors are with truths combined.
Your tortured truths, which Moses seemed to know,
He could not unto inspiration owe;   110
But if from God one error you admit,
How dubious is the rest of holy writ!

What knotty difficulties fancy solves!
The heavens irradiate, and the earth revolves;
But here imagination is allowed
To clear this voucher from its mantling cloud:
From the same word we different meanings quote,
As David wears a many-coloured coat.

O inspiration, ever hid in night,
Reflecting various each adjacent light!   120
If Moses caught thee in the parted flood;
If David found thee in a sea of blood;
If Mahomet with slaughter drenched thy soil,
On loaded asses bearing off thy spoil;
If thou hast favoured Pagan, Turk, or Jew,
Say, had not Broughton inspiration too?
Such rank absurdities debase his line,
I almost could have sworn he copied thine.

EPISTLE

Confute with candour, where you can confute,
Reason and arrogance but poorly suit.   130
Yourself may fall before some abler pen,
Infallibility is not for men.
With modest diffidence new schemes indite,
Be not too positive, though in the right.
What man of sense would value vulgar praise,
Or rise on Penny's prose, or duller lays?
Though pointed fingers mark the man of fame,
And literary grocers chant your name ;
Though in each tailor's bookcase Catcott shines,
With ornamental flowers and gilded lines ;   140
Though youthful ladies, who by instinct scan
The natural philosophy of man,
Can every reason of your work repeat,
As sands in Africa retain the heat ;
Yet check your flowing pride : will all allow
To wreathe the laboured laurel round your brow?
Some may with seeming arguments dispense,
Tickling your vanity to wound your sense :
But Clayfield censures, and demonstrates too,
Your theory is certainly untrue.   150
On reason and Newtonian rules he proves
How distant your machine from either moves.
But my objections may be reckoned weak,
As nothing but my mother-tongue I speak ;
Else would I ask, by what immortal power
All nature was dissolved as in an hour ?
How, when the earth acquired a solid state,
And rising mountains saw the waves abate,
Each particle of matter sought its kind,
All in a strata regular combined ?   160
When instantaneously the liquid heap
Hardened to rocks, the barriers of the deep,

EPISTLE

Why did not earth unite a stony mass,
Since stony filaments through all must pass?
If on the wings of air the planets run,
Why are they not impelled into the sun?
Philosophy, nay, common sense, will prove
All passives with their active agents move.
If the diurnal motion of the air
Revolves the planets in their destined sphere,   170
How are the secondary orbs impelled?
How are the moons from falling headlong held?

'Twas the Eternal's fiat, you reply;
And who will give Eternity the lie?
I own the awful truth, that God made all,
And by His fiat worlds and systems fall;
But study nature; not an atom there
Will, unassisted by her powers, appear.
The fiat, without agents, is, at best,
For priestcraft or for ignorance a vest.   180

Some fancy God is what we nature call,
Being itself material, all in all;
The fragments of the Deity we own,
Is vulgarly as various matter known.
No agents could assist creation's birth:
We trample on our God, for God is earth.
'Tis past the power of language to confute
This latitudinary attribute.

How lofty must imagination soar,
To reach absurdities unknown before!   190
Thanks to thy pinions, Broughton, thou hast brought
From the moon's orb a novelty of thought.
Restrain, O muse! thy unaccomplished lines,
Fling not thy saucy satire at divines;
This single truth thy brother bards must tell,
Thou hast one excellence, of railing well;

EPISTLE

But disputations are befitting those
Who settle Hebrew points, and scold in prose.

   O learning ! where are all thy fancied joys,
Thy empty pleasures and thy solemn toys?   200
Proud of thy own importance, though we see
We've little reason to be proud of thee:
Thou putrid fœtus of a barren brain,
Thou offspring illegitimate of pain.

   Tell me, sententious mortals, tell me whence
You claim the preference to men of sense?
[Burgum] wants learning: see the lettered throng
Banter his English in a Latin song.
Oxonian sages hesitate to speak
Their native language, but declaim in Greek.   210
If in his jests a discord should appear,
A dull lampoon is innocently clear.
Ye classic dunces, self-sufficient fools,
Is this the boasted justice of your schools?
[Burgum] has parts, parts which would set aside
The laboured acquisitions of your pride;
Uncultivated now his genius lies,
Instruction sees his latent beauties rise;
His gold is bullion, yours debased with brass,
Impressed with folly's head to make it pass.   220

   But [Burgum] swears so loud, so indiscreet,
His thunders rattle through the listening street.
Ye rigid Christians, formally severe,
Blind to his charities, his oaths you hear;
Observe his virtues: calumny must own
A noble soul is in his actions shown.
Though dark this bright original you paint,
I'd rather be a [Burgum] than a saint.

EPISTLE

Excuse me, Catcott, if from you I stray,
The muse will go where merit leads the way : 230
The owls of learning may admire the night,
But [Burgum] shines with reason's glowing light.

Still admonition presses to my pen,
The infant muse would give advice to men.
But what avails it, since the man I blame
Owns no superior in the paths of fame?
In springs, in mountains, stratas, mines, and rocks,
Catcott is every notion orthodox.
If to think otherwise you claim pretence,
You're a detested heretic in sense. 240
But oh ! how lofty your ideas roar,
In showing wondering cits the fossil store !
The ladies are quite ravished, as he tells
The short adventures of the pretty shells ;
Miss Biddy sickens to indulge her touch,
Madam more prudent thinks 'twould seem too much.
The doors fly open, instantly he draws
The spary lode, and wonders of applause ;
The full-dressed lady sees with envying eye
The sparkle of her diamond pendants die ; 250
Sage natural philosophers adore
The fossil whimsies of the numerous store.
But see ! the purple stream begins to play ;
To shew how fountains climb the hilly way :
Hark what a murmur echoes through the throng.
Gods ! that the pretty trifle should be wrong !
Experience in the voice of reason tells,
Above its surface water never swells.

Where is the priestly soul of Catcott now ?
See what a triumph sits upon his brow. 260
And can the poor applause of things like these,
Whose souls and sentiments are all disease,

THE EXHIBITION

Raise little triumphs in a man like you,
Catcott, the foremost of the judging few?
So at Llewellyn's your great brother sits,
The laughter of his tributary wits;
Ruling the noisy multitude with ease,
Empties his pint, and sputters his decrees.

20th December 1769

M<small>R</small> C<small>ATCOTT</small> will be pleased to observe that I admire many things in his learned Remarks. This poem is an innocent effort of poetical vengeance, as Mr Catcott has done me the honour to criticise my trifles. I have taken great poetical liberties, and what I dislike in verse possibly deserves my approbation in the plain prose of truth.—The many admirers of Mr Catcott may, on perusal of this, rank me as an enemy: but I am indifferent in all things; I value neither the praise nor the censure of the multitude.

[EXTRACT FROM] THE EXHIBITION: A PERSONAL SATIRE

T<small>HIS</small> truth, this mighty truth—if truth can shine
In the smooth polish of a laboured line—
Catcott by sad experience testifies;
And who shall tell a sabled priest he lies?
Bred to the juggling of the spacious band
Predestinated to adorn the land,
The selfish Catcott ripened to a priest,
And wore the sable livery of the Beast.

By birth to prejudice and whim allied,
And heavy with hereditary pride, 10
He modelled pleasure by a fossil rule,
And spent his youth to prove himself a fool ;
Buried existence in a lengthened cave,
And lost in dreams whatever nature gave.

1st May 1770

FABLES FOR THE COURT

Addressed to Mr Michael Clayfield, of Bristol

THE SHEPHERDS

MORALS, as critics must allow,
Are almost out of fashion now ;
And, if we credit Dodsley's word,
All applications are absurd.
What has the author to be vain in
Who knows his fable wants explaining,
And substitutes a second scene
To publish what the first should mean?
Besides, it saucily reflects
Upon the reader's intellects, 10
When, armed in metaphors and dashes,
The bard some noble villain lashes,
'Tis a direct affront, no doubt,
To think he cannot find it out.
The sing-song trifles of the stage,
The happy favourites of the age,
Without a meaning crawl along,
And, for a moral, gives a song.
The tragic muse, once pure and chaste,
Is turned a whore, debauched by taste : 20

Poor Juliet never claims the tear
Till borne triumphant on the bier;
And Ammon's son is never great
Till seated in his chair of state.
And yet the harlot scarce goes down,
She's been so long upon the town,
Her morals never can be seen.
Not rigid Johnson seems to mean,
A tittering epilogue contains
The cobweb of a poet's brains.   30
If what the muse prepares to write
To entertain the public sight
Should in its characters be known,
The knowledge is the reader's own.
When villany and vices shine,
You won't find Sandwich in the line;
When little rascals rise to fame,
Sir Fletcher cannot read his name;
Nor will the muse digressive run
To call the king his mother's son,   40
But, plodding on the beaten way,
With honest North prepares the lay:
And should the meaning figures please
The dull reviews of laughing ease,
No politician can dispute
My knowledge of the Earl of Bute.

A flock of sheep, no matter where,
Was all an aged shepherd's care;
His dogs were watchful, and he took
Upon himself the ruling crook.   50
His boys who wattled-in the fold
Were never bought and never sold.
'Tis true, by strange affection led,
He visited a turnip-bed;

And, fearful of a winter storm,
Employed his wool to keep it warm.
But that, comparatively set
Against the present heavy debt,
Was but a trifling piece of state,
And hardly make a villain great.　　　　60
The shepherd died—the dreadful toll
Entreated masses for his soul :
The pious bosom and the back
Shone in the farce of courtly black.
The weeping laureate's ready pen
Lamented o'er the best of men ;
And Oxford sent her load of rhyme
In all varieties of chime,
Administering due consolation,
Well seasoned with congratulation.　　　70
Cambridge her ancient lumber wrote,
And what could Cambridge do but quote?
All sung, though very few could read,
And none but mercers mourned indeed.
The younger shepherd caught the crook,
And was a monarch in his look.
The flock rejoiced, and could no less
 Than pay their duty and address ;
And Edinburgh was heard to sing,
' Now heaven be praised for such a king ! '　80
All joined in joy and expectation,
And ' Union ! ' echoed through the nation.
A council called ——— * * *

JOURNAL SIXTH

'Tis mystery all, in every sect
You find this palpable defect,
The axis of the dark machine
Is enigmatic and unseen.
Opinion is the only guide
By which our senses are supplied ;
Mere grief's conjecture, fancy's whim,
Can make our reason side with him.
But this discourse perhaps will be
As little liked by you as me ;   10
I'll change the subject for a better,
And leave the doctor, and his letter.
A priest, whose sanctimonious face
Became a sermon, or a grace,
Could take an orthodox repast,
And left the knighted loin the last ;
To fasting very little bent,
He'd pray indeed till breath was spent.
Shrill was his treble as a cat,
His organs being choked with fat ;   20
In college quite as graceful seen
As Camplin or the lazy dean,
(Who sold the ancient cross to Hoare
For one church-dinner, nothing more ;
The dean who, sleeping on the book,
Dreams he is swearing at his cook)
This animated hill of oil
Was to another dean the foil.
They seemed two beasts of different kind,
Contra in politics and mind ;   30

The only sympathy they knew,
They both loved turtle *à la* stew.
The dean was empty, thin and long,
As Fowler's back or head or song.
He met the rector in the street,
Sinking a canal with his feet.
'Sir', quoth the dean, with solemn nod,
'You are a minister of God;
And, as I apprehend, should be
About such holy works as me. 40
But, cry your mercy, at a feast
You only shew yourself a priest.
No sermon politic you preach,
No doctrine damnable you teach.
Did not we few maintain the fight,
Mystery might sink, and all be light.
From house to house your appetite
In daily sojourn paints ye right.
Nor lies, true-orthodox, you carry,
You hardly ever hang or marry. 50
Good Mr Rector, let me tell ye
You've too much tallow in this belly.
Fast, and repent of every sin,
And grow like me, upright and thin;
Be active, and assist your mother,
And then I'll own ye for a brother'.

'Sir', quoth the rector in a huff,
'True, you're diminutive enough,
And let me tell ye, Mr Dean,
You are as worthless too as lean; 60
This mountain, strutting to my face,
Is an undoubted sign of grace.
Grace, though you ne'er on turtle sup,
Will like a bladder blow you up,

A tun of claret swells your case
Less than a single ounce of grace'.

'You're wrong', the bursting dean replied,
'Your logic's on the rough-cast side,
The minor's right, the major falls,
Weak as his modern honour's walls.
A spreading trunk, with rotten skin,
Shews very little's kept within;
But when the casket's neat, not large,
We guess the importance of the charge'.

'Sir', quoth the rector, ' I've a story
Quite apropos to lay before ye.
A sage philosopher, to try
What pupil saw with reason's eye,
Prepared three boxes, gold, lead, stone,
And bid three youngsters claim each one.
The first, a Bristol merchant's heir,
Loved pelf above the charming fair;
So 'tis not difficult to say,
Which box the dolthead took away.
The next, as sensible as me,
Desired the pebbled one, d'ye see.
The other having scratched his head,
Considered, though the third was lead,
'Twas metal still surpassing stone,
So claimed the leaden box his own.
Now to unclose they all prepare,
And hope alternate laughs at fear.
The golden case does ashes hold,
The leaden shines with sparkling gold,
But in the outcast stone they see
A jewel, such pray fancy me'.

'Sir', quoth the dean, ' I truly say
You tell a tale a pretty way ;
But the conclusion to allow—
'Fore Gad, I scarcely can tell how.   100
A jewel ! Fancy must be strong
To think you keep your water long.
I preach, thank gracious heaven ! as clear
As any pulpit-stander here,
But may the devil claw my face
If e'er I prayed for puffing grace,
To be a mountain, and to carry
Such a vile heap—I'd rather marry !
Each day to sweat three gallons full
And span a furlong on my skull.   110
Lost to the melting joys of love—
Not to be borne—like justice move'.

And here the dean was running on,
Through half a couplet having gone :
Quoth rector peevish, ' I shan't stay
To throw my precious time away.
The generous Burgum having sent
A ticket as a compliment,
I think myself in duty bound
Six pounds of turtle to confound'.   120

'That man you mention', answers Dean,
' Creates in priests of sense the spleen,
His soul's as open as his hand,
Virtue distressed may both command ;
That ragged virtue is a whore,
I always beat her from my door.
But Burgum gives, and giving shews
His honour leads him by the nose.
Ah ! how unlike the church divine,
Whose feeble lights on mountains shine,   130

And being placed so near the sky,
Are lost to every human eye.
His luminaries shine around
Like stars in the Cimmerian ground'.

'Invidious slanderer!' quoth priest,
'O may I never scent a feast,
If thy cursed conscience is as pure
As underlings in Whitefield's cure!
The church, as thy display has shewn,
Is turned a bawd to lustful town;   140
But what against the Church you've said,
Shall soon fall heavy on your head.
Is Burgum's virtue then a fault?
Venison and heaven forbid the thought!
He gives, and never eyes return,
O may paste altars to him burn!
But whilst I talk with worthless you,
Perhaps the dinner waits—adieu'.

This said, the rector trudged along,
As heavy as Fowlerian song.   150
The hollow dean, with fairy feet,
Stepped lightly through the dirty street.
At last, arrived at destined place,
The bulky doctor squeaks the grace:
'Lord bless the many-flavoured meat,
And grant us strength enough to eat!
May all and every mother's son
Be drunk before the dinner's done.
When we give thanks for dining well, oh!
May each grunt out in Ritornello'.   160
'Amen!' resounds to distant tide,
And weapons clang on every side,
The oily rivers burn around,
And gnashing teeth make doleful sound.

Now is the busy president
In his own fated element,
In every look and action great,
His presence doubly fills the plate ;
Nobly invited to the feast,
They all contribute gold at least.   170
The duke and president collected,
Alike beloved, alike respected.

SAY, Baker, if experience hoar
Has yet unbolted wisdom's door,
What is this phantom of the mind,
This love, when sifted and refined ?
When the poor lover, fancy-frighted,
Is with shadowy joys delighted ;
A frown shall throw him in despair,
A smile shall brighten up his air.   180
Jealous without a seeming cause,
From flattering smiles he misery draws ;
Again, without his reason's aid,
His bosom's still, the devil's laid.
If this is love, my callous heart
Has never felt the rankling dart.
Oft have I seen the wounded swain
Upon the rack of pleasing pain,
Full of his flame, upon his tongue
The quivering declaration hung,   190
When lost to courage, sense, and reason,
He talked of weather and the season.
Such tremors never cowered me,
I'm flattering, impudent, and free,
Unmoved by frowns and lowering eyes,
'Tis smiles I only ask and prize ;

JOURNAL SIXTH

And when the smile is freely given,
You're in the highway-road to heaven.
These coward lovers seldom find
That whining makes the ladies kind.   200
They laugh at silly silent swains
Who're fit for nothing but their chains.
'Tis an effrontery and tongue
On very oily hinges hung
Must win the blooming, melting fair,
And show the joys of heaven here.

A rake, I take it, is a creature
Who winds through all the folds of nature;
Who sees the passions, and can tell
How the soft beating heart shall swell;   210
Who, when he ravishes the joy,
Defies the torments of the boy.
Who with the soul the body gains,
And shares love's pleasures, not his pains.
Who holds his charmer's reputation
Above a tavern veneration;
And when a love-repast he makes,
Not even prying fame partakes.
Who looks above a prostitute, he
Thinks love the only price of beauty,   220
And she that can be basely sold
Is much beneath or love or gold.
Who thinks the almost dearest part
In all the body is the heart:
Without it, rapture cannot rise,
Nor pleasures wanton in the eyes;
The sacred joy of love is dead,
Witness the sleeping marriage bed.
This is the picture of a rake,
Show it the ladies—won't it take?   230

A buck's a beast of the other side,
And real but in hoofs and hide:
To nature and the passions dead,
A brothel is his house and bed;
To fan the flame of warm desire,
And after wanton in the fire,
He thinks a labour; and his parts
Were not designed to conquer hearts.
Serene with bottle, pox and whore,
He's happy and requires no more. 240
The girls of virtue when he views,
Dead to all converse but the stews,
Silent as death, he's nought to say,
But sheepish steals himself away.
This is a buck to life displayed,
A character to charm each maid.
Now, prithee, friend, a choice to make,
Wouldst choose the buck before the rake?
The buck, as brutal as the name,
Invenoms every charmer's fame, 250
And though he never touched her hand,
Protests he had her at command.
The rake, in gratitude for pleasure,
Keeps reputation dear as treasure.
  * * *

But hudibrastics may be found
To tire ye with repeated sound;
So, changing for a Shandeyan style,
I ask your favour and your smile.

ODE

Recitative

In his wooden palace jumping,
 Tearing, sweating, bawling, thumping, 260

'Repent, repent, repent',
　　The mighty Whitefield cries,
　　Oblique lightning in his eyes,
'Or die and be damned!'　All around
The long-eared rabble grunt in dismal sound.
　　'Repent, repent, repent',
　　Each concave mouth replies.
The comet of gospel, the lanthorn of light,
Is rising and shining like candles at night.
　　　　He shakes his ears,　　　　　　270
　　　　He jumps, he stares;
　　　　Hark, he's whining!
The short-hand saints prepare to write,
　　　　And high they mount their ears.

Air

　　　'Now the devil take ye all,
Saints or no saints, all in a lump;
　　　Here must I labour and bawl,
And thump, and thump, and thump;
　　　And never a souse to be got.
Unless—I swear by jingo,　　　　　　280
　　　A greater profit's made,
　　　I'll forswear my trade,
My gown and market-lingo,
　　　And leave ye all to pot'.

Recitative

Now he raves like brindled cat,
　　　Now 'tis thunder,
　　　　　Rowling,
　　　　　Growling,
　　　　　Rumbling,
　　　　　Grumbling,　　　　　　　290

Noise and nonsense, jest and blunder.
  Now he chats of this and that,
    No more the soul-jobber,
    No more the sly robber,
He's now an old woman who talks to her cat.
Again he starts, he beats his breast,
He rolls his eyes, erects his crest ;
    Hark ! hark ! the sound begins,
'Tis a bargain and sale for remission of sins.

Air

'Say, beloved congregation,   300
  In the hour of tribulation,
Did the power of man affray me?
  Say, ye wives, and say, ye daughters,
  Ha'n't I staunched your running waters,
I have laboured, pay me, pay me !

  I have given absolution,
  Don't withhold your contribution ;
Men and angels should obey me—
  Give but freely, you've remission
  For all sins without condition ;   310
You're my debtors, pay me, pay me !'

Recitative

Again he's lost, again he chatters
Of lace and bobbin and such matters.
  A thickening vapour swells—
  Of Adam's fall he tells ;
  Dark as twice ten thousand hells
Is the gibberish which he spatters.
Now a most dismal elegy he sings,
  Groans, doleful groans are heard about;
  The Issacharian rout   320
Swell the sharp howl, and loud the sorrow rings.

He sung a modern buck, whose end
  Was blinded prejudice and zeal;
In life, to every vice a friend,
  Unfixed as fortune on her wheel.
He lived a buck, he died a fool,
  So let him to oblivion fall,
  Who thought a wretched body all,
  Untaught in nature's or the passions'
    school.
  Now he takes another theme, 330
  Thus he tells his waking dream.

Air

' After fasting and praying and grunting and weeping,
My guardian angel beheld me fast sleeping;
And instantly capering into my brain,
Relieved me from prison of bodily chain.
The soul can be everything, as you all know,
And mine was transformed to the shape of a crow '.
(The preacher or metre has surely mistook,
For all must confess that a parson's a rook).

' Having wings, as I think I informed ye before, 340
I shot through a cavern and knocked at hell's door.
    Out comes Mr Porter Devil,
    And, I'll assure ye, very civil.
" Dear sir ", quoth he, " pray step within,
    The company is drinking tea;
We have a stranger just come in,
    A brother from the triple tree ",

' Well, in I walked, and what d'ye think?
Instead of sulphur, fire, and stink,
    'Twas like a masquerade, 350
    All grandeur, all parade.
Here stood an amphitheatre,
There stood the small Haymarket-house,

With devil-actors, very clever,
  Who without blacking did Othello.
  And truly, a huge horned fellow
  Told me, he hoped I would endeavour
  To learn a part, and get a souse ;
For pleasure was the business there.
  A lawyer asked me for a fee,   360
  To plead my right to drinking tea :
I begged his pardon ; to my thinking,
  I'd rather have a cheering cup,
For tea was but insipid drinking,
  And brandy raised the spirits up.
    So having seen each place in hell,
    I straight awoke, and found all well '.

Recitative

Now again his cornet's sounding,
Sense and harmony confounding ;
  Reason tortured, scripture twisted   370
    Into every form of fancy ;
  Forms which never yet existed,
    And but his oblique optics can see.
      He swears,
      He tears,
With sputtered nonsense now he breaks the ears ;
At last the sermon and the paper ends ;
He whines, and hopes his well-beloved friends
    Will contribute their sous
To pay the arrears for building a house ;   380
With spiritual doctors, and doctors for poxes,
Who all must be satisfied out of the boxes.
    Hark ! hark !—his cry resounds,
' Fire and thunder, blood and wounds,
    Contribute, contribute,
    And pay me my tribute,

Or the devil, I swear,
Shall hunt ye as sportsmen would hunt a poor hare.
Whoever gives, unto the Lord he lends '.
The saint is melted, pays his fee, and wends ;   390
And here the tedious lengthening Journal ends.

Ended Sat. evening, 30th Sept. 1769

KEW GARDENS

HAIL KEW ! thou darling of the tuneful nine,
Thou eating-house of verse, where poets dine ;
The temple of the idol of the great,
Sacred to council-mysteries of state ;
Sir Gilbert oft, in dangerous trials known,
To make the shame and felony his own,
Burns incense on thy altars, and presents
The grateful sound of clamorous discontents :
In the bold favour of thy goddess vain,
He brandishes his sword and shakes his chain.   10
He knows her secret workings and desires,
Her hidden attributes and vestal fires ;
Like an old oak has seen her god-head fall
Beneath the wild descendant of Fingal,
And happy in the view of promised store
Forgot his dignity and held the door.
* * * * happy genius, comes along,
Humming the music of a Highland song :
Rough and unpolished in the tricks of state,
He plots by instinct, is by nature great.   20
Who, not a mantled herald, can dispute
The native grandeur of the house of Bute ?
Who, not a Caledonian, can deny
By instinct all its noble branches lie ?

'Tis an entailed estate upon the name,
To plunder, plot, and pillage into fame ;
To live in splendour, infamy, and pride,
The guiders of the tools who seem to guide
Or starve on honesty, in state their own,
And marshal sheep unnoticed and unknown.　　30
* * * * versed in juntos and intrigues,
The fool and statesmen in close union leagues ;
Sits at the council's head ; esteemed at most
An useful kind of circulating post,
Through whose short stage each future measure's
　　laid,
And all the orders of the thane conveyed.
He gives the written text by fortune wrote,
Sir Gilbert adds his necessary note.
Dyson, a plodding animal of state,
Who's classically little, to be great ;　　40
An instrument, made use of to record
The future witty speeches of his lord :
To write epistles to his powerful dame,
And in the dark supply his loss of flame ;
To sell preferment ; grovel in the dust,
The slave of interest and the slave of lust ;
To lick his lordship's shoes, and find a flaw
In every statute that opposed his law ;
To carry orders to the guiding tool,
To flatter * * * * with the hopes of rule ;　　50
To send congratulations to the man,
Who stands so well affected to the clan—
(To [Barrington] whose conscientious mind
Does universal service to mankind,
When, red with justice and the royal cause,
His bloody musket shook with court-applause :
When monarchs, representatives of God,
Honoured the rascal with a gracious nod,

Three ghosts in George's sanguine field were seen,
And two struck horror into Bethnal Green ;   60
Soft pity's voice, unnoticed by the crown,
Stole in a murmur through the weeping town ;
And freedom, wandering restless and alone,
Saw no redress expected from the throne,
Then bade remonstrance wear a bolder dress,
And loudly supplicate, and force success :
* * * * heard, and, resting on his mace,
'The usual fees, my lord, and state the case'.
' Three thousand, and reversion to your son ' :
'The seals, my lord, are mine, the matter's
    done '.   70
'This house of foolish cits, and drunken boys,
Offends my ears, like Broderip's horrid noise :
'Tis a flat riot by the statute made,
Destructive to our happiness and trade'.
' Thy action, * * * * is just in law,
In the defence of ministry *I'll* draw ;
Nor doubt I when in solemn pomp arrayed,
To act as bravely, be as richly paid'.
So * * * * spoke, and in his usual way
When giving out his syllables for pay,   80
With happy fluency he scattered round
His nicely culled varieties of sound,
Unmeaning, unconnected, false, unfair :
All he can boast is modulated air)—
To bribe the common council to protest ;
To learn a witless alderman to jest ;
The father of the city to deprave,
And add the hummed apostate to the knave,
Who wisely disinherits his first-born,
And doats upon the blossom of his horn ;   90
To fill up places by preferment void,
Is Dyson by the quadruples employed ;

He bears the message of the gartered fate,
The running footmen to the favoured great:
When spent with labour, overgrown with spoil,
Some barony or earldom pays his toil.

   Whilst two chief actors wisely keep away,
And two before the mystic curtain play;
The goddess, mourning for her absent god,
Approves the flying measures with a nod.   100
Her approbation, with her power combined,
Exalts her tools above the common kind.
She turns the movements of the dark machine,
Nor is her management of state unseen;
Regardless of the world, she still turns round,
And tumbles * * * * to his native ground.
Great in possession of a mystic ring,
She leads the Lords and Commons in a string.
Where is the modest muse of Jones retired,
So bashful, so impatiently admired?   110
Ah! is that noble emulation dead,
Which bade the laurels blossom on his head,
When Kew's enchanting heap of stones was sung
In strains superior to a mortal tongue,
And kitchen-gardens most luxurious glowed
With flowers which ne'er in Mayor's window blowed;
Where cabbages, exotic'ly divine,
Were tagged in feet, and measured with a line?
Ah! what invention graced the happy strain;
Well might the laureate bard of Kew be vain!   120
Thy Clifton too! how justly is the theme
As much the poet's as his jingling dream.
Who but a muse inventive, great, like thine,
Could honour Bristol with a nervous line?
What generous, honest genius would have sold
To knaves and catamites his praise for gold?

To leave alone the notions which disgrace
This hawking, peddling, catamitish place,
Did not thy iron conscience blush to write
This Tophet of the gentle arts polite? 130
Lost to all learning, elegance, and sense,
Long had the famous city told her pence;
Avarice sat brooding in her white-washed cell,
And pleasure had a hut at Jacob's Well.
Poor Hickey, ruined by his fine survey,
Perpetuates Elton in the saving lay.
A mean assembly-room, absurdly built,
Boasted one gorgeous lamp of copper gilt;
With fartbing candles, chandeliers of tin,
And services of water, rum, and gin. 140
There, in the dull solemnity of wigs,
The dancing bears of commerce murder jigs.
Here dance the dowdy belles of crooked trunk,
And often, very often, reel home drunk;
Here dance the bucks with infinite delight,
And club to pay the fiddlers for the night,
While Broderip's hum-drum symphonies of flats
Rival tbe harmony of midnight cats.
What charms has music, when great Broderip sweats
To torture sound to what his brother sets! 150
With scraps of ballad tunes, and *gude Scotch sangs*,
Which god-like Ramsay to his bagpipe twangs,
With tattered fragments of forgotten plays,
With Playford's melody to Sternhold's lays,
This pipe of science, mighty Broderip, comes,
And a strange, unconnected jumble thrums.
Roused to devotion in a sprightly air,
Danced into piety, and jigged to prayer;
A modern hornpipe's murder greets our ears,
The heavenly music of domestic spheres; 160

The flying band in swift transition hops
Through all the tortured, vile burlesque of stops.
Sacred to sleep, in superstitious key
Dull, doleful diapasons die away;
Sleep spreads his silken wings, and, lulled by sound,
The vicar slumbers, and the snore goes round:
Whilst Broderip at his passive organ groans
Through all his slow variety of tones.
How unlike Allen! Allen is divine!
His touch is sentimental, tender, fine;   170
No little affectations e'er disgraced
His more refined, his sentimental taste:
He keeps the passions with the sound in play,
And the soul trembles with the trembling key.

The groves of Kew, however misapplied
To serve the purposes of lust and pride,
Were, by the greater monarch's care, designed
A place of conversation for the mind;
Where solitude and silence should remain,
And conscience keep her sessions and arraign.   180
But ah! how fallen from that better state!
'Tis now a heathen temple of the great,
Where sits the female pilot of the helm,
Who shakes oppression's fetters through the realm.
Her name is Tyranny, and in a string
She leads the shadow of an infant king;
Dispenses favours with a royal hand,
And marks, like destiny, what lord shall stand;
Her four-fold representative displays
How future statesmen may their fortune raise;   190
While thronging multitudes their offerings bring,
And bards, like Jones, their panegyrics sing.
The loyal aldermen, a troop alone,
Protest their infamy, to serve the throne;

The merchant-tailor minister declares
He'll mutilate objections with his shears.
Sir Robert, in his own importance big,
Settles his potent, magisterial wig;
Having another legacy in view,
Accepts the measure and improves it too.   200
Before the altar all the suppliants bow,
And would repeat a speech if they knew how;
A gracious nod the speaking image gave,
And scattered honours upon every knave.
The loyal sons of Caledonia came,
And paid their secret homage to the dame;
Then swore, by all their hopes of future reign,
Each measure of the junto to maintain,
The orders of the ministry to take,
And honour * * * for his father's sake.   210
Well pleased, the goddess dignified his grace,
And scattered round the benefits of place;
With other pensions blessed his lordship's post,
And smiled on murdered * * * * injured ghost.
Through all the happy lovers' numerous clan
The inexhausted tides of favour ran :
* * *, * * *, happy in a name,
Emerged from poverty to wealth and fame;
And English taxes paid (and scarcely too)
The noble generosity of Kew.   220
Kew ! happy subject for a lengthened lay,
Though thousands write, there's something still to say;
Thy garden's elegance, thy owner's state,
The highest in the present list of fate,
Are subjects where the muse may wildly range,
Unsatiate, in variety of change;
But hold, my dedication is forgot :
Now—shall I praise some late-ennobled Scot
Exalt the motto of a Highland lord,

And prove him great, like Guthrie, by record? 230
(Though were the truth to all the nobles known,
The vouchers he refers to are his own.)
Shall I trace * * *'s powerful pedigree,
Or show him an attorney's clerk, like me?
Or shall I rather give to * * * * its due,
And to a Burgum recommend my Kew?
Why sneers the sapient Broughton at the man?
Broughton can't boast the merit Burgum can.
How lofty must imagination soar,
To reach absurdities unknown before! 240
Thanks to thy pinions, Broughton, thou hast brought
From the moon's orb a novelty of thought.

Burgum wants learning—see the lettered throng
Banter his English in a Latin song.
If in his jests a discord should appear,
A dull lampoon is innocently dear.
Ye sage, Broughtonian, self-sufficient fools,
Is this the boasted justice of your schools?
Burgum has parts, parts which will set aside
The laboured acquisitions of your pride; 250
Uncultivated now his genius lies,
Instruction sees his latent talents rise;
His gold is bullion, yours debased with brass,
Impressed with folly's head to make it pass.
But Burgum swears so loud, so indiscreet,
His thunders echo through the listening street;
Ye rigid Christians, formally severe,
Blind to his charities, his oaths you hear;
Observe his actions—calumny must own
A noble soul is in these actions shown: 260
Though dark this bright original you paint,
I'd rather be a Burgum than a saint.

Hail, inspiration! whose Cimmerian night
Gleams into day with every flying light:

If Moses caught thee at the parted flood;
If David found thee in a sea of blood;
If Mahomet with slaughter drenched thy soil,
On loaded asses bearing off the spoil;
If thou hast favoured Pagan, Turk, or Jew,
Say, had not Broughton inspiration too? 270
Such rank absurdities debase his line,
I almost could have sworn he copied thine.
Hail, inspiration! whose auspicious ray
Immortalised great Armstrong in a day:
Armstrong, whose Caledonian genius flies
Above the reach of humble judgment's ties;
Whose lines prosaic regularly creep,
Sacred to dulness and congenial sleep.
Hail, inspiration! whose mysterious wings
Are strangers to what rigid [Johnson] sings: 280
By him thy airy voyages are curbed,
Nor moping wisdom's by thy flight disturbed;
To ancient lore and musty precepts bound,
Thou art forbid the range of fairy ground.
Irene creeps so classical and dry,
None but a Greek philosopher can cry;
Through five long acts unlettered heroes sleep,
And critics by the square of learning weep.
Hark! what's the horrid bellowing from the stage?
Oh! 'tis the ancient chorus of the age; 290
Grown wise, the judgment of the town refines,
And in a philosophic habit shines;
Models each pleasure in scholastic taste,
And heavenly Greece is copied and disgraced.
The *False Alarm*, in style and subject great,
The mighty Atlas of a falling state,
Which makes us happy, insolent, and free,
O god-like inspiration! came from thee.

* * * * whose brazen countenance, like mine,
Scorns in the polish of a blush to shine, 300
Scrupled to vindicate his fallen grace,
Or hint he acted right—till out of place.
Why will the lovers of the truth deplore
That miracles and wonders are no more?
Why will the deists, impudently free,
Assert what cannot now, could never be?
Why will religion suffer the reproach,
Since * * * * dresses well and keeps a coach?
Bristol and * * * * have bestowed their pence,
And * * * after * * * echoed sense. 310
Since * * * * once by providence, or chance,
Tumbled his lengthening quavers in a dance :
Since Catcott seemed to reason, and display
The meaning of the words he meant to say :
Since Warburton, his native pride forgot,
Bowed to the garment of the ruling Scot ;
And offered * * * * ghost (a welcome gift)
And hoped, in gratitude, to have a lift ;
An universal primacy, at least,
A fit reward for such a stirring priest : 320
Since Horne imprudently displayed his zeal,
And made his foe the powerful reasons feel :
Since * * * has meaning in his last discourse :
Since * * * * borrowed honesty by force,
And trembled at the measures of the friend
His infant conscience shuddered to defend :
Since * * * in his race of vice outrun,
Scrupled to do what * * * * since hath done.
Hail, inspiration ! Catcott learns to preach,
And classic Lee attempts by thee to teach ; 330
By inspiration North directs his tools,
And [Bute] above by inspiration rules,

Distils the thistle of the gartered crew,
And drains the sacred reservoirs of Kew.
Inspired with hopes of rising in the kirk,
Here * * * * whines his Sunday's journey-work;
Soft * * * * undeniably a saint,
Whimpers in accent so extremely faint,
You see the substance of his empty prayer,
His nothing to the purpose in his air; 340
His sermons have no arguments, 'tis true,
Would you have sense and pretty figures too?
With what a swimming elegance and ease
He scatters out distorted similes!
It matters not how wretchedly applied,
Saints are permitted to set sense aside.
This oratorial novelty in town
Dies into fame, and ogles to renown;
The dowdy damsels of his chosen tribe
Are fee'd to heaven, his person is the bribe; 350
All who can superficial talk admire,
His vanity, not beauty, sets on fire:
Enough of * * * * let him ogle still,
Convince with nonsense, and with foppery kill,
Pray for the secret measures of the great,
And hope the Lord will regulate the state:
Florid as Klopstock, and as quick as me
At double epithet or simile;
His despicable talents cannot harm
Those who defy a Johnson's *False Alarm*. 360
Hail, inspiration! piously I kneel,
And call upon thy sacred name with zeal;
Come, spread thy sooty pinions o'er my pen,
Teach me the secrets of the lords of men;
In visionary prospects let me see
How [Bute] employs his sense, derived from thee;
Display the mystic sibyl of the isle,
And dress her wrinkled features in a smile;

Of past and secret measures let me tell,
How [Grafton] pilfered power, and Chatham fell: 370
Chatham, whose patriotic actions wear
One single brand of infamy—the peer;
Whose popularity again thinks fit
To loose the coronet, revive the Pitt;
And in the upper house (where leading peers
Practise a minuet step, or scratch their ears)
He warmly undertakes to plead the cause
Of injured liberty, and broken laws.
Hail, inspiration! from whose fountain flow
The strains which circulate through all the Row, 380
With humblest reverence thy aid I ask,
For this laborious and herculean task.
How difficult to make a piece go down
With booksellers, reviewers, and the town;
None with a Christian, charitable love,
A kind and fixed intention to approve,
The wild excursions of the muse will read.
Alas! I was not born beyond the Tweed!
To public favour I have no pretence,
If public favour is the child of sense: 390
To paraphrase on Home in Armstrong's rhymes,
To decorate Fingal in sounding chimes,
The self-sufficient muse was never known,
But shines in trifling dulness all her own.
Where, rich with painted bricks and lifeless white,
Four dirty alleys in a cross unite,
Where avaricious sons of commerce meet
To do their public business in the street;
There stands a dome to dulness ever dear,
Where * * * * models justice by the square; 400
Where bulky aldermen display their sense,
And Bristol patriots wager out their pence:
Here, in the malice of my stars confined,
I call the muses to divert my mind;

KEW GARDENS

Come, inspiration ! mysticly instil
The spirit of a [Junius] in my quill,
An equal terror to the small and great,
To lash an alderman or knave of state.

  Here * * * thundering through the spacious court,
Grounds equity on Jeffries's report ; 410
And oft, explaining to the lords of trade,
Proves himself right by statutes never made ;
In * * * * able politicians see
Another * * * * in epitome.
If good Sir * * * * did not bawl so loud,
What has he else superior to the crowd ?
His peruke boasts solemnity of law :
E'en there might counsellors detect a flaw.
But Providence is just, as doctors tell,
That triple mystery's a good sentinel ; 420
Was * * * * not so noisy, and more wise,
The body corporate would close its eyes.
Useless the satire, stoically wise,
Bristol can literary rubs despise ;
You'll wonder whence the wisdom may proceed,
'Tis doubtful if her aldermen can read ;
This as a certainty the muse may tell,
None of her common-councilmen can spell :
Why, busy * * * * wilt thou trouble * * *
Their worships hear, and understand like thee. 430

  Few beings absolutely boast the man,
Few have the understanding of a Spanne ;
Every idea of a city mind
Is to commercial incidents confined :
True ! some exceptions to this general rule
Can show the merchant blended with the fool.
* * * * with magisterial air commits ;
* * * * presides the chief of city wits ;

In jigs and country-dances * * * * shines,
And * * * * slumbers over Mallet's lines: 440
His ample visage, oft on nothing bent,
Sleeps in vacuity of sentiment.
When in the venerable gothic hall,
Where fetters rattle, evidences bawl,
Puzzled in thought by equity or law,
Into their inner room his senses draw;
There, as they snore in consultation deep,
The foolish vulgar deem him fast asleep.
    If silent * * * * senatorial pride
Rose into being as his avarice died, 450
Scattering his hundreds, rattling in his coach,
What mortal wonders at the fair * * * *
Though royal horners burn in powdered flames,
When fell the pretty nymph of many names?
Still we behold her fiery virtue stand,
As firm as * * * * regulating band.
* * * * within whose sacerdotal face,
Add all the honorary signs of grace;
Great in his accent, greater in his size,
But mightier still in turtle and mince-pies: 460
Whose entertaining flows of eloquence,
In spite of affectation, will be sense.
Why, patriotic [Johnson], art thou still?
What pensioned lethargy has seized thy quill?
Hast thou forgot the murmurs of applause
Which buzzed about the leader of the cause;
When, dressed in metaphors, the fluent [Creech]
Rose from his chair, and slumbering drawled his
    speech?
When * * * * fired with loyalty and place,
Forsook his breeding to defend his grace! 470
And saving * * * * from a furious blow,
  sisted on his plan, a double row?

KEW GARDENS

Rise * * * * bid remonstrance tell the throne,
When freedom suffers, London's not alone:
Take off the load of infamy and shame
Which lies on Bristol's despicable name;
Revive thy ardour for thy country's cause,
And live again in honour and applause.
Alas! the patriot listens to his whore,
And popularity is heard no more;   480
The dying voice of liberty's forgot,
No more he drinks damnation to the Scot.
* * * * no longer in his quarrel fights;
No further dulness witty * * * * writes:
In organs and an organist renowned,
He rises into notice by a sound,
Commemorates his spirit in a tone,
By * * * * created, rival of a groan:
O be his taste immortal as the lays!
For * * * invents and tuneful [Broderip] plays;   490
And this harmonious jangling of the spheres,
To give the whole connection, Bristol hears.

Hail, Kew! thy more important powers I sing,
Powers which direct the conscience of a king;
The English number daringly would soar
To thy first power, [the Babylonish whore.]
Come, Newton, and assist me to explain
The hidden meanings of the present reign.
Newton, accept the tribute of a line
From one whose humble genius honours thine;   500
Mysterious shall the mazy numbers seem,
To give thee matter for a future dream;
Thy happy talent, meanings to untie,
My vacancy of meaning may supply;
And where the muse is witty in a dash,
Thy explanations may enforce the lash.

How shall the line, grown servile in respect
To North or Sandwich infamy direct?
Unless a wise ellipsis intervene,
How shall I satirise the sleepy dean? 510
Perhaps the muse might fortunately strike
A highly finished picture, very like;
But deans are all so lazy, dull, and fat,
None could be certain worthy Barton sat.
Come then, my Newton, leave the musty lines
Where revelation's farthing candle shines;
In search of hidden truths let others go—
Be thou the fiddler to my puppet-show:
What are these hidden truths but secret lies,
Which from diseased imaginations rise? 520
What if our politicians should succeed
In fixing up the ministerial creed,
Who could such golden arguments refuse,
Which melts and proselytes the hardened Jews?
When universal reformation bribes
With words and wealthy metaphors, the tribes.
To empty pews the brawny chaplain swears,
Whilst none but trembling superstition hears.
When ministers, with sacerdotal hands,
Baptize the flock in streams of golden sands, 530
Through every town conversion wings her way,
And conscience is a prostitute for pay.

 Faith removes mountains; like a modern dean.
Faith can see virtues which were never seen:
Our pious ministry this sentence quote,
To prove their instrument's superior vote;
Whilst Luttrell, happy in his lordship's voice,
Bids faith persuade us 'tis the people's choice.
This mountain of objections to remove,
This knotty, rotten argument to prove, 540

Faith insufficient, Newton caught the pen,
And proved by demonstration, one was ten:
What boots it if he reasoned right or no?
'Twas orthodox—the thane would have it so.
Whoe'er shall doubts and false conclusions draw
Against the inquisition of the law,
With gaolers, chains, and pillories must plead,
And Mansfield's conscience settle right his creed.
'Is Mansfield's conscience then', will freedom cry,
'A standard-block to dress our notions by?   550
Why, what a blunder has the fool let fall!
That Mansfield has no conscience, none at all!'
Pardon me, freedom, this and something more
The knowing writer might have known before;
But, bred in Bristol's mercenary cell,
Compelled in scenes of avarice to dwell,
What generous passion can my dross refine?
What besides interest can direct the line?
And should a galling truth, like this, be told
By me, instructed here to slave for gold,   560
My prudent neighbours (who can read) would see
Another Savage to be starved in me.
Faith is a powerful virtue everywhere;
By this once Bristol dressed, for Cato, Clare;
But now the blockheads grumble, Nugent's made
Lord of this idol, being lord of trade.
They bawled for Clare, when little in their eyes,
But cannot to the titled villain rise:
This state-credulity, a bait for fools,
Employs his lordship's literary tools;   570
Murphy, a bishop of the chosen sect,
A ruling pastor of the Lord's elect,
Keeps journals, posts, and magazines in awe,
And parcels out his daily statute-law.

Would you the bard's veracity dispute?
He borrows persecution's scourge of Bute,
An excommunication-satire writes,
And the slow mischief trifles till it bites.
This faith, the subject of a late divine,
Is not as unsubstantial as his line ;   580
Though, blind and dubious to behold the right,
Its optics mourn a fixed Egyptian night,
Yet things unseen are seen so very clear,
She knew fresh muster would begin the year ;
She knows that North, by Bute and conscience led,
Will hold his honours till his favour's dead,
She knows that Martin, ere he can be great,
Must practise at the target of the state :
If then his erring pistol should not kill,
Why Martin must remain a traitor still.   590
His gracious mistress, generous to the brave,
Will not neglect the necessary knave ;
Since pious Chudleigh is become his grace,
Martin turns pimp, to occupy her place.
Say, Rigby, in the honours of the door,
How properly a rogue succeeds a whore !
She knows (the subject almost slipt my quill
Lost in that pistol of a woman's will)—
She knows that Bute will exercise his rod,
The worthiest of the worthy sons of God.   600

'Ah !' (exclaims Catcott) 'this is saying much ;
The Scripture tells us peace-makers are such '.
Who can dispute this title?   Who deny
What taxes and oppressions testify ?
Who of the thane's beatitude can doubt?
Oh ! was but North as sure of being out !
And (as I end whatever I begin)
Was Chatham but as sure of being in !

Bute, foster-child of fate, dear to a dame
Whom satire freely would, but dare not, name— 610
(Ye plodding barristers, who hunt a flaw,
What treason would you from the sentence draw?
Tremble, and stand attentive as a dean,
Know, Royal Favour is the dame I mean.
To sport with royalty my muse forbears,
And kindly takes compassion on my ears.
When once Shibbeare in glorious triumph stood
Upon a rostrum of distinguished wood,
Who then withheld his guinea or his praise,
Or envied him his crown of English bays? 620
But now Modestus, truant to the cause,
Assists the pioneers who sap the laws,
Wreaths infamy around a sinking pen,
Who could withhold the pillory again?)—
Bute, lifted into notice by the eyes
Of one whose optics always setting rise—
Forgive a pun, ye rationals, forgive
A flighty youth, as yet unlearnt to live;
When I have conned each sage's musty rule,
I may with greater reason play the fool; 630
Burgum and I, in ancient lore untaught,
Are always with our natures in a fault;
Though Camplin would instruct us in the part,
Our stubborn morals will not err by art.
Having in various starts from order strayed,
We'll call imagination to our aid—
See Bute astride upon a wrinkled hag,
His hand replenished with an opened bag,
Whence fly the ghosts of taxes and supplies,
The sales of places, and the last excise! 640
Upon the ground, in seemly order laid,
The Stuarts stretch the majesty of plaid;

Rich with poor dependence bow the head,
And saw their hopes arising from the dead.
His countrymen were mustered into place,
And a Scotch piper rose above his grace.
But say, astrologers, could this be strange?
The lord of the ascendant ruled the change;
And music, whether bagpipes, fiddles, drums,
All that has sense or meaning overcomes.   650
See now this universal favourite Scot,
His former native poverty forgot,
The highest member of the car of state,
Where well he plays at blindman's buff with fate;
If fortune condescends to bless his play,
And drop a rich Havannah in his way,
He keeps it, with intention to release
All conquests at the general day of peace:
When first and foremost to divide the spoil,
Some millions down might satisfy his toil;   660
To guide the car of war he fancied not,
Where honour and no money could be got.
The Scots have tender honours to a man:
Honour's the tie that bundles up the clan:
They want one requisite to be divine,
One requisite in which all others shine,
They're very poor; then who can blame the hand
Which polishes by wealth its native land?
And to complete the worth possessed before,
Gives every Scotchman one perfection more;   670
Nobly bestows the infamy of place,
And Campbell struts about in doubled lace?
Who says Bute bartered peace, and wisely sold
His king, his unioned countrymen, for gold?
When ministerial hirelings proofs deny,
If Musgrave could not prove it, how can I?
No facts unwarranted shall soil my quill,
Suffice it there's a strong suspicion still.

When Bute his iron rod of favour shook,
And bore his haughty temper in his look ;   680
Not yet contented with his boundless sway,
Which all perforce must outwardly obey,
He thought to throw his chain upon the mind ;
Nor would he leave conjecture unconfined.
We saw his measures wrong, and yet, in spite
Of reason, we must think those measures right ;
Whilst curbed and checked by his imperious reign,
We must be satisfied, and not complain.
Complaints are libels, as the present age
Are all instructed by a law-wise sage,   690
Who, happy in his eloquence and fees,
Advances to preferment by degrees :
Trembles to think of such a daring step
As from a tool to Chancellor to leap ;
But, lest his prudence should the law disgrace,
He keeps a longing eye upon the mace.
Whilst Bute was suffered to pursue his plan,
And ruin freedom as he raised the clan ;
Could not his pride, his universal pride,
With working undisturbed be satisfied?   700
But when we saw the villany and fraud,
What conscience but a Scotchman's could applaud?
But yet 'twas nothing—cheating in our sight,
We should have hummed ourselves, and thought him right !
This faith, established by the mighty thane,
Will long outlive the system of the Dane ;
This faith—but now the number must be brief,
All human things are centred in belief ;
And (or the philosophic sages dream)
All our most true ideas only seem :   710
Faith is a glass to rectify our sight,
And teach us to distinguish wrong from right.

By this corrected, Bute appears a Pitt,
And candour marks the lines which Murphy writ;
Then let this faith support our ruined cause,
And give us back our liberties and laws :
No more complain of favourites made by lust,
No more think Chatham's patriot reasons just,
But let the Babylonish harlot see
We to her Baal bow the humble knee.   720
Lost in the praises of that favourite Scot,
My better theme, my Newton, was forgot :
Blessed with a pregnant wit, and never known
To boast of one impertinence his own,
He warped his vanity to serve his God,
And in the paths of pious fathers trod.
Though genius might have started something new,
He honoured lawn, and proved his scripture true ;
No literary work presumed upon,
He wrote, the understrapper of St John ;   730
Unravelled every mystic simile,
Rich in the faith, and fanciful as me ;
Pulled revelation's secret robes aside,
And saw what priestish modesty would hide.
Then seized the pen, and, with a good intent,
Discovered hidden meanings never meant.
The reader who, in carnal notions bred,
Has Athanasius without reverence read,
Will make a scurvy kind of lenten feast
Upon the tortured offals of The Beast :   740
But if, in happy superstition taught,
He never once presumed to doubt in thought ;
Like Catcott, lost in prejudice and pride,
He takes the literal meaning for his guide ;
Let him read Newton, and his bill of fare :
What prophecies unprophesied are there !
In explanations he's so justly skilled,
The pseudo-prophet's mysteries are fulfilled ;

No superficial reasons have disgraced
The worthy prelate's sacerdotal taste ;   750
No flimsy arguments he holds to view,
Like Camplin, he affirms it, and 'tis true.
Faith, Newton, is the tottering churchman's crutch,
On which our blest religion builds so much ;
Thy fame would feel the loss of this support,
As much as Sawney's instruments at court ;
For secret services without a name,
And mysteries in religion, are the same.
But to return to state, from whence the muse
In wild digression smaller themes pursues ;   760
And rambling from his grace's magic rod,
Descends to lash the ministers of God.
Both are adventures perilous and hard,
And often bring destruction on the bard ;
For priests, and hireling ministers of state,
Are priests in love, infernals in their hate :
The church, no theme for satire, scorns the lash,
And will not suffer scandal in a dash :
Not Bute so tender in his spotless fame,
Not Bute so careful of his lady's name.   770

Has sable lost its virtue ?   Will the bell
No longer scare a straying sprite to hell?
Since souls, when animating flesh, are sold
For benefices, bishoprics, and gold ;
Since mitres, nightly laid upon the breast,
Can charm the nightmare conscience into rest,
And learned exorcists very lately made
Greater improvements in the living trade ;
Since Warburton (of whom in future rhymes)
Has settled reformation on the times ;   780
Whilst from the teeming press his numbers fly,
And, like his reasons, just exist and die ;

Since, in the steps of clerical degree,
All through the telescope of fancy see;
(Though fancy under reason's lash may fall,
Yet fancy in religion's all in all):
Amongst these cassocked worthies, is there one
Who has the conscience to be freedom's son?
Horne, patriotic Horne, will join the cause,
And tread on mitres to procure applause.   790
Prepare thy book and sacerdotal dress
To lay a walking spirit of the press,
Who knocks at midnight at his lordship's door,
And roars in hollow voice—' A hundred more!'
' A hundred more!' his rising greatness cries,
Astonishment and terror in his eyes;
' A hundred more! by God, I won't comply!'
' Give', quoth the voice, ' I'll raise a hue and cry;
On a wrong scent the leading beagle's gone,
Your interrupted measures may go on;   800
Grant what I ask, I'll witness to the thane,
I'm not another Fanny of Cock Lane'.
' Enough', says Mungo, ' re-assume the quill;
And what we can afford to give, we will'.

When Bute, the ministry and people's head,
With royal favour pensioned Johnson dead;
His works, in undeserved oblivion sunk,
Were read no longer, and the man was drunk.
Some blockhead, ever envious of his fame,
Massacred Shakespeare in the doctor's name: 810
The public saw the cheat, and wondered not—
Death is of all mortality the lot.
Kenrick has wrote his elegy, and penned
A piece of decent praise for such a friend;
And universal cat-calls testified
How mourned the critics when the genius died.

But now, though strange the fact to deists seem,
His ghost is risen in a vernal theme,
And emulation maddened all the Row
To catch the strains which from a spectre flow, 820
And print the reasons of a bard deceased,
Who once gave all the town a weekly feast.
As beer, to every drinking purpose dead,
Is to a wondrous metamorphose led,
And opened to the actions of the winds,
In vinegar a resurrection finds ;
His genius dead, and decently interred,
The clamorous noise of duns sonorous heard,
Soured into life, assumed the heavy pen,
And saw existence for an hour again ; 830
Scattered his thoughts spontaneous from his brain,
And proved we had no reason to complain ;
Whilst from his fancy figures budded out,
As hair on humid carcases will sprout.
Horne ! set this restless shallow spirit still,
And from his venal fingers snatch the quill.
If, in defiance of the priestly word,
He still will scribble floridly absurd,
North is superior in a potent charm
To lay the terrors of a *False Alarm* : 840
Another hundred added to his five,
No longer is the stumbling-block alive ;
Fixed in his chair, contented and at home,
The busy 'Rambler' will no longer roam.
Released from servitude (such 'tis to think)
He'll prove it perfect happiness to drink :
Once (let the lovers of *Irene* weep)
He thought it perfect happiness to sleep.
Irene, wondrous composition, came,
To give the audience rest, the author fame ; 850

A snore was much more grateful than a clap,
And pit, box, gallery, proved it in a nap.
Hail Johnson ! chief of bards, thy rigid laws
Bestowed due praise, and critics snored applause.

If from the humblest station, in a place
By writers fixed eternal in disgrace,
Long in the literary world unknown
To all but scribbling blockheads of its own ;
Then only introduced, unhappy fate !
The subject of a satire's little hate ;   860
Whilst equally the butt of ridicule,
The town was dirty, and the bard a fool :
If from this place, where catamites are found
To swarm like Scots on honorary ground,
I may presume to exercise the pen,
And write a greeting to the best of men :
Health to the ruling minister I send,
Nor has that minister a better friend.
Greater, perhaps, in titles, pensions, place,
He inconsiderately prefers his grace.   870
Ah, North ! a humble bard is better far,
Friendship was never found near Grafton's star ;
Bishops are not by office orthodox :
Who'd wear a title, when they've titled Fox ?
Nor does the honorary shame stop here,
Have we not Weymouth, Barrington, and Clare ?
If noble murders, as in tale we're told,
Made heroes of the ministers of old,
In noble murders Barrington's divine,
His merit claims the laureated line.   880
Let officers of train-bands wisely try
To save the blood of citizens, and fly
When some bold urchin beats his drum in sport,
Or tragic trumpets entertain the court ;

KEW GARDENS

The captain flies through every lane in town,
And safe from danger wears his civic crown:
Our noble secretary scorned to run,
But with his magic word discharged the gun.
I leave him to the comforts of his breast,
And midnight ghosts, to howl him into rest. 890
Health to the minister, of [Bute] the tool,
Who with the little vulgar seems to rule.
But since the wiser maxims of the age
Mark for a noddy Ptolemy the sage;
Since Newton and Copernicus have taught
Our blundering senses ever are in fault;
The wise look further, and the wise can see
The hands of Sawney actuating thee;
The clock-work of thy conscience turns about,
Just as his mandates wind thee in and out. 900
By this political machine, my rhymes
Conceive an estimation of the times;
And, as the wheels of state in measures move,
See how time passes in the world above:
Whilst tottering on the slippery edge of doubt,
Sir Fletcher sees his train-bands flying out:
Thinks the minority, acquiring state,
Will undergo a change, and soon be great.
North issues out his hundreds to the crew,
Who catch the atoms of the golden dew; 910
The etiquette of wise Sir Robert takes,
The doubtful stand resolved, and one forsakes;
He shackles every vote in golden chains,
And Johnson in his list of slaves maintains.
Rest, Johnson, hapless spirit, rest and drink,
No more defile thy claret glass with ink:
In quiet sleep repose thy heavy head,
[Kenrick] disdains to piss upon the dead:

Administration will defend thy fame,
And pensions add importance to thy name. 920
When sovereign judgment owns thy works divine,
And every writer of reviews is thine,
Let busy Kenrick vent his little spleen,
And spit his venom in a magazine.
Health to the minister ! nor will I dare
To pour out flattery in his noble ear ;
His virtue, stoically great, disdains
Smooth adulation's entertaining strains,
And, red with virgin modesty, withdraws
From wondering crowds and murmurs of applause. 930
Here let no disappointed rhymer say,
Because his virtue shuns the glare of day,
And, like the conscience of a Bristol dean,
Is never by the subtlest optic seen,
That virtue is with North a priestish jest,
By which a mere nonentity's expressed.
No, North is strictly virtuous, pious, wise,
As every pensioned Johnson testifies.
But, reader, I had rather you should see
His virtues from another than from me : 940
Bear witness, Bristol, nobly prove that I
By thee or North was never paid to lie.
Health to the minister ! his vices known,
(As every lord has vices of his own,
And all who wear a title think to shine
In forming follies foreign to his line ;)
His vices shall employ my ablest pen,
And mark him out a miracle of men.
Then let the muse the healing strain begin, 950
And stamp repentance upon every sin.
Why this recoil ?—And will the dauntless muse
To lash a minister of state refuse ?
What ! is his soul so black, thou canst not find
Aught like a human virtue in his mind ?

Then draw him so, and to the public tell
Who owns this representative of hell:
Administration lifts her iron chain,
And truth must abdicate her lawful reign.

  Oh, Prudence! if, by friends or counsel swayed,
I had thy saving institutes obeyed,   960
And, lost to every love but love of self,
A wretch like Harris, living but in pelf;
Then, happy in a coach or turtle-feast,
I might have been an alderman at least.
Sage are the arguments by which I'm taught
To curb the wild excursive flights of thought:
Let Harris wear his self-sufficient air,
Nor dare remark, for Harris is a mayor;
If Catcott's flimsy system can't be proved,
Let it alone, for Catcott's much beloved;   970
If Burgum bought a Bacon for a Strange,
The man has credit, and is great on 'change;
If Camplin ungrammatically spoke,
'Tis dangerous on such men to break a joke;
If you from satire could withhold the line,
At every public hall perhaps you'd dine.
'I must confess,' exclaims a prudent sage,
'You're really something clever for your age:
Your lines have sentiment, and now and then
A dash of satire stumbles from your pen: 980
But ah! that satire is a dangerous thing,
And often wounds the writer with its sting;
Your infant muse should sport with other toys,
Men will not bear the ridicule of boys.
Some of the aldermen, (for some, indeed,
For want of education cannot read;
And those who can, when they aloud rehearse
What Collins, happy genius! 'titles verse,

So spin the strains sonorous through the nose,
The hearer cannot call it verse or prose,)   990
Some of the aldermen may take offence
At your maintaining them devoid of sense ;
And if you touch their aldermanic pride,
Bid dark reflection tell how Savage died !
Go to * * * * and copy worthy * * * *'
Ah ! what a sharp experienced genius that :
Well he prepares his bottle and his jest,
An alderman is no unwelcome guest ;
Adulterate talents and adulterate wine
May make another drawling rascal shine ;   1000
His known integrity outvies a court,
His the dull tale, original the port :
Whilst loud he entertains the sleepy cits,
And rates his wine according to his wits,
Should a trite pun by happy error please,
His worship thunders at the laughing Mease ;
And * * * inserts this item in his bill,
Five shillings for a jest with every gill.
How commendable this, to turn at once
To good account the vintner and the dunce,   1010
And, by a very hocus-pocus hit,
Dispose of damaged claret and bad wit,
Search through the ragged tribe who drink small beer,
And sweetly echo in his worship's ear,—
' What are the wages of the tuneful nine,
What are their pleasures when compared to mine?
Happy I eat, and tell my numerous pence,
Free from the servitude of rhyme or sense :
The sing-song Whitehead ushers in the year
With joy to Briton's king and sovereign dear,   1020
And, in compliance to an ancient mode,
Measures his syllables into an ode ;

Yet such the sorry merit of his muse,
He bows to deans and licks his lordship's shoes.
Then leave the wicked, barren way of rhyme,
Fly far from poverty—be wise in time—
Regard the office more—Parnassus less—
Put your religion in a decent dress;
Then may your interest in the town advance,
Above the reach of muses or romance. 1030
Besides, the town (a sober, honest town,
Which smiles on virtue, and gives vice a frown)
Bids censure brand with infamy your name,
I, even I, must think you are to blame.
Is there a street within this spacious place
That boasts the happiness of one fair face,
Where conversation does not turn on you,
Blaming your wild amours, your morals too?
Oaths, sacred and tremendous oaths you swear,
Oaths that might shock a Luttrell's soul to hear; 1040
These very oaths, as if a thing of joke,
Made to betray, intended to be broke;
Whilst the too tender and believing maid,
(Remember pretty Fanny) is betrayed;
Then your religion—ah, beware! beware!
Although a deist is no monster here,
Yet hide your tenets—priests are powerful foes,
And priesthood fetters justice by the nose:
Think not the merit of a jingling song
Can countenance the author's acting wrong; 1050
Reform your manners, and with solemn air
Hear Catcott bray, and Robins squeak in prayer:
Robins, a reverend, cully-mully puff,
Who thinks all sermons, but his own, are stuff;
When harping on the dull, unmeaning text,
By disquisitions he's so sore perplexed,

He stammers, instantaneously is drawn
A bordered piece of inspiration-lawn,
Which being thrice unto his nose applied,
Into his pineal gland the vapours glide ;   1060
And now we hear the jingling doctor roar
On subjects he dissected thrice before.
Honour the scarlet robe, and let the quill
Be silent when old Isaac eats his fill.
Regard thy interest, ever love thyself,
Rise into notice as you rise in pelf ;
The muses have no credit here, and fame
Confines itself to the mercantile name.
Then clip imagination's wing, be wise,
And, great in wealth, to real greatness rise.   1070
Or if you must persist to sing and dream,
Let only panegyric be your theme ;
With pulpit adulation tickle Cutts,
And wreathe with ivy Garden's tavern-butts ;
Find sentiment in Dampier's empty look,
Genius in Collins, harmony in Rooke ;
Swear Broderip's horrid noise the tuneful spheres,
And rescue Pindar from the songs of Shears.
Would you still further raise the fairy ground,
Praise Broughton,—for his eloquence profound,   1080
His generosity, his sentiment,
His active fancy, and his thoughts on Lent :
Make North a Chatham, canonise his grace,
And beg a pension, or procure a place'.

  Damned narrow notions ! notions which disgrace
The boasted reason of the human race :
Bristol may keep her prudent maxims still,
I scorn her prudence, and I ever will :
Since all my vices magnified are here,
She cannot paint me worse than I appear ;   1090

When raving in the lunacy of ink,
I catch my pen, and publish what I think.

[The poem was afterwards made to end as follows.]

Damned narrow notions! tending to disgrace
The boasted reason of the human race.
Bristol may keep her prudent maxims still,
But know, my saving friends, I never will.
The composition of my soul is made
Too great for servile, avaricious trade;
When raving in the lunacy of ink,
I catch the pen, and publish what I think.   1100
North is a creature, and the king's misled;
Mansfield and Norton came as justice fled;
Few of our ministers are over wise:—
Old Harpagon's a cheat, and Taylor lies.
When cooler judgment actuates my brain,
My cooler judgment still approves the strain;
And if a horrid picture greets your view,
Where it continues still, if copied true.
Though in the double infamy of lawn
The future bishopric of Barton's drawn,   1110
Protect me, fair ones, if I durst engage
To serve ye in this catamitish age,
To exercise a passion banished hence,
And summon satire into your defence.
Woman, of every happiness the best,
Is all my heaven,—religion is a jest.
Nor shall the muse in any future book
With awe upon the chains of favour look:
North shall in all his vices be displayed,
And Warburton in lively pride arrayed;   1120
Sandwich shall undergo the healing lash,
And read his character without a dash;

Mansfield, surrounded by his dogs of law,
Shall see his picture drawn in every flaw;
Luttrell (if satire can descend so low)
Shall all his native little vices show;
And Grafton, though prudentially resigned,
Shall view a striking copy of his mind;
Whilst iron justice, lifting up her scales,
Shall weigh the Princess Dowager of Wales. 1130

THE WHORE OF BABYLON

The lines of this poem, somewhat differently arranged, are contained in the above, and are not reprinted. The satire refers to the Princess Dowager of Wales. See also "Kew Gardens", and "Resignation".

THE PROPHECY

'When times are at the worst they will certainly mend'.

THIS truth of old was sorrow's friend,
'Times at the worst will surely mend'.
The difficulty's then, to know
How long oppression's clock can go;
When Britain's sons may cease to sigh,
And hope that their redemption's nigh.

When vice exalted takes the lead,
And vengeance hangs but by a thread;
Gay peeresses turned out o' doors;
Whoremasters peers, and sons of whores; 10
Look up, ye Britons! cease to sigh,
For your redemption draweth nigh.

THE PROPHECY

When vile corruption's brazen face
At council-board shall take her place;
And lords and commoners resort
To welcome her at Britain's court:
Look up, ye Britons! cease to sigh,
For your redemption draweth nigh.

See pension's harbour, large and clear,
Defended by St Stephen's pier!
The entrance safe, by current led,
Tiding round G[rafton's] jetty-head;
Look up, ye Britons! cease to sigh,
For your redemption draweth nigh.

When civil-power shall snore at ease,
While soldiers fire—to keep the peace;
When murders sanctuary find,
And petticoats can justice blind;
Look up, ye Britons! cease to sigh,
For your redemption draweth nigh.

Commerce o'er bondage will prevail,
Free as the wind that fills her sail;
When she complains of vile restraint,
And power is deaf to her complaint;
Look up, ye Britons! cease to sigh,
For your redemption draweth nigh.

When raw projectors shall begin
Oppression's hedge, to keep her in;
She in disdain will take her flight,
And bid the Gotham fools good-night.
Look up, ye Britons! cease to sigh,
For your redemption draweth nigh.

When tax is laid, to save debate,
By prudent ministers of state;

And what the people did not give
Is levied by prerogative ;
Look up, ye Britons ! cease to sigh,
For your redemption draweth nigh.

When popish bishops dare to claim
Authority, in George's name ; 50
By treason's hand set up, in spite
Of George's title, William's right ;
Look up, ye Britons ! cease to sigh,
For your redemption draweth nigh.

When popish priest a pension draws
From starved exchequer, for the cause ;
Commissioned proselytes to make
In British realms, for Britain's sake ;
Look up, ye Britons ! cease to sigh,
For your redemption draweth nigh. 60

When snug in power, sly recusants
Make laws for British protestants ;
And damning William's revolution
As justices, claim execution ;
Look up, ye Britons ! cease to sigh,
For your redemption draweth nigh.

When soldiers, paid for our defence,
In wanton pride slay innocence ;
Blood from the ground for vengeance reeks,
Till Heaven the inquisition makes ; 70
Look up, ye Britons ! cease to sigh,
For your redemption draweth nigh.

When at Bute's feet poor freedom lies,
Marked by the priest for sacrifice,
And doomed a victim for the sins
Of half the *outs*, and all the *ins* ;

THE PROPHECY

Look up, ye Britons! cease to sigh,
For your redemption draweth nigh.

When stewards pass a *boot* account,
And credit for the gross amount;
Then, to replace exhausted store,
Mortgage the land to borrow more;
Look up, ye Britons! cease to sigh,
For your redemption draweth nigh.

When scrutineers, for private ends,
Against the vote declare their friends;
Or judge, as you stand there alive,
That five is more than forty-five;
Look up, ye Britons! cease to sigh,
For your redemption draweth nigh.

When George shall condescend to hear
The modest suit, the humble prayer;
A prince, to purpled pride unknown!
No favourites disgrace the throne!
Look up, ye Britons! sigh no more,
For your redemption's at the door.

When time shall bring your wish about,
Or, seven-years lease, *you sold*, is out,
No future contract to fulfil;
Your tenants holding at your will;
Raise up your heads! your right demand!
For your redemption's in your hand.

Then is your time to strike the blow,
And let the *slaves* of mammon know
Briton's true sons a bribe can scorn,
And die as *free* as they were born.
Virtue again shall take her seat,
And your redemption stand complete.

RESIGNATION

Hail, resignation ! hail, ambiguous dame,
Thou Parthian archer in the fight of fame !
When thou hast drawn the mystic veil between,
'Tis the poor minister's concluding scene.
Sheltered beneath thy pinions he withdraws,
And tells us his integrity's the cause.
Sneaking to solitude, he rails at state,
And rather would be virtuous than be great ;
Laments the impotence of those who guide,
And wishes public clamours may subside.   10
But while such rogues as North or Sandwich steer,
Our grievances will never disappear.

Hail, resignation ! 'tis from thee we trace
The various villanies of power and place ;
When rascals, once but infamy and rags,
Rich with a nation's ruin, swell their bags,
Purchase a title and a royal smile,
And pay to be distinguishably vile ;
When big with self-importance thus they shine,
Contented with their gleanings, they resign !   20
When ministers, unable to preside,
The tottering vehicle no longer guide,
The powerful thane prepares to kick his grace
From all his glorious dignities of place ;
But still the honour of the action's thine,
And Grafton's tender conscience can resign.
Lament not, Grafton, that thy hasty fall
Turns out a public happiness to all ;
Still by your emptiness of look appear
The ruins of a man who used to steer ;   30

Still wear that insignificance of face,
Which dignifies you more than power or place.

 Whilst now the constitution tottering stands,
And needs the firm support of able hands,
Your grace stood foremost in the glorious cause
To shake the very basis of our laws ;
But, thanks to Camden and a noble few,
They stemmed oppression's tide, and conquered you.
How can your prudence be completely praised
In flying from the storm yourself had raised? 40
When the black clouds of discord veiled the sky,
'Twas more than prudence in your grace to fly ;
For had the thunders burst upon your head,
Soon had you mingled with the headless dead ;
Not Bute, though here the deputy of fate,
Could save so vile a minister of state.

 Oft has the Carlton sibyl prophesied
How long each minister of state should guide,
And from the dark recesses of her cell,
When Bute was absent, would to Stuart tell 50
The secret fates of senators and peers,
What lord's exalted but to lose his ears,
What future plans the junto have designed,
What wretches are with Rockingham combined,
Who should accept a privy seal or rod,
Who's lord-lieutenant of the land of Nod,
What pensioned nobleman should hold his post,
What poor dependant scored without his host,
What patriot big with popular applause
Should join the ministry and prop the cause ; 60
With many secrets of a like import,
The daily tittle-tattle of a court,
By common fame retailed as office news
In coffee-houses, taverns, cellars, stews.

Oft from her secret casket would she draw
A knotty plan to undermine the law;
But though the council sat upon the scheme,
Time has discovered that 'tis all a dream:
Long had she known the date of Grafton's power,
And in her tablet marked his flying hour; 70
Rumour reports, a message from her cell
Arrived but just three hours before he fell.
Well knew the subtle minister of state
Her knowledge in the mysteries of fate,
And catching every pension he could find,
Obeyed the fatal summons—and resigned!

Far in the north, amidst whose dreary hills
None hear the pleasant murmuring sound of rills,
Where no soft gale in dying raptures blows,
Or aught which bears the look of verdure grows, 80
Save where the north wind cuts the solemn yew,
And russet rushes drink the noxious dew,
(Dank exhalations drawn from stagnant moors,
The morning dress of Caledonia's shores),
Upon a bleak and solitary plain,
Exposed to every storm of wind and rain,
A humble cottage reared its lowly head,
Its roof with matted reeds and rushes spread.
The walls were osiers daubed with slimy clay,
One narrow entrance opened to the day. 90
Here lived a laird, the ruler of his clan,
Whose fame through every northern mountain ran;
Great was his learning, for he long had been
A student at the town of Aberdeen,
Professor of all languages at once;
To him, some reckoned Chappelow a dunce.
With happy fluency he learned to speak
Syriac or Latin, Arabic or Greek.

RESIGNATION

Not any tongue in which Oxonians sing,
When they rejoice or blubber with the king, 100
To him appeared unknown : with sapient look
He taught the highland meaning of each crook.
But often when to pastimes he inclined,
To give some relaxation to his mind,
He laid his books aside, forgot to read,
To hunt wild goslings down the river Tweed,
To chase a starving weasel from her bed,
And wear the spoil triumphant on his head.
'Tis true his rent-roll just maintained his state,
But some, in spite of poverty, are great. 110
Though famine sunk her impress on his face,
Still you might there his haughty temper trace.
Descended from a catalogue of kings
Whose warlike arts Mac Pherson sweetly sings,
He bore the majesty of monarchs past,
Like a tall pine rent with the winter's blast,
Whose spreading trunk and withered branches show
How glorious once the lordly tree might grow.

Of all the warring passions in his breast,
Ambition still presided o'er the rest ; 120
This is the spur which actuates us all,
The visionary height whence thousands fall,
The author's hobby-horse, the soldier's steed
Which aids him in each military deed,
The lady's dresser, looking-glass, and paint,
The warm devotion of the seeming saint.

Sawney, the noble ruler of the clan,
Had numbered o'er the riper years of man ;
Graceful in stature, ravishing his mien,
To make a conquest was but to be seen. 130
Fired by ambition, he resolved to roam
Far from the famine of his native home,

To seek the warmer climate of the south,
And at one banquet feast his eyes and mouth.
In vain the amorous highland lass complained,
The son of monarchs would not be restrained.
Clad in his native many-coloured suit,
Forth struts the walking majesty of Bute.
His spacious sword, to a large wallet strung,
Across his broad capacious shoulders hung.   140
As from the hills the land of promise rose,
A secret transport in his bosom glows ;
A joy prophetic, until then unknown,
Assured him all he viewed would be his own.
New scenes of pleasure recreate his sight,
He views the fertile meadows with delight ;
Still in soliloquy he praised the view,
Nor was more pleased with future scenes at Kew.
His wonder broke in murmurs from his tongue,
No more the praise of highland hills he sung,   150
Till now a stranger to the cheerful green
Where springing flowers diversify the scene.
The lofty elm, the oak of lordly look,
The willow shadowing the bubbling brook,
The hedges, blooming with the sweets of May,
With double pleasure marked his gladsome way.
Having through varying rural prospects past,
He reached the great metropolis at last.
Here fate beheld him as he trudged the street,
Bare was his buttocks and unshod his feet ;   160
A lengthening train of boys displayed him great,
He seemed already minister of state.
The Carlton sibyl saw his graceful mien,
And straight forgot her hopes of being queen.
The little urchin chose a piercing dart
And * * * * gored her heart.

She sighed, she wished ; swift virtuous Chudleigh flew
To bring the Caledonian swain to Kew ;
Then introduced him to her secret cell—
What further can the modest numbers tell ?   170
Suffice it that, among the youth of fire
Whom widows strong and amorous dames admire,

                  [Line omitted]

None could with Sawney's never ceasing heat
None rode the broomstaff with so good a grace,
Or pleased her with such majesty of face.
Enraptured with her incubus, she sought
How to reward his merit as she ought.
Resolved to make him greatest of the great,
She led him to her hidden cave of state.
There spurs and coronets were placed around,   180
And privy seals were scattered on the ground ;
Here piles of honorary truncheons lay,
And gleaming stars made artificial day.
With mystic rods, whose magic power is such
They metamorphose parties with a touch.
Here hung the princely prize of gartered blue,
With flags of all varieties of hue.
'These', said the sibyl, 'from this present hour
Are thine, with every dignity of power.
No statesman shall be titularly great,   190
None shall obtain an office in the state
But such whose principles and manners suit
The virtuous temper of the Earl of Bute.
All shall pursue thy interest, none shall guide
But such as you repute are qualified.
No more on Scotland's melancholy plain
Your starving countrymen shall drink the rain,
But hither hasting on their naked feet,
Procure a place, forget themselves, and eat.

No southern patriot shall oppose my will, 200
If not my look, my treasurer can kill ;
His pistol never fails in time of need,
And who dares contradict my power shall bleed.
A future Barrington will also rise
With blood and death to entertain my eyes.
But this forestalls futurity and fate,
I'll choose the present hour to make thee great'.
He bowed submission, and with eager view
Gazed on the withered oracle of Kew.
She seized a pendant garter, and began 210
To elevate the ruler of the clan ;
Girt round his leg the honoured trifle shone,
And gathered double lustre from the throne.
With native dignity he filled the stall,
The wonder, jest, and enmity of all.
Not yet content with honorary grace,
The sibyl, busy for the sweets of place,
Kicked out a minister, the people's pride,
And lifted Sawney in his place to guide.
The leader of the treasury, he rose, 220
Whilst fate marked down the nation's future woes.
Mad with ambition, his imperious hand
Scattered oppression through a groaning land ;
Still taxes followed taxes, grants, supplies,
With every ill resulting from excise.
Not satisfied with this unjust increase,
He struck a bolder stroke, and sold the peace ;
The Gallic millions so convinced his mind,
On honourable terms the treaty's signed.

But who his private character can blame, 230
Or brand his titles with a villain's name?
Upon an estimation of the gains,
He stooped beneath himself to take the reins.

RESIGNATION

A good economist, he served the crown,
And made his master's interest his own.
His starving friends and countrymen applied
To share the ministry, assist to guide,
Nor asked in vain : his charitable hand
Made plenty smile in Scotland's barren land ;
Her wandering sons, for poverty renowned,   240
Places and pensions, bribes or titles found.
Far from the south was humble merit fled,
And on the northern mountains reared her head ;
And genius, having ranged beyond the Tweed,
Sat brooding upon bards who could not read ;
Whilst courage, boasting of his highland might,
Mentions not Culloden's inglorious flight.
But whilst his lordship fills the honoured stall,
Ample provision satisfies them all.
The genius sings his praise, the soldier swears   250
To mutilate each murmuring caitiff's ears ;
The father of his country they adore,
And live in elegance unknown before.

Nor yet unthankful he for power and place,
He praised the sibyl with distinguished grace.
And oft repairing to [the] cell of hate,
He laid aside the dignity of state.
* * * * the withered hag
Repaid his ardour with a wealthy bag.
Oft, when replenished with superior might,   260
The thane has * three millions in a night.
Or, when the treasury was sunk with spoil,
Three coronets have recompensed his toil ;
And had not virtuous Chudleigh held the door,
She to this moment might have been a whore.
Around this mystic sun of liquid gold
A swarm of planetary statesmen rolled ;

Though some have since as ministers been known,
They shone with borrowed lustre not their own:
In every revolution, day and night,   270
From Bute they caught each particle of light;
He destined out the circles they fulfil,
Hung on the bulky nothing of his will.

How shall I brand with infamy a name
Which bids defiance to all sense of shame?
How shall I touch his iron soul with pain,
Who hears unmoved a multitude complain?
A multitude made wretched by his hand,
The common curse and nuisance of the land.
Holland, of thee I sing—infernal wretch!   280
Say, can thy power of mischief further stretch?
Is there no other army to be sold,
No town to be destroyed for bribes and gold?
Or wilt thou rather sit contented down,
And starve the subject to enrich the crown?
That when the treasury can boast supplies,
Thy pilfering genius may have exercise;
Whilst unaccounted millions pay thy toil,
Thou art secure if Bute divides the spoil;
Catching his influence from the best of kings,   290
Vice broods beneath the shadow of his wings;
The vengeance of a nation is defied,
And liberty and justice set aside.
Distinguished robber of the public, say,
What urged thy timid spirit's hasty way?
Sheltered in the protection of a king,
Did recollection paint the fate of Byng?
Did conscience hold that mirror to thy sight,
Or Aylyffe's ghost accompany thy flight?
Is Bute more powerful than the sceptred hand,   300
Or art thou safer in a foreign land?

RESIGNATION

In vain, the scene relinquished, now you grieve,
Cursing the moment you were forced to leave
The ruins on the Isle of Thanet built,
The fruits of plunder, villany, and guilt.
When you presume on English ground to tread,
Justice will lift her weapon at your head.
Contented with the author of your state,
Maintain the conversation of the great.
Be busy in confederacy and plot, 310
And settle what shall be on what is not;
Display the statesman in some wild design,
Foretell when North will tumble and resign,
How long the busy Sandwich, mad for rule,
Will lose his labour and remain a fool.
But your accounts, the subject of debate,
Are much beneath the notice of the great.
Let bribed exchequer-tellers find 'em just,
Which, on the penalty of place, they must ;
Before they're seen your honesty is clear, 320
And all will evidently right appear.

When as a minister you had your day,
And gathered light from Bute's superior ray,
His striking representative you shone,
And seemed to glimmer in yourself alone ;
The lives of thousands bartered for a bribe,
With villanies too shocking to describe.
Your system of oppression testified
None but the conscientious Fox could guide.
As Bute is fixed eternal in his sphere, 330
And ministers revolved around in air,
Your infamy with such a lasting ray
Glowed through your orb in one continual day.
Still ablest politicians hold dispute,
Whether you gave or borrowed light from Bute.

Lost in the blaze of his superior parts,
We often have descried your little arts.
But at a proper distance from his sphere
We saw the little villain disappear;
When dressed in titles, the burlesque of place, 340
A more illustrious rascal shewed his face;
Your destined sphere of ministry now run,
You dropped like others in the parent sun;
There as a spot you purpose to remain,
And seek protection in the sibyl's swain.
Grafton his planetary life began,
Though foreign to the system of the clan;
Slowly he rolled around the fount of light,
Long was his day, but longer was his night.
Irregular, unequal in his course, 350
Now languid he revolves, now rolls with force;
His scarce-collected light obliquely hurled
Was scattered ere it reached his frozen world.
Through all his under offices of place,
All had conspired to represent his grace;
Lifeless and dull the wheels of state were driven,
Slow as a courtier on his road to heaven.
If expedition urged the dull machine.
He knew so little of the golden mean,
Swift hurry and confusion wild began 360
To discompose the thane's determined plan.
Error, his secretary, lent his aid
To undermine each plot his cunning laid;
He wrote despatches in his grace's name,
And ruined every project North could frame:
Yet as he blundered through the lengthened night,
He seriously protested all was right.

 Since dissipation is thy only joy,
Go, Grafton, join the dance, and act the boy;

RESIGNATION

'Tis not for fops in cabinets to shine,
And justice must confess that title's thine.
Dress to excess, and powder into fame,
In drums and hurricanes exalt your name.
There you may glitter, there your worth may rise
Above the little reach of vulgar eyes.
But in the high departments of the state
Your talents are too trifling to be great;
There all your imperfections rise to view,
Not Sandwich so contemptible as you.
Bute, from the summit of his power, descried
Your glaring inability to guide,
And mustering every rascal in his gang,
Who might for merit altogether hang,
From the black catalogue and worthy crew,
The jesuitical and scheming few,
Selected by the leader of the clan,
Received instructions for their future plan;
And, after proper adoration paid,
Were to their destined sphere of state conveyed,
To shine the minister's satéllites,
Collect his light, and give his lordship ease,
Reform his crooked politics, and draw
A more severe attack upon the law;
Settle his erring revolutions right,
And give in just proportion day and night.

Alas! the force of Scottish pride is such,
These mushrooms of a day presumed too much;
Conscious of cunning and superior arts,
They scorned the minister's too trifling parts;
Grafton resents a treatment so unjust,
And damns the Carlton sibyl's fiery lust,
By which a scoundrel Scot oppressed the realm,
And rogues, below contempt, disgraced the helm.

Swift scandal caught the accents as they fell,
And bore them to the sibyl's secret cell.
Enraged, she winged a messenger to Bute,
Some minister more able to depute;
Her character and virtue was a jest,
Whilst Grafton was of useless power possessed.
This done, her just desire of vengeance warm,   410
She gave him notice of the bursting storm;
Timid and dubious, Grafton faced about,
And trembled at the thoughts of being out;
But as no laws the sibyl's power confined,
He dropped his blushing honours, and resigned!

Step forward, North! and let the doubtful see
Wonders and miracles revived in thee.
Did not the living witness haunt the court,
What ear had given faith to my report?
Amidst the rout of ministerial slaves,   420
Rogues who want genius to refine to knaves,
Who could imagine that the wretch most base
Should fill the highest infamy of place?
That North, the vile domestic of a peer
Whose name an Englishman detests to hear,
Should leave his trivial share of Bedford's gains,
Become a minister, and take the reins;
And from the meanest of the gang ascend
Above his worthy governor and friend?
This wondrous metamorphose of an hour   430
Sufficiently evinced the sibyl's power.
To ruin nations, little rogues to raise,
A virtue supernatural displays;
What but a power infernal or divine
Could honour North, or make his grace resign?

Some superficial politicians tell,
When Grafton from his gilded turret fell,

RESIGNATION

The sibyl substituted North, a blank,
A mustered fagot to complete the rank,
Without a distant thought that such a tool   440
Would change its being and aspire to rule.
But such the humble North's indulgent fate,
When striding in the saddle of the state,
He caught by inspiration statesmanship,
And drove the slow machine and smacked his whip:
Whilst Bedford, wondering at his sudden skill,
With reverence viewed the packhorse of his will.

His majesty (the buttons thrown aside)
Declared his fixed intention to preside.
No longer sacrificed to every knave,   450
He'd show himself discreet as well as brave;
In every cabinet and council-cause
He'd be dictator and enforce the laws;
Whilst North should in his present office stand
As understrapper to direct his hand.

Now, expectation, now extend thy wing!
Happy the land whose minister's a king;
Happy the king, who, ruling each debate,
Can peep through every roguery of state!
See, hope, arrayed in robes of virgin white,   460
Trailing an arched variety of light,
Comes showering blessings on a ruined realm,
And shews the crowned director of the helm!
Return, fair goddess, till some future day,
The king has seen the error of his way,
And by his smarting shoulders seems to feel
The wheel of state is not a Catherine wheel.
Wise by experience, general nurse of fools,
He leaves the ministry to venal tools;
And finds his happy talents better suit   470
The making buttons for his favourite Bute;

In countenancing the unlawful views
Which North, the delegate of Bute, pursues
In glossing with authority a train
Whose names are infamy, and objects gain.

Hail, filial duty ! great, if rightly used,
How little when mistaken and abused !
Viewed from one point, how glorious art thou seen,
From others, how degenerate and mean !
A seraph or an idiot's head we see :   480
Often the latter stands the type of thee,
And, bowing at his parent's knee, is dressed
In a long hood and many-coloured vest.
The sceptred king, who dignifies a throne,
Should be in private life himself alone ;
No friend or mother should his conscience scan,
Or with the nation's head confound the man.
Like juggling Melchizideck's priestish plea,
Collected in himself, a king should be.
But truths may be unwelcome, and the lay,   490
Which shall to royal ears such truths convey,
The conflagrations of the hangman's ire
May roast, and execute with foreign fire.
The muse who values safety shall return,
And sing of subjects where she cannot burn.
Continue, North, thy vile burlesque of power,
And reap the harvest of the present hour ;
Collect, and fill thy coffers with the spoil,
And let thy gatherings recompense thy toil.
Whilst the rogues out revile the rascals in, 500
Repeat the proverb, ' Let those laugh that win ' :
Fleeting and transitory is the date
Of sublunary ministers of state ;
Then whilst thy summer lasts prepare thy hay,
Nor trust to autumn and a future day.

RESIGNATION

I leave thee now, but with intent to trace
The villains and the honest men of place.
The first are still assisting in thy train
To aid the pillage and divide the gain ;
The last, of known integrity of mind,   510
Forsook a venal party, and resigned !
Come, satire ! aid me to display the first,
Of every honest Englishman accursed ;
Come, truth, assist me to prepare the lays,
Where worth demands, and give the latter praise.
Ingenious Sandwich, whither dost thou fly
To shun the censure of the public eye?
Dost thou want matter for another speech,
Or other works of genius to impeach ?
Or would thy insignificance and pride   520
Presume above thyself and seek to guide ?
Pursue thy *ignis-fatuus* of power,
And call to thy assistance virtuous Gower ;
Set Rigby's happy countenance in play
To vindicate whatever you can say.
Then, when you totter into place and fame,
With double infamy you brand your name.

Say, Sandwich, in the winter of your date,
Can you ascend the hobby-horse of state ?
Do titles echo grateful in your ear,   530
Or is it mockery to call you peer ?
In fifty's silvered age to play the fool,
And bide with rascals infamous a tool,
Plainly denote your judgment is no more ;
Your honour was extinguished long before.

Say, if reflection ever blest thy mind,
Hast thou one real friend among mankind ?
Thou hadst one once, free, generous, and sincere,
Too good a senator for such a peer ;

Him thou hadst offered as a sacrifice   540
To lewdness, immorality, and vice ;
Your patronising scoundrels set the gin,
And friendship was the bait to draw him in.
What honourable villain could they find
Of Sandwich's latitudinary mind ?
Though intimacy seemed to stop the way,
You they employed to tempt him and betray.
Full well you executed their commands,
Well you deserved the pension at their hands.
For you, in hours of trifling, he compiled   550
A dissertation blasphemous and wild.
Be it recorded, 'twas at your desire
He called for demons to assist his lyre ;
Relying on your friendship, soon he found
How dangerous the support of rotten ground.
In your infernal attributes arrayed,
You seized the wished-for poem, and betrayed.

Hail, mighty Twitcher ! can my feeble line
Give due reward to merit such as thine ?
Not Churchill's keenest satire ever reached   560
The conscience of the rascal who impeached.
My humble numbers and untutored lay
On such a hardened wretch are thrown away ;
I leave thee to the impotent delight
Of visiting the harlots of the night ;
Go, hear thy nightingale's enchanting strain,
My satire shall not dart a sting in vain.
There you may boast one sense is entertained,
Though age present your other senses pained :
Go, Sandwich, if thy fire of lust compel,   570
Regale at Harrington's religious cell,
With loss of impotence, and dire disease ;
Exert your poor endeavours as you please,

RESIGNATION

The jest and bubble of the harlot crew;
What entertained your youth, in age pursue.

 When Grafton shook oppression's iron rod,
Like Egypt's lice, the instrument of God;
When Camden, driven from his office, saw
The last weak efforts of expiring law;
When Bute, the regulator of the state,   580
Preferred the vicious, to transplant the great;
When rank corruption through all orders ran,
And infamy united Sawney's clan;
When every office was with rogues disgraced,
And the Scotch dialect became the taste,
Could Beaufort with such creatures stay behind?
No, Beaufort was a Briton, and resigned.
Thy resignation, Somerset, shall shine
When time hath buried the recording line,
And, proudly glaring in the rolls of fame,   590
With more than titles decorate thy name.
Amidst the gartered rascals of the age,
Who murder noble parts, the court their stage,
One nobleman of honesty remains,
Who scorns to draw in ministerial chains;
Who honours virtue and his country's peace,
And sees with pity grievances increase;
Who bravely left all sordid views of place,
And lives the honour of the Beaufort race.

 Deep in the secret, Barrington and Gower,   600
Raised upon villany, aspire to power;
Big with importance, they presume to rise
Above a minister they must despise;
Whilst Barrington, as secretary, shows
How many pensions paid his blood and blows.
And Gower, the humbler creature of the two,
Has only future prospects in his view.

But North requires assistance from the great,
To work another button in the state,
That Weymouth may complete the birthday-suit, 610
Full-trimmed by Twitcher, and cut out by Bute :
So many worthy schemers must produce
A statesman's coat of universal use ;
Some system of economy, to save
Another million for another knave ;
Some plan to make a duty, large before,
Additionally great, to grind the poor :
For 'tis a maxim with the guiding wise,
Just as the commons sink, the rich arise.

If ministers and privy-council knaves 620
Would rest contented with their being slaves,
And not with anxious infamy pursue
Those measures which will fetter others too,
The swelling cry of liberty would rest,
Nor Englishmen complain, nor knaves protest.
But courtiers have a littleness of mind,
And, once enslaved, would fetter all mankind.
'Tis to this narrowness of soul we owe
What further ills our liberties shall know ;
'Tis from this principle our feuds began, 630
Fomented by the Scots, ignoble clan :
Strange that such little creatures of a tool,
By lust and not by merit raised to rule,
Should sow contention in a noble land,
And scatter thunders from a venal hand.
Gods ! that these fly-blows of a stallion's day,
Warmed into being by the sibyl's ray,
Should shake the constitution, rights, and laws,
And prosecute the man of freedom's cause !
Whilst Wilkes to every Briton's right appealed, 640
With loss of liberty that right he sealed :

RESIGNATION

Imprisoned and oppressed he persevered,
Nor Sawney or his powerful sibyl feared.
The hag, replete with malice, from above
Shot poison on the screech-owl of her love ;
Unfortunately to his pen it fell,
And flowed in double rancour to her cell ;
Madly she raved ; to ease her tortured mind,
The object of her hatred is confined :
But he, supported by his country's laws,   650
Bid her defiance, for 'twas freedom's cause.
Her treasurer and Talbot fought in vain,
Though each attained his favourite object—gain.
She sat as usual when a project fails,
Damned Chudleigh's phiz, and dined upon her nails.
Unhappy land ! whose governed monarch sees
Through glasses and perspectives such as these ;
When, juggling to deceive his untried sight,
He views the ministry all trammelled right ;
Whilst, to his eye the other glass applied,   660
His subjects' failings are all magnified.
Unheeded the petitions are received,
Nor one report of grievances believed ;
'Tis but the voice of faction in disguise
That blinds with liberty the people's eyes :
'Tis riot and licentiousness pursues
Some disappointed placeman's private [views].
And shall such venal creatures steer the helm,
Waving oppression's banners round the realm ?
Shall Britons to the vile detested troop,   670
Forgetting ancient honour, meanly stoop ?
Shall we our rights and liberties resign,
To lay those jewels at a woman's shrine ?
No : let us still be Britons !. Be it known,
The favours we solicit are our own.

Engage, ye Britons, in the glorious task,
And stronger still enforce the things you ask :
Assert your rights, remonstrate with the throne,
Insist on liberty, and that alone.

Alas ! America, thy ruined cause 680
Displays the ministry's contempt of laws.
Unrepresented thou art taxed, excised,
By creatures much too vile to be despised ;
The outcast of an outed gang are sent
To bless thy commerce with [a] government.
Whilst pity rises to behold thy fate,
We saw thee in this worst of troubles great ;
Whilst anxious for thy wavering dubious cause,
We give thy proper spirit due applause.
If virtuous Grafton's sentimental taste 690
Is in his measures or his mistress placed,
In either 'tis originally rare,
One shews the midnight cully, one the peer :
Review him, Britons, with a proper pride,
Was this a statesman qualified to guide ?
Was this the minister whose mighty hand
Has scattered civil discord through the land ?
Since smallest trifles, when ordained by fate,
Rise into power and counteract the great,
What shall we call thee, Grafton ? Fortune's whip, 700
Or rather the burlesque of statesmanship ?
When, daring in thy insolence of place,
Bold in an empty majesty of face,
We saw thee exercise thy magic rod,
And form a titled villain with a nod ;
Turn out the virtuous, airily advance
The members of the council in a dance,
And honouring Sandwich with a serious [air],
Commend the fancy of his solitaire ?

RESIGNATION

These were thy actions, worthy of record, 710
Worthy the bubbled wretch and venal lord.
Since villainy is meritorious grown,
Step forward, for thy merit's not unknown.
What Mansfield's conscience shuddered to receive,
Thy mercenary temper cannot leave.
Reversions, pensions, bribes and titled views,
What mortal scoundrel can such things refuse?
If Dunning's nice integrity of mind
Will not in pales of interest be confined,
Let his uncommon honesty resign, 720
And boast the empty pension of the nine :
A Thurlow, grasping every offered straw,
Shines his successor, and degrades the law.
How like the ministry who linked his chains !
His measures tend incessantly to gains.
If Weymouth dresses to the height of taste,
At once with fifty places laced,
Can such a summer insect of the state
Be otherwise than in externals great?
Thou bustling marplot of each hidden plan, 730
How wilt thou answer to the sibyl's man?
Did thy own shallow politics direct
To treat the mayor with purposed disrespect ;
Or did it come in orders from above,
From her who sacrificed her soul to love?

Rigby, whose conscience is a perfect dice,
A just epitome of every vice,
Replete with what accomplishments support
The empty admiration of a court,
Yet wants a barony to grace record, 740
And hopes to lose the rascal in the lord.
His wish is granted, and the king prepares
A title of renown, to brand his heirs.

When vice creates the patent for a peer,
What lord so nominally great as Clare?
Whilst Chatham from his coroneted oak
Unheeded shook the senate with his croak,
The minister, too powerful to be right,
Laughed at his prophecy and second sight,
Since Mother Shipton's oracle of state   750
Forestalled the future incidents of fate.
Grafton might shake his elbows, dance, and dream,
'Twere labour lost to strive against the stream.
If Grafton in his juggling statesman's game
Bubbled for interest, betted but for fame,
The leader of the treasury could pay
For every loss in politics and play.

   Sir Fletcher's noisy eloquence of tongue
Is on such pliant oily hinges hung,
Turned to all points of politics and doubt,   760
But though for ever worsted, never out.
Can such a wretched creature take the chair
And exercise his new-made power with air?
This worthy speaker of a worthy crew
Can write long speeches and repeat them too;
A practised lawyer in the venal court,
From higher powers he borrows his report;
Above the scandalous aspersion 'tool',
He only squares his conscience by a rule.
Granby, too great to join the hated cause,   770
Throws down his useless truncheon and withdraws;
Whilst, unrenowned for military deeds,
A youthful branch of royalty succeeds.
Let Coventry, Yonge, Palmerston, and Brett,
With resignation pay the crown a debt;
If, in return for offices of trust,
The ministry expect you'll prove unjust,

What soul that values freedom could with ease
Stoop under obligations such as these?
If you're a Briton (every virtue dead) 780
That would upon your dying freedom tread,
'List in the gang, and piously procure.
To make your calling and election sure.
Go, flatter Sawney for his jockeyship,
Assist in each long shuffle, hedge, and slip;
Thus rising on the stilts of favour, see
What Grafton was, and future dukes will be:
How Rigby, Weymouth, Barrington began
To juggle into fame and play the man.

Amidst this general rage of turning out 790
What officer will stand, remains a doubt.
If virtue's an objection at the board,
With what propriety the council's stored!
Where could the Caledonian minion find
Such striking copies of his venal mind?
Search through the winding labyrinths of place,
See all alike politically base.
If virtues, foreign to the office, shine,
How fast the prodigies of state resign!
Still as they drop, the rising race begin 800
To boast the infamy of being in;
And generous Bristol, constant to his friend,
Employs his lifted crutches to ascend.
Look round thee, North! see, what glorious scene!
O let no thought of vengeance intervene:
Throw thy own insignificance aside,
And swell in self-importance, power, and pride.
See Holland easy with his pilfered store,
And Bute intriguing how to pilfer more,
See Grafton's coffers boast the wealth of place, 810
A providence reserve to hedge and race.

New to oppression and the servile chain,
Hark how the wronged Americans complain ;
Whilst unregarded the petitions lie,
And liberty unnoticed swells her cry.
Yet, yet reflect, thou despicable thing,
How wavering is the favour of a king ;
Think, since that feeble fence and Bute is all,
How soon thy humbug farce of state may fall ;
Then catch the present moment while 'tis thine,   820
Implore a noble pension, and resign !

THE ART OF PUFFING

BY A BOOKSELLER'S JOURNEYMAN

VERSED by experience in the subtle art,
The mysteries of a title I impart :
Teach the young author how to please the town,
And make the heavy drug of rhyme go down.
Since Curl, immortal never-dying name !
A double pica in the book of fame,
By various arts did various dunces prop,
And tickled every fancy to his shop,
Who can, like Pottinger, ensure a book?
Who judges with the solid taste of Cooke?   10
Villains, exalted in the midway sky,
Shall live again to drain your purses dry :
Nor yet unrivalled they ; see Baldwin comes,
Rich in inventions, patents, cuts, and hums :
The honourable Boswell writes, 'tis true,
What else can Paoli's supporter do?
The trading wits endeavour to attain,
Like booksellers, the world's first idol—gain.

THE DEFENCE 163.

For this they puff the heavy Goldsmith's line,
And hail his sentiment, though trite, divine ; 20.
For this the patriotic bard complains,
And Bingley binds poor liberty in chains :
For this was every reader's faith deceived,
And Edmunds swore what nobody believed :
For this the wits in close disguises fight ;
For this the varying politicians write ;
For this each month new magazines are sold,
With dulness filled and transcripts of the old.
The *Town and Country* struck a lucky hit,
Was novel, sentimental, full of wit : 30.
Aping her walk the same success to find,
The *Court and City* hobbles far behind.
Sons of Apollo, learn : merit's no more
Than a good frontispiece to grace the door :
The author who invents a title well
Will always find his covered dulness sell :
Flexney and every bookseller will buy—
Bound in neat calf, the work will never die.
                                        PAMP.
22*nd July* 1770

THE DEFENCE

                    25*th December* 1769.
No more, dear Smith, the hackneyed tale renew ;
I own their censure, I approve it too.
For how can idiots, destitute of thought,
Conceive or estimate, but as they're taught ?
Say, can the satirising pen of Shears
Exalt his name, or mutilate his ears ?
None but a Lawrence can adorn his lays,
Who in a quart of claret drinks his praise.

Taylor repeats what Catcott told before,
But lying Taylor is believed no more.   10
If in myself I think my notion just,
The church and all her arguments are dust.

Religion's but opinion's bastard son,
A perfect mystery, more than three in one.
'Tis fancy all, distempers of the mind ;
As education taught us, we're inclined.
Happy the man, whose reason bids him see
Mankind are by the state of nature free ;
Who, thinking for himself despises those
That would upon his better sense impose ;   20
Is to himself the minister of God,
Nor treads the path where Athanasius trod.
Happy (if mortals can be) is the man,
Who, not by priest but reason, rules his span :
Reason, to its possessor a sure guide,
Reason a thorn in revelation's side.
If reason fails, incapable to tread
Through gloomy revelation's thickening bed,
On what authority the church we own?
How shall we worship deities unknown?   30
Can the Eternal Justice, pleased, receive
The prayers of those who, ignorant, believe?

Search the thick multitudes of every sect,
The church supreme, with Whitfield's new elect;
No individual can their God define,
No, not great Penny, in his nervous line.
But why must Chatterton selected sit
The butt of every critic's little wit?
Am I alone for ever in a crime,
Nonsense in prose, or blasphemy in rhyme?   40
All monosyllables a line appears :
Is it not very often so in Shears?

See generous Eccas lengthening out my praise,
Enraptured with the music of my lays ;
In all the arts of panegyric graced,
The cream of modern literary taste.

' Why, to be sure, the metaphoric line
Has something sentimental, tender, fine ;
But then how hobbling are the other two ;
There are some beauties, but they're very few. 50
Besides the author, 'faith 'tis something odd,
Commends a reverential awe of God.
Read but another fancy of his brain,
He's atheistical in every strain '.
Fallacious is the charge : 'tis all a lie,
As to my reason I can testify.
I own a God, immortal, boundless, wise,
Who bid our glories of creation rise ;
Who formed His varied likeness in mankind,
Centering His many wonders in the mind ; 60
Who saw religion a fantastic night,
But gave us reason to obtain the light.
Indulgent Whitfield scruples not to say,
He only can direct to heaven's high-way ;
While bishops with as much vehemence tell,
All sects heterodox are food for hell.
Why then, dear Smith, since doctors disagree,
Their notions are not oracles to me :
What I think right I ever will pursue,
And leave you liberty to do so too. 70

HAPPINESS

SINCE happiness was not ordained for man,
Let's make ourselves as easy as we can ;
Possessed with fame or fortune, friend or whore,
But think it happiness—we want no more.

    Hail, revelation ! sphere-enveloped dame,
To some divinity, to most a name,
Reason's dark-lantern, superstition's sun,
Whose cause mysterious and effect are one—
From thee, ideal bliss we only trace,
Fair as ambition's dream, or beauty's face,   10
But, in reality, as shadowy found
As seeming truth in twisted mysteries bound.
What little rest from over-anxious care
The lords of nature are designed to share.
To wanton whim and prejudice we owe.
Opinion is the only god we know.
Our furthest wish, the deity we fear,
In different subjects, differently appear.
Where's the foundation of religion placed?
On every individual's fickle taste.   20
The narrow way the priest-rid mortals tread,
By superstitious prejudice misled.
This passage leads to heaven—yet, strange to tell !
Another's conscience finds it lead to hell.
Conscience, the soul-chameleon's varying hue,
Reflects all notions, to no notion true.
The bloody son of Jesse, when he saw
The mystic priesthood kept the Jews in awe,
He made himself an ephod to his mind,
And sought the Lord, and always found him kind : 30

In murder, horrid cruelty, and lust,
The Lord was with him, and his actions just.

   Priestcraft, thou universal blind of all,
Thou idol, at whose feet all nations fall ;
Father of misery, origin of sin,
Whose first existence did with fear begin !
Still sparing deal thy seeming blessings out,
Veil thy Elysium with a cloud of doubt.
Since present blessings in possession cloy,
Bid hope in future worlds expect the joy ;   40
Or, if thy sons the airy phantoms slight,
And dawning reason would direct them right,
Some glittering trifle to their optics hold ;
Perhaps they'll think the glaring spangle gold,
And, madded in the search of coins and toys,
Eager pursue the momentary joys.

   Mercator worships mammon, and adores
No other deity but gold and whores.
Catcott is very fond of talk and fame :
His wish, a perpetuity of name ;   50
Which to procure, a pewter altar's made,
To bear his name and signify his trade ;
In pomp burlesqued the rising spire to head,
To tell futurity a pewterer's dead.
Incomparable Catcott, still pursue
The seeming happiness thou hast in view.
Unfinished chimneys, gaping spires complete,
Eternal fame on oval dishes beat ;
Ride four-inch bridges, clouded turrets climb,
And bravely die—to live in after-time.   60
Horrid idea ! if on rolls of fame
The twentieth century only find thy name,
Unnoticed this, in prose or tagging flower,
He left his dinner to ascend the tower !

Then, what avails thy anxious spitting pain?
Thy laugh-provoking labours are in vain.
On matrimonial pewter set thy hand,
Hammer with every power thou canst command,
Stamp thy whole self, original as 'tis,
To propagate thy whimsies, name, and phiz—   70
Then, when the tottering spires or chimneys fall,
A Catcott shall remain admired by all.

Eudo, who has some trifling couplets writ,
Is only happy when he's thought a wit—
Thinks I've more judgment than the whole reviews,
Because I always compliment his muse.
If any mildly would reprove his faults,
They're critics envy-sickened at his thoughts.
To me he flies, his best-belovèd friend,
Reads me asleep, then wakes me to commend.   80

Say, sages—if not sleep-charmed by the rhyme—
Is flattery, much-loved flattery, any crime?
Shall dragon satire exercise his sting,
And not insinuating flattery sing?
Is it more noble to torment than please?
How ill that thought with rectitude agrees!

Come to my pen, companion of the lay,
And speak of worth where merit cannot say;
Let lazy Barton undistinguished snore,
Nor lash his generosity to Hoare;   90
Praise him for sermons of his curate bought,
His easy flow of words, his depth of thought
His active spirit, ever in display;
His great devotion when he drawls to pray;
His sainted soul distinguishably seen,
With all the virtues of a modern dean.

HAPPINESS

Varo, a genius of peculiar taste,
His misery in his happiness is placed;
When in soft calm the waves of fortune roll,
A tempest of reflection storms the soul;
But what would make another man distressed
Gives him tranquility and thoughtless rest:
No disappointment can his peace invade,
Superior to all troubles not self-made.
This character let gray Oxonians scan,
And tell me of what species he's a man;
Or be it by young Yeatman criticised,
Who damns good English if not Latinised.
In Aristotle's scale the muse he weighs,
And damps her little fire with copied lays!
Versed in the mystic learning of the schools,
He rings bob-majors by Leibnitzian rules.

Pulvis, whose knowledge centres in degrees,
Is never happy but when taking fees.
Blessed with a bushy wig and solemn grace,
Catcott admires him for a fossil face.

When first his farce of countenance began,
Ere the soft down had marked him almost man,
A solemn dulness occupied his eyes,
And the fond mother thought him wondrous wise;
But little had she read in nature's book,
That fools assume a philosophic look.

O! education, ever in the wrong,
To thee the curses of mankind belong;
Thou first great author of our future state,
Chief source of our religion, passions, fate:
On every atom of the doctor's frame
Nature has stamped the pedant with his name;

But thou hast made him (ever wast thou blind)
A licensed butcher of the human kind.   130
Mouldering in dust the fair Lavinia lies;
Death and our doctor closed her sparkling eyes.
O all ye powers, the guardians of the world!
Where is the useless bolt of vengeance hurled?
Say, shall this leaden sword of plague prevail,
And kill the mighty where the mighty fail?
Let the red bolus tremble o'er his head,
And with his cordial julep strike him dead!

But to return: in this wide sea of thought,
How shall we steer our notions as we ought?   140
Content is happiness, as sages say—
But what's content? The trifle of a day.
Then, friend, let inclination be thy guide,
Nor be by superstition led aside.
The saint and sinner, fool and wise attain
An equal share of easiness and pain.
1770

CHATTERTON'S WILL

ALL this wrote between 11 and 2 o'clock Saturday, in the utmost distress of mind. *14th April* 1770.

Burgum, I thank thee, thou hast let me see
That Bristol has impressed her stamp on thee,
Thy generous spirit emulates the Mayor's,
Thy generous spirit with thy Bristol's pairs.
Gods! What would Burgum give to get a name,
And snatch his blundering dialect from shame!
What would he give, to hand his memory down
To time's remotest boundary?—A crown.

Would you ask more, his swelling face looks blue ;
Futurity he rates at two pound two.   10
Well, Burgum, take thy laurel to thy brow ;
With a rich saddle decorate a sow,
Strut in iambics, totter in an ode,
Promise, and never pay, and be the mode.

Catcott, for thee, I know thy heart is good,
But ah ! thy merit's seldom understood ;
Too bigoted to whimsies, which thy youth
Received to venerate as gospel truth,
Thy friendship never could be dear to me,
Since all I am is opposite to thee.   20
If ever obligated to thy purse,
Rowley discharges all ; my first, chief curse !
For had I never known the antique lore,
I ne'er had ventured from my peaceful shore
To be the wreck of promises and hopes,
A Boy of Learning, and a Bard of Tropes ;
But happy in my humble sphere had moved,
Untroubled, unrespected, unbeloved.

To Barrett next, he has my thanks sincere
For all the little knowledge I had here.   30
But what was knowledge ? Could it here succeed
When scarcely twenty in the town can read ?
Could knowledge bring in interest to maintain
The wild expenses of a poet's brain ?
Disinterested Burgum never meant
To take my knowledge for his gain per cent.
When wildly squandering everything I got
On books and learning, and the Lord knows what,
Could Burgum then, my critic, patron, friend,
Without security attempt to lend ?   40
No, that would be imprudent in the man ;
Accuse him of imprudence if you can.

He promised, I confess, and seemed sincere;
Few keep an honorary promise here.
I thank thee, Barrett: thy advice was right,
But 'twas ordained by fate that I should write.
Spite of the prudence of this prudent place,
I wrote my mind, nor hid the author's face.
Harris ere long, when, reeking from the press,
My numbers make his self-importance less,   50
Will wrinkle up his face, and damn the day,
And drag my body to the triple way.
Poor superstitious mortals! wreak your hate
Upon my cold remains——

[The remainder of this remarkable effusion is in prose.]

FRAGMENT

Far from the reach of critics and reviews,
Brush up thy pinions and ascend, my muse!
Of conversation sing an ample theme,
And drink the tea of Heliconian stream.
Hail, matchless linguist! prating Delia, hail!
When scandal's best materials, hackneyed, fail,
Thy quick invention lends a quick supply,
And all thy talk is one continued lie.
Know, thou eternal babbler, that my song
Could shew a line as venomed as thy tongue.   10
In pity to thy sex, I cease to write
Of London journeys and the marriage-night.
The conversation which in taverns ring
Descends below my satire's soaring sting.
Upon his elbow-throne great Maro sits,
Revered at Forster's by the would-be wits;
Deliberately the studied jest he breaks,
And long and loud the polished table shakes;

Retailed in every brothel-house in town,
Each dancing booby vends it as his own. 20
Upon the emptied jelly-glass reclined,
The laughing Maro gathers up his wind ;
The tail-bud 'prentice rubs his hands and grins,
Ready to laugh before the tale begins :
' To talk of freedom, politics, and Bute,
And knotty arguments in law confute,
I leave to blockheads, for such things designed,
Be it my task divine to ease the mind '.

'To-morrow', says a Church of England priest,
' Is of good St Epiphany the feast. 30
It nothing matters whether he or she,
But be all servants from their labour free '.
The laugh begins with Maro, and goes round,
And the dry jest is very witty found.
In every corner of the room are seen
Round altars covered with eternal green,
Piled high with offerings to the goddess fame,
Which mortals, chronicles and journals name ;
Where in strange jumble flesh and spirit lie,
And illustration sees a jest-book nigh ; 40
Anti-venereal medicine cheek by jowl
With Whitfield's famous physic for the soul ;
The patriot Wilkes's ever-famed essay,
With Bute and justice in the self-same lay :
Which of the two deserved (ye casuists, tell)
The conflagrations of a hangman's hell?

The clock strikes eight ; the taper dully shines ;
Farewell, my muse, nor think of further lines :
Nine leaves, and in two hours, or something odd,
Shut up the book,—it is enough, by God ! 50
  28*th October* [1769]

Sage Gloster's bishop sits supine between
His fiery floggers and a cure for spleen ;
The son of flame, enthusiastic Law.
Displays his bigot blade, and thunders draw,
Unconscious of his neighbours, some vile plays,
Directing-posts to Beelzebub's highways ;
Fools are philosophers in Jones's line,
And, bound in gold and scarlet, Dodsleys shine ;
These are the various offerings fame requires,
For ever rising to her shrines in spires ; 60
Hence all Avaro's politics are drained,
And Evelina's general scandal's gained.

Where Satan's temple rears its lofty head,
And muddy torrents wash their shrinking bed ;
Where the stupendous sons of commerce meet,
Sometimes to scold indeed, but oft to eat ;
Where frugal Cambria all her poultry gives,
And where the insatiate Messalina lives,
A mighty fabric opens to the sight ;
With four large columns, five large windows dight ; 70
With four small portals, 'tis with much ado
A common-council lady can pass through :
Here Hare first teaches supple limbs to bend,
And faults of nature never fails to mend.

Here conversation takes a nobler flight,
For nature leads the theme, and all is right ;
The little god of love improves discourse,
And sage discretion finds his thunder hoarse ;
About the flame the gilded trifles play,
Till, lost in forge unknown, they melt away, 80
And, cherishing the passion in the mind,
Their each idea's brightened and refined.

Ye painted guardians of the lovely fair,
Who spread the saffron bloom, and tinge the hair ;

FRAGMENT

Whose deep invention first found out the art
Of making rapture glow in every part;
Of wounding by each varied attitude—
Sure 'twas a thought divinity endued.

* * * *

FRAGMENT

INTEREST, thou universal god of men,
Wait on the couplet and reprove the pen;
If aught unwelcome to thy ears shall rise,
Hold jails and famine to the poet's eyes;
Bid satire sheathe her sharp avenging steel,
And lose a number rather than a meal.
Nay, prithee, honour, do not make us mad,
When I am hungry something must be had.
Can honest consciousness of doing right
Provide a dinner or a bed at night? 10
What though Astrea decks my soul in gold,
My mortal lumber trembles with the cold;
Then, cursed tormentor of my peace, begone!
Flattery's a cloak, and I will put it on.

In a low cottage, shaking with the wind,
A door in front, a span of light behind,
Tervono's lungs their mystic play began,
And nature in the infant marked the man.
Six times the youth of morn, the golden sun,
Through the twelve stages of his course had run, 20
Tervono rose, the merchant of the plain,
His soul was traffic, his elysium gain;
The ragged chapman found his word a law,
And lost in barter every favourite taw.

FRAGMENT

Through various scenes Tervono still ascends,
And still is making, still forgetting friends;
Full of this maxim, often heard in trade,
Friendship with none but equals should be made.
His soul is all the merchant. None can find
The shadow of a virtue in his mind.   30
Nor are his vices reason misapplied;
Mean as his spirit, sneaking as his pride.
At city dinner, or a turtle feast,
As expeditious as a hungry priest:
No foe to Bacchanalian brutal rites,
In vile confusion dozing off the nights.

Tervono would be flattered; shall I then
In stigmatising satire shake the pen?
Muse, for his brow the laurel wreath prepare,
Though soon 'twill wither when 'tis planted there.   40
Come, panegyric; adulation, haste,
And sing this wonder of mercántile taste.
And whilst his virtue rises in my lines,
The patron's happy, and the poet dines.
Some, philosophically cased in steel,
Can neither poverty or hunger feel;
But that is not my case: the muses know
What water-gruel stuff from Phœbus flow.
Then if the range of satire seize my brain,
May none but brother poets meet the strain.   50
May bulky aldermen nor vicars rise,
Hung *in terrorem* to their brothers' eyes:
When, lost in trance by gospel or by law,
In to their inward room the senses draw,
There as they snore in consultation deep,
Are by the vulgar reckoned fast asleep.

FEBRUARY

AN ELEGY

BEGIN, my muse, the imitative lay,
  Aonian doxies sound the thrumming string;
Attempt no number of the plaintive Gay,
  Let me like midnight cats, or Collins sing.

If, in the trammels of the doleful line,
  The bounding hail, or drilling rain descend;
Come, brooding melancholy, power divine,
  And every unformed mass of words amend.

Now the rough Goat withdraws his curling horns,
  And the cold Waterer twirls his circling mop.   10
Swift sudden anguish darts through altering corns,
  And the spruce mercer trembles in his shop.

Now infant authors, maddening for renown,
  Extend the plume, and hum about the stage,
Procure a benefit, amuse the town,
  And proudly glitter in a title-page.

Now, wrapped in ninefold fur, his squeamish grace
  Defies the fury of the howling storm;
And, whilst the tempest whistles round his face,
  Exults to find his mantled carcase warm.   20

Now rumbling coaches furious drive along,
  Full of the majesty of city dames,
Whose jewels, sparkling in the gaudy throng,
  Raise strange emotions and invidious flames.

Now merit, happy in the calm of place,
  To mortals as a Highlander appears,
And, conscious of the excellence of lace,
  With spreading frogs and gleaming spangles glares;

Whilst envy, on a tripod seated nigh,
    In form a shoe-boy, daubs the valued fruit,   30
And, darting lightnings from his vengeful eye,
    Raves about Wilkes, and politics, and Bute.

Now Barry, taller than a grenadier,
    Dwindles into a stripling of eighteen;
Or, sabled in Othello, breaks the ear,
    Exerts his voice, and totters to the scene.

Now Foote, a looking-glass for all mankind,
    Applies his wax to personal defects;
But leaves untouched the image of the mind,
    His art no mental quality reflects.   40

Now Drury's potent king extorts applause,
    And pit, box, gallery, echo ' How divine!'
Whilst, versed in all the drama's mystic laws,
    His graceful action saves the wooden line.

Now—but what further can the muses sing?
    Now dropping particles of water fall;
Now vapours, riding on the north wind's wing,
    With transitory darkness shadow all.

Alas! how joyless the descriptive theme,
    When sorrow on the writer's quiet preys;   50
And, like a mouse in Cheshire cheese supreme,
    Devours the substance of the lessening bays.

Come, February, lend thy darkest sky,
    There teach the wintered muse with clouds to soar;
Come, February, lift the number high;
    Let the sharp strain like wind through alleys roar.

Ye channels, wandering through the spacious street,
    In hollow murmurs roll the dirt along,
With inundations wet the sabled feet,
    Whilst gouts, responsive, join the elegiac song.   60

ELEGY

Ye damsels fair, whose silver voices shrill
  Sound through meandering folds of echo's horn,
Let the sweet cry of liberty be still,
  No more let smoking cakes awake the morn.

O, Winter! put away thy snowy pride;
  O, Spring! neglect the cowslip and the bell;
O, Summer! throw thy pears and plums aside;
  O, Autumn! bid the grape with poison swell.

The pensioned muse of Johnson is no more!
  Drowned in a butt of wine his genius lies: 70
Earth! Ocean! Heaven! the wondrous loss deplore,
  The dregs of nature with her glory dies.

What iron stoic can suppress the tear?
  What sour reviewer reads with vacant eye?
What bard but decks his literary bier?
  Alas! I cannot sing—I howl—I cry—

                                      D.

Bristol, 12*th February* [1770]

ELEGY

HASTE, haste! ye solemn messengers of night,
  Spread the black mantle on the shrinking plain;
But, ah! my torments still survive the light,
  The changing seasons alter not my pain.

Ye variegated children of the spring;
  Ye blossoms blushing with the pearly dew;
Ye birds that sweetly in the hawthorn sing;
  Ye flowery meadows, lawns of verdant hue;

Faint are your colours, harsh your love-notes thrill,
  To me no pleasure nature now can yield: 10
Alike the barren rock and woody hill,
  The dark-brown blasted heath, and fruitful field.

Ye spouting cataracts; ye silver streams;
  Ye spacious rivers, whom the willow shrouds,
Ascend the bright-crowned sun's far-shining beams,
  To aid the mournful tear-distilling clouds.

Ye noxious vapours, fall upon my head;
  Ye writhing adders, round my feet entwine;
Ye toads, your venom in my foot-path spread;
  Ye blasting meteors, upon me shine.   20

Ye circling seasons, intercept the year;
  Forbid the beauties of the spring to rise;
Let not the life-preserving grain appear;
  Let howling tempests harrow up the skies.

Ye cloud-girt, moss-grown turrets, look no more
  Into the palace of the god of day;
Ye loud tempestuous billows, cease to roar,
  In plaintive numbers through the valleys stray.

Ye verdant-vested trees, forget to grow,
  Cast off the yellow foliage of your pride;   30
Ye softly tingling rivulets, cease to flow,
  Or, swelled with certain death and poison, glide.

Ye solemn warblers of the gloomy night,
  That rest in lightning-blasted oaks the day,
Through the black mantles take your slow-paced flight,
  Rending the silent wood with shrieking lay.

Ye snow-crowned mountains, lost to mortal eyes,
  Down to the valleys bend your hoary head;
Ye livid comets, fire the peopled skies—
  For—Lady Betty's tabby cat is dead!   40

ELEGY WRITTEN AT STANTON DREW

JOYLESS I hail the solemn gloom,
    Joyless I view the pillars vast and rude
Where erst the fool of superstition trod,
    In smoking blood imbrued,
And rising from the tomb,
    Mistaken homage to an unknown god.
    Fancy, whither dost thou stray,
    Whither dost thou wing thy way?
    Check the rising wild delight,
    Ah! what avails this awful sight?   10
    Maria is no more!
Why, cursed remembrance, wilt thou haunt my mind?
    The blessings past are misery now;
    Upon her lovely brow
    Her lovelier soul she wore.
    Soft as the evening gale
    When breathing perfumes through the rose-hedged vale,
She was my joy, my happiness refined.
    All hail, ye solemn horrors of this scene,
    The blasted oak, the dusky green.   20
    Ye dreary altars, by whose side
    The druid priest, in crimson dyed,
        The solemn dirges sung,
    And drove the golden knife
    Into the palpitating seat of life,
    When, rent with horrid shouts,
        The distant valleys rung.

    The bleeding body bends,
    The glowing purple stream ascends,
    Whilst the troubled spirit near   30
    Hovers in the steamy air ;
Again the sacred dirge they sing,
Again the distant hill and coppice valley ring.
    Soul of my dear Maria, haste,
    Whilst my languid spirits waste ;
    When from this my prison free,
    Catch my soul, it flies to thee ;
    Death had doubly armed his dart,
    In piercing thee, it pierced my heart.

ELEGY

JOYLESS I seek the solitary shade,
  Where dusky contemplation veils the scene,
The dark retreat, of leafless branches made,
  Where sickening sorrow wets the yellowed green.

The darksome ruins of some sacred cell,
  Where erst the sons of superstition trod,
Tottering upon the mossy meadow, tell
  We better know, but less adore, our God.

Now, as I mournful tread the gloomy cave,
  Through the wide window, once with mysterious dight,   10
The distant forest, and the darkened wave
  Of the swollen Avon ravishes my sight.

But see, the thickening veil of evening's drawn,
  The azure changes to a sabled blue ;
The rapturing prospects fly the lessening lawn,
  And nature seems to mourn the dying view.

Self-frighted fear creeps silent through the gloom,
    Starts at the rustling leaf, and rolls his eyes;
Aghast with horror, when he views the tomb,
    With every torment of a hell, he flies.   20

The bubbling brooks in plaintive murmurs roll,
    The bird of omen, with incessant scream,
To melancholy thoughts awakes the soul,
    And lulls the mind to contemplation's dream.

A dreary stillness broods o'er all the vale,
    The clouded moon emits a feeble glare;
Joyless I seek the darkling hill and dale,
    Where'er I wander, sorrow still is there.
    Bristol, 17*th November* 1769

ELEGY

WHY blooms the radiance of the morning sky?
    Why springs the beauties of the season round?
Why buds the blossom with the glossy dye?
    Ah! why does nature beautify the ground?

Whilst, softly floating on the zephyr's wing,
    The melting accents of the thrushes rise,
And all the heavenly music of the spring,
    Steal on the sense, and harmonise the skies;

When the racked soul is not attuned to joy,
    When sorrow an internal monarch reigns: 10
In vain the choristers their powers employ,
    'Tis hateful music, and discordant strains.

The velvet mantle of the skirted mead,
    The rich varieties of Flora's pride,
Till the full bosom is from trouble freed,
    Disgusts the eye, and bids the big tear glide.

Once, ere the gold-haired sun shot the new ray
    Through the grey twilight of the dubious morn,
To woodlands, lawns, and hills, I took my way,
    And listened to the echoes of the horn ;   20

Dwelt on the prospect, sought the varied view,
    Traced the meanders of the bubbling stream :
From joy to joy uninterrupted flew,
    And thought existence but a fairy dream.

Now through the gloomy cloister's lengthening way,
    Through all the terror superstition frames,
I lose the minutes of the lingering day,
    And view the night light up her pointed flames.

I dare the danger of the mouldering wall,
    Nor heed the arch that totters o'er my head ;   30
O ! quickly may the friendly ruin fall,
    Release me of my love, and strike me dead.

M———— ! cruel, sweet, inexorable fair,
    O ! must I unregarded seek the grave?
Must I, from all my bosom holds, repair,
    When one indulgent smile from thee would save?

Let mercy plead my cause ; and think, oh ! think !
    A love like mine but ill deserves thy hate :
Remember, I am tottering on the brink,
    Thy smile or censure seals my final fate.   40

                                            C.

Shoreditch, 20*th May* 1770

AN ELEGY

On the Much Lamented DEATH of WILLIAM BECKFORD Esq., Late LORD-MAYOR of, and REPRESENTATIVE in PARLIAMENT FOR, THE CITY OF LONDON. [Died 21st June 1770.]

WEEP on, ye Britons—give your general tear ;
    But hence, ye venal—hence, each titled slave ;
An honest pang should wait on Beckford's bier,
    And patriot anguish mark the patriot's grave.

When, like the Roman, to his field retired,
    'Twas you, (surrounded by unnumbered foes)
Who called him forth, his services required,
    And took from age the blessing of repose.

With soul impelled by virtue's sacred flame,
    To stem the torrent of corruption's tide,   10
He came, heaven-fraught with liberty ! he came,
    And nobly in his country's service died.

In the last awful, the departing hour,
    When life's poor lamp more faint, and fainter grew ;
As memory feebly exercised her power,
    He only felt for liberty and you.

He viewed death's arrow with a Christian eye,
    With firmness only to a Christian known ;
And nobly gave your miseries that sigh
    With which he never gratified his own.   20

Thou breathing sculpture, celebrate his fame,
    And give his laurel everlasting bloom ;
Record his worth while gratitude has name,
    And teach succeeding ages from his tomb.

The sword of justice cautiously he swayed,
   His hand for ever held the balance right;
Each venial fault with pity he surveyed,
   But murder found no mercy in his sight.

He knew, when flatterers besiege a throne,
   Truth seldom reaches to a monarch's ear;   30
Knew, if oppressed a loyal people groan,
   'Tis not the courtier's interest he should hear.

Hence, honest to his prince, his manly tongue,
   The public wrong and loyalty conveyed,
While titled tremblers, every nerve unstrung,
   Looked all around, confounded and dismayed;

Looked all around, astonished to behold
   (Trained up to flattery from their early youth)
An artless, fearless citizen unfold
   To royal ears a mortifying truth.   40

Titles to him no pleasure could impart,
   No bribes his rigid virtue could control;
The star could never gain upon his heart,
   Nor turn the tide of honour in his soul.

For this his name our history shall adorn,
   Shall soar on fame's wide pinions, all sublime,
Till heaven's own bright and never-dying morn
   Absorbs our little particle of time.

Far other fate the venal crew shall find,
   Who sigh for pomp, or languish after strings;   50
And sell their native probity of mind,
   For bribes from statesmen, or for smiles from kings.

And here a long inglorious list of names
   On my disturbed imagination crowd;
'Oh! let them perish' (loud the muse exclaims)
   'Consigned for ever to oblivion's cloud.

White be the page that celebrates his fame,
  Nor let one mark of infamy appear;
Let not the villain's mingle with his name,
  Lest indignation stop the swelling tear.   60

The swelling tear should plenteously descend,
  The deluged eye should give the heart relief;
Humanity should melt for nature's friend,
  In all the richest luxury of grief'.

He, as a planet with unceasing ray,
  Is seen in one unvaried course to move,
Through life pursued but one illustrious way,
  And all his orbit was his country's love.

But he is gone! And now, alas! no more
  His generous hand neglected worth redeems;   70
No more around his mansion shall the poor
  Bask in his warm, his charitable beams.

No more his grateful countrymen shall hear
  His manly voice, in martyred freedom's cause;
No more the courtly sycophant shall fear
  His poignant lash for violated laws.

Yet say, stern virtue, who'd not wish to die,
  Thus greatly struggling, a whole land to save?
Who would not wish, with ardour wish to lie,
  With Beckford's honour, in a Beckford's grave?   80

Not honour, such as princes can bestow,
  Whose breath a reptile to a lord can raise;
But far the brightest honour here below,
  A grateful nation's unabating praise.

But see! where liberty, on yonder strand,
  Where the cliff rises, and the billows roar,
Already takes her melancholy stand,
  To wing her passage to some happier shore.

Stay, goddess ! stay, nor leave this once-blessed isle,
   So many ages thy peculiar care,   90
O ! stay, and cheer us ever with thy smile,
   Lest quick we sink in terrible despair.

And lo ! she listens to the muse's call ;
   She comes, once more, to cheer a wretched land ;
Thou, tyranny, shall tremble to thy fall !
   To hear her high, her absolute command :

' Let not, my sons, the laws your fathers bought,
   With such rich oceans of undaunted blood,
By traitors, thus be basely set at nought,
   While at your hearts you feel the purple flood.   100

Unite in firm, in honourable bands ;
   Break every link of slavery's hateful chain :
Nor let your children, at their fathers' hands,
   Demand their birthright, and demand in vain.

Where'er the murderers of their country hide,
   Whatever dignities their names adorn :
It is your duty—let it be your pride,
   To drag them forth to universal scorn.

So shall your loved, your venerated name,
   O'er earth's vast convex gloriously expand ;   110
So shall your still accumulating fame
   In one bright story with your Beckford stand '.

ELEGY

TO THE MEMORY OF MR THOMAS PHILLIPS OF FAIRFORD

No more I hail the morning's golden gleam,
  No more the wonders of the view I sing;
Friendship requires a melancholy theme,
  At her command the awful lyre I string!

Now as I wander through this leafless grove,
  Where the dark vapours of the evening rise,
How shall I teach the chorded shell to move,
  Or stay the gushing torrent from my eyes?

Phillips! great master of the boundless lyre,
  Thee would the grateful muse attempt to paint: 10
Give me a double portion of thy fire,
  Or all the powers of language are too faint.

Say what bold number, what immortal line,
  The image of thy genius can reflect?
Oh, lend my pen what animated thine,
  To shew thee in thy native glories decked!

The joyous charms of spring delighted saw
  Their beauties doubly glaring in thy lay;
Nothing was spring which Phillips did not draw,
  And every image of his muse was May. 20

So rose the regal hyacinthal star,
  So shone the pleasant rustic daisied bed,
So seemed the woodlands lessening from afar;
  You saw the real prospect as you read.

Majestic summer's blooming flowery pride
    Next claimed the honour of his nervous song;
He taught the stream in hollow trills to glide,
    And led the glories of the year along.

When golden autumn, wreathed in ripened corn,
    From purple clusters pressed the foamy wine,   30
Thy genius did his sallow brows adorn,
    And made the beauties of the season thine.

Pale rugged winter bending o'er his tread,
    His grizzled head bedropt with icy dew;
His eyes, a dusky light congealed and dead;
    His robe, a tinge of bright ethereal blue;

His train a motleyed, sanguine, sable cloud,
    He limps along the russet, dreary moor,
Whilst rising whirlwinds, blasting, keen and loud,
    Roll the white surges to the sounding shore.   40

Nor were his pleasures unimproved by thee;
    Pleasures he has, though horribly deformed;
The silvered hill, the polished lake we see,
    Is by thy genius fixed, preserved, and warmed.

The rough November has his pleasures too;
    But I'm insensible to every joy:
Farewell the laurel! now I grasp the yew,
    And all my little powers of grief employ.

In thee each virtue found a pleasing cell,
    Thy mind was honour, and thy soul divine;   50
With thee did every power of genius dwell,
    Thou wast the Helicon of all the nine.

Fancy, whose various figure-tinctured vest
    Was ever changing to a different hue;
Her head, with varied bays and flowerets dressed,
    Her eyes, two spangles of the morning dew.

In dancing attitude she swept thy string;
  And now she soars, and now again descends;
And now, reclining on the zephyr's wing,
  Unto the velvet-vested mead she bends.

Peace, decked in all the softness of the dove,
  Over thy passions spread her silver plume;
The rosy veil of harmony and love
  Hung on thy soul in one eternal bloom.

Peace, gentlest, softest of the virtues, spread
  Her silver pinions, wet with dewy tears,
Upon her best distinguished poet's head,
  And taught his lyre the music of the spheres.

Temperance, with health and beauty in her train,
  And massy-muscled strength in graceful pride,
Pointed at scarlet luxury and pain,
  And did at every cheerful feast preside.

Content, who smiles at all the frowns of fate,
  Fanned from idea every seeming ill;
In thy own virtues and thy genius great,
  The happy muse laid every trouble still.

But see, the sickened glare of day retires,
  And the meek evening shades with dusky grey;
The west faint glimmers with the saffron fires,
  And like thy life, O Phillips! flies away.

Here, stretched upon this heaven-ascending hill,
  I'll wait the horrors of the coming night,
I'll imitate the gently-plaintive rill,
  And by the glare of lambent vapours write.

Wet with the dew, the yellow hawthorns bow;
  The loud winds whistle through the echoing dell;
Far o'er the lea the breathing cattle low,
  And the shrill shrieking of the screech-owl swell.

With whistling sound the dusky foliage flies,
    And wantons with the wind in rapid whirls;   90
The gurgling rivulet to the valley hies,
    And, lost to sight, in dying murmurs curls.

Now, as the mantle of the evening swells
    Upon my mind, I feel a thickening gloom.
Ah! could I charm by friendship's potent spells
    The soul of Phillips from the deathy tomb!

Then would we wander through this darkened vale,
    In converse such as heavenly spirits use,
And, borne upon the plumage of the gale,
    Hymn the Creator, and exhort the muse.   100

But, horror to reflection! now no more
    Will Phillips sing, the wonder of the plain!
When, doubting whether they might not adore,
    Admiring mortals heard his nervous strain.

A maddening darkness reigns through all the lawn,
    Nought but a doleful bell of death is heard,
Save where, into a hoary oak withdrawn,
    The scream proclaims the cursed nocturnal bird.

Now rest, my muse, but only rest to weep
    A friend made dear by every sacred tie;   110
Unknown to me be comfort, peace, or sleep:
    Phillips is dead—'tis pleasure then to die.
D. B.

    Bristol, 5*th December* [1769]

ELEGY
ON THE DEATH OF MR PHILLIPS

ASSIST me, powers of heaven! what do I hear?
Surprise and horror check the burning tear,
Is Phillips dead, and is my friend no more,
Gone like the sand divested from the shore?
And is he gone?—Can then the nine refuse
To sing with gratitude a favoured muse?

ELEGY

No more I hail the morning's golden gleam,
    No more the wonders of the view I sing;
Friendship requires a melancholy theme,
    At her command the awful lyre I string!   10

Now as I wander through this leafless grove,
    Where tempests howl, and blasts eternal rise,
How shall I teach the chorded shell to move,
    Or stay the gushing torrent from my eyes?

Phillips! great master of the boundless lyre,
    Thee would my soul-racked muse attempt to paint;
Give me a double portion of thy fire,
    Or all the powers of language are too faint.

Say, soul unsullied by the filth of vice,
    Say, meek-eyed spirit, where's thy tuneful shell,   20
Which when the silver stream was locked with ice,
    Was wont to cheer the tempest-ravaged dell?

Oft as the filmy veil of evening drew
    The thickening shade upon the vivid green,
Thou, lost in transport at the dying view,
    Bid'st the ascending muse display the scene.

When golden autumn, wreathed in ripened corn,
　From purple clusters pressed the foamy wine,
Thy genius did his sallow brows adorn,
　And made the beauties of the season thine.　30

With rustling sound the yellow foliage flies,
　And wantons with the wind in rapid whirls ;
The gurgling rivulet to the valley hies,
　Whilst on its bank the spangled serpent curls.

The joyous charms of spring delighted saw
　Their beauties doubly glaring in thy lay ;
Nothing was spring which Phillips did not draw,
　And every image of his muse was May.

So rose the regal hyacinthal star,
　So shone the verdure of the daisied bed,　40
So seemed the forest glimmering from afar ;
　You saw the real prospect as you read.

Majestic summer's blooming flowery pride
　Next claimed the honour of his nervous song ;
He taught the stream in hollow trills to glide,
　And led the glories of the year along.

Pale rugged winter bending o'er his tread,
　His grizzled hair bedropt with icy dew ;
His eyes, a dusky light congealed and dead ;
　His robe, a tinge of bright ethereal blue ;　50

His train a motleyed, sanguine, sable cloud,
　He limps along the russet, dreary moor,
Whilst rising whirlwinds, blasting, keen, and loud,
　Roll the white surges to the sounding shore.

Nor were his pleasures unimproved by thee ;
　Pleasures he has, though horribly deformed ;
The polished lake, the silvered hill we see,
　Is by thy genius fired, preserved, and warmed.

ELEGY

The rough October has his pleasures too;
  But I'm insensible to every joy: 60
Farewell the laurel! now I grasp the yew,
  And all my little powers in grief employ.

Immortal shadow of my much-loved friend!
  Clothed in thy native virtue meet my soul,
When on the fatal bed, my passions bend,
  And curb my floods of anguish as they roll.

In thee each virtue found a pleasing cell,
  Thy mind was honour, and thy soul divine;
With thee did every god of genius dwell,
  Thou wast the Helicon of all the nine. 70

Fancy, whose various figure-tinctured vest
  Was ever changing to a different hue;
Her head, with varied bays and flowerets dressed,
  Her eyes, two spangles of the morning dew.

With dancing attitude she swept thy string;
  And now she soars, and now again descends;
And now, reclining on the zephyr's wing,
  Unto the velvet-vested mead she bends.

Peace, decked in all the softness of the dove,
  Over thy passions spread her silver plume; 80
The rosy veil of harmony and love
  Hung on thy soul in one eternal bloom.

Peace, gentlest, softest of the virtues, spread
  Her silver pinions, wet with dewy tears,
Upon her best distinguished poet's head,
  And taught his lyre the music of the spheres.

Temperance, with health and beauty in her train,
  And massy-muscled strength in graceful pride,
Pointed at scarlet luxury and pain,
  And did at every frugal feast preside. 90

Black melancholy, stealing to the shade,
  With raging madness, frantic, loud, and dire,
Whose bloody hand displays the reeking blade,
  Were strangers to thy heaven-directed lyre.

Content, who smiles in every frown of fate,
  Wreathed thy pacific brow and soothed thy ill:
In thy own virtues and thy genius great,
  The happy muse laid every trouble still.

But see! the sickening lamp of day retires,
  And the meek evening shades the dusky grey; 100
The west faint glimmers with the saffron fires,
  And like thy life, O Phillips! flies away.

Here, stretched upon this heaven-ascending hill,
  I'll wait the horrors of the coming night,
I'll imitate the gently-plaintive rill,
  And by the glare of lambent vapours write.

Wet with the dew the yellow hawthorn bows;
  The rustic whistles through the echoing cave;
Far o'er the lea the breathing cattle low,
  And the full Avon lifts the darkened wave. 110

Now, as the mantle of the evening swells
  Upon my mind, I feel a thickening gloom!
Ah! could I charm by necromantic spells
  The soul of Phillips from the deathy tomb!

Then would we wander through this darkened vale,
  In converse such as heavenly spirits use,
And, borne upon the pinions of the gale,
  Hymn the Creator, and exert the muse.

But, horror to reflection! now no more
  Will Phillips sing, the wonder of the plain! 120
When, doubting whether they might not adore,
  Admiring mortals heard his nervous strain.

See! see! the pitchy vapour hides the lawn,
   Nought but a doleful bell of death is heard,
Save where into a blasted oak withdrawn
   The scream proclaims the cursed nocturnal bird.
Now rest, my muse, but only rest to weep
   A friend made dear by every sacred tie;
Unknown to me be comfort, peace, or sleep:
   Phillips is dead—'tis pleasure then to die.   130
Few are the pleasures Chatterton e'er knew,
   Short were the moments of his transient peace;
But melancholy robbed him of those few,
   And this hath bid all future comfort cease.
And can the muse be silent, Phillips gone?
   And am I still alive? My soul, arise!
The robe of immortality put on,
   And meet thy Phillips in his native skies.

TO THE READER
Observe, in favour of a hobbling strain,
   Neat as exported from the parent brain,   140
And each and every couplet I have penned,
   But little laboured, and I never mend.
                                 T. C.

ON THOMAS PHILLIPS'S DEATH
To Clayfield, long renowned the muse's friend,
Presuming on his goodness, this I send;
Unknown to you, tranquility, and fame,
In this address perhaps I am to blame.
This rudeness let necessity excuse;
And anxious friendship for a much-loved muse.
Twice have the circling hours unveiled the east,
Since horror found me, and all pleasures ceased;
Since every number tended to deplore;
Since fame asserted Phillips was no more.   10

Say, is he mansioned in his native spheres,
Or is't a vapour that exhales in tears?
Swift as idea, rid me of my pain,
And let my dubious wretchedness be plain.
It is too true: the awful lyre is strung,
His elegy the sister muses sung.
O may he live, and useless be the strain!
Fly, generous Clayfield, rid me of my pain.
Forgive my boldness, think the urgent cause;
And who can bind necessity with laws? 20
I wait, the admirer of your noble parts,
You, friend to genius, sciences, and arts.
                    THOS. CHATTERTON
Bristol, *Monday Evening*, 30*th October* 1769.

ELEGY

ON MR WM. SMITH

ASCEND, my muse, on sorrow's sable plume,
   Let the soft number meet the swelling sigh;
With laureated chaplets deck the tomb,
   The blood-stained tomb where Smith and comfort lie.

I loved him with a brother's ardent love,
   Beyond the love which tenderest brothers bear;
Though savage kindred bosoms cannot move,
   Friendship shall deck his urn and pay the tear.

Despised, an alien to thy father's breast,
   Thy ready services repaid with hate; 10
By brother, father, sisters, all distressed,
   They pushed thee on to death, they urged thy fate.

Ye callous-breasted brutes in human form,
  Have you not often boldly wished him dead?
He's gone, ere yet his fire of man was warm,
  O may his crying blood be on your head!
    12*th August* 1769.

ELEGY

ON THE DEATH OF MR JOHN TANDEY, SEN.

A sincere Christian friend. He died 5th January 1769, aged 76.

  YE virgins of the sacred choir,
  Awake the soul-dissolving lyre,
    Begin the mournful strain;
  To deck the much-loved Tandey's urn,
  Let the poetic genius burn,
    And all Parnassus drain.

  Ye ghosts! that leave the silent tomb
  To wander in the midnight gloom,
    Unseen by mortal eye;
  Garlands of yew and cypress bring,   10
  Adorn his tomb, his praises sing,
    And swell the general sigh.

  Ye wretches, who could scarcely save
  Your starving offspring from the grave,
    By God afflicted sore,
  Vent the big tear, the soul-felt sigh,
  And swell your meagre infants' cry,
    For Tandey is no more.

  To you his charity he dealt,
  His melting soul your miseries felt,   20
    And made your woes his own.

ON THE LAST EPIPHANY

A common friend to all mankind;
His face the index of his mind,
  Where all the saint was shown.

In him the social virtues joined,
His judgment sound, his sense refined,
  His actions ever just.
Who can suppress the rising sigh,
To think such saint-like men must die,
  And mix with common dust?   30

Had virtue power from death to save,
The good man ne'er would see the grave,
  But live immortal here:
Hawksworth and Tandey are no more;
Lament, ye virtuous and ye poor,
  And drop the unfeigned tear.

ON THE LAST EPIPHANY; OR, CHRIST COMING TO JUDGMENT

Behold! just coming from above,
The Judge, with majesty and love!
The sky divides, and rolls away,
T'admit Him through the realms of day!
The sun, astonished, hides its face,
The moon and stars with wonder gaze
At Jesu's bright superior rays!
Dread lightnings flash, and thunders roar,
And shake the earth and briny shore;
The trumpet sounds at heaven's command,   10
And pierceth through the sea and land;

The dead in each now hear the voice,
The sinners fear and saints rejoice;
For now the awful hour is come,
When every tenant of the tomb
Must rise, and take his everlasting doom.

A HYMN FOR CHRISTMAS DAY

ALMIGHTY Framer of the skies!
O let our pure devotion rise,
　　Like incense in Thy sight!
Wrapped in impenetrable shade
The texture of our souls were made,
　　Till Thy command gave light.

The sun of glory gleamed: the ray
Refined the darkness into day,
　　And bid the vapours fly.
Impelled by His eternal love,　　　　10
He left His palaces above
　　To cheer our gloomy sky.

How shall we celebrate the day,
When God appeared in mortal clay,
　　The mark of worldly scorn;
When the archangel's heavenly lays
Attempted the Redeemer's praise,
　　And hailed salvation's morn?

A humble form the Godhead wore,
The pains of poverty He bore,　　　　20
　　To gaudy pomp unknown:
Though in a human walk He trod,
Still was the man Almighty God,
　　In glory all His own.

Despised, oppressed, the Godhead bears
The torment of this vale of tears,
   Nor bid His vengeance rise ;
He saw the creature He had made
Revile His power, His peace invade ;
   He saw with mercy's eyes.   30

How shall we celebrate His name,
Who groaned beneath a life of shame,
   In all afflictions tried?
The soul is raptured to conceive
A truth, which Being must believe,
   The God Eternal died.

My soul, exert thy powers, adore,
Upon devotion's plumage soar
   To celebrate the day.
The God from whom creation sprung   40
Shall animate my grateful tongue ;
   From Him I'll catch the lay !

                X. Y.

SLY DICK

SHARP was the frost, the wind was high,
And sparkling stars bedecked the sky ;
Sly Dick, in arts of cunning skilled,
Whose rapine all his pockets filled,
Had laid him down to take his rest
And soothe with sleep his anxious breast.
'Twas thus a dark infernal sprite,
A native of the blackest night,
Portending mischief to devise,
Upon Sly Dick he cast his eyes.   10
Then straight descends the infernal sprite,
And in his chamber does alight :

SLY DICK

In visions he before him stands,
And his attention he commands.
Thus spake the sprite : 'Hearken, my friend,
And to my counsels now attend.
Within the garret's spacious dome
There lies a well stored wealthy room,
Well stored with cloth and stockings too,
Which I suppose will do for you ;　　　　　20
First from the cloth take thou a purse,
For thee it will not be the worse,
A noble purse rewards thy pains,
A purse to hold thy filching gains ;
Then, for the stockings, let them reeve,
And not a scrap behind thee leave ;
Five bundles for a penny sell,
And pence to thee will come pell-mell ;
See it be done with speed and care'.
Thus spake the sprite and sunk in air.　　　30

When in the morn, with thoughts erect,
Sly Dick did on his dream reflect,
'Why, faith', thinks he, ''tis something too,
It might—perhaps—it might—be true,
I'll go and see'. Away he hies,
And to the garret quick he flies,
Enters the room, cuts up the clothes,
And after that reeves up the hose ;
Then of the cloth he purses made,
Purses to hold his filching trade.　　　　　40
　　　　　Cætera desunt.

THE CHURCHWARDEN AND THE APPARITION

A FABLE

The night was cold, the wind was high,
And stars bespangled all the sky;
Churchwarden Joe had lain him down,
And slept secure on bed of down;
But still the pleasing hope of gain,
That never left his active brain,
Exposed the churchyard to his view,
That seat of treasure wholly new.
'Pull down that cross', he quickly cried,
The mason instantly complied:　　　　　10
When lo! behold, the golden prize
Appears—joy sparkles in his eyes!
The door now creaks, the window shakes,
With sudden fear he starts and wakes.
Quaking and pale, in eager haste
His haggard eyes around he cast;
A ghastly phantom, lean and wan,
That instant rose, and thus began:
'Weak wretch—to think to blind my eyes
Hypocrisy's a thin disguise;　　　　　20
Your humble mien and fawning tongue
Have oft deceived the old and young.
On this side now, and now on that,
The very emblem of the bat:
Whatever part you take, we know
'Tis only interest makes it so,

And though with sacred zeal you burn,
Religion's only for your turn ;
I'm Conscience called !' Joe greatly feared ;
The lightning flashed—it disappeared.   30

APOSTATE WILL

In days of old, when Wesley's power
Gathered new strength by every hour,
Apostate Will, just sunk in trade,
Resolved his bargain should be made.
Then straight to Wesley he repairs,
And puts on grave and solemn airs,
Then thus the pious man addressed :
'Good sir, I think your doctrine best,
Your servant will a Wesley be,
Therefore the principles teach me '.   10
The preacher then instructions gave,
How he in this world should behave.
He hears, assents, and gives a nod,
Says every word's the word of God,
Then lifting his dissembling eyes,
' How blessèd is the sect !' he cries,
' Nor Bingham, Young, nor Stillingfleet,
Shall make me from this sect retreat'.
He then his circumstance declared,
How hardly with him matters fared,   20
Begged him next morning for to make
A small collection for his sake.
The preacher said, ' Do not repine,
The whole collection shall be thine '.
With looks demure and cringing bows,
About his business straight he goes.

His outward acts were grave and prim,
The Methodist appeared in him.
But, be his outward what it will,
His heart was an apostate's still.   30
He'd oft profess an hallowed flame,
And everywhere preached Wesley's name;
He was a preacher, and what not,
As long as money could be got;
He'd oft profess, with holy fire,
'The labourer's worthy of his hire'.

It happened once upon a time,
When all his works were in their prime,
A noble place appeared in view;
Then—to the Methodists, adieu!   40
A Methodist no more he'll be,
The Protestants serve best for *he*.
Then to the curate straight he ran,
And thus addressed the reverend man:
'I was a Methodist, 'tis true;
With penitence I turn to you.
O that it were your bounteous will
That I the vacant place might fill!
With justice I'd myself acquit,
Do every thing that's right and fit'.   50
The curate straightway gave consent—
To take the place he quickly went.
Accordingly he took the place,
And keeps it with dissembled grace.

14th April 1764

THE METHODIST
May 1770.

SAYS Tom to Jack, "'Tis very odd,
These representatives of God,
In colour, way of life, and evil,
Should be so very like the devil'.
Jack, understand, was one of those
Who mould religion in the nose,
A red-hot Methodist; his face
Was full of puritanic grace,
His loose lank hair, his slow gradation,
Declared a late regeneration;   10
Among the daughters long renowned,
For standing upon holy ground;
Never in carnal battle beat,
Though sometimes forced to a retreat.
But Catcott, hero as he is,
Knight of incomparable phiz,
When pliant doxy seems to yield,
Courageously forsakes the field.
Jack, or to write more gravely, John,
Through hills of Wesley's works had gone;   20
Could sing one hundred hymns by rote,
Hymns which will sanctify the throat:
But some indeed composed so oddly,
You'd swear 'twas bawdy songs made godly.

COLIN INSTRUCTED

YOUNG Colin was as stout a boy
As ever gave a maiden joy;
But long in vain he told his tale
To black-eyed Biddy of the Dale.

'Ah why', the whining shepherd cried,
'Am I alone your smiles denied?
I only tell in vain my tale
To black-eyed Biddy of the Dale'.

'True, Colin', said the laughing dame,
'You only whimper out your flame;   10
Others do more than sigh their tale
To black-eyed Biddy of the Dale'.

He took the hint, etc.

A BURLESQUE CANTATA

Recitative

MOUNTED aloft in Bristol's narrow streets,
Where pride and luxury with meanness meets,
A sturdy collier pressed the empty sack,
A troop of thousands swarming on his back;
When sudden to his rapt ecstatic view
Rose the brown beauties of his red-haired Sue.
Music spontaneously echoed from his tongue,
And thus the lover rather bawled, than sung.

Air

Zounds! Pri'thee, pretty Zue, is it thee?
  Odzookers, I mun have a kiss!   10
A sweetheart should always be free,
  I whope you wunt take it amiss.

Thy peepers are blacker than a coal,
  Thy carcase is sound as a sack,
Thy visage is whiter than ball,
  Odzookers, I mun have a smack.

Recitative

The swain descending, in his raptured arms
Held fast the goddess, and despoiled her charms.
Whilst, locked in Cupid's amorous embrace,
His jetty skin met her red bronzed face,
It seemed the sun when labouring in eclipse;
And on her nose he stamped his sable lips,
Pleased * * * * *

CLIFTON

CLIFTON, sweet village! now demands the lay,
The loved retreat of all the rich and gay;
The darling spot which pining maidens seek,
To give health's roses to the pallid cheek.
Warm from its font the holy water pours,
And lures the sick to Clifton's neighbouring bowers.
Let bright Hygeia her glad reign resume,
And o'er each sickly form renew her bloom.
Me, whom no fell disease this hour compels
To visit Bristol's celebrated wells,
Far other motives prompt my eager view;
My heart can here its favourite bent pursue;
Here can I gaze, pause, and muse between,
And draw some moral truth from every scene.
Yon dusky rocks that from the stream arise,
In rude rough grandeur threat the distant skies,
Seem as if nature, in a painful throe,
With dire convulsions labouring to and fro,
(To give the boiling waves a ready vent)
At one dread stroke the solid mountain rent;
The huge cleft rocks transmit to distant fame
The sacred gilding of a good saint's name.

Now round the varied scene attention turns
Her ready eye—my soul with ardour burns;
For on that spot my glowing fancy dwells,
Where cenotaph its mournful story tells—
How Britain's heroes, true to honour's laws,
Fell, bravely fighting in their country's cause.
But though in distant fields your limbs are laid,
In fame's long list your glories ne'er will fade ; 30
But, blooming still beyond the grip of death,
Fear not the blast of time's inclouding breath.
Your generous leader raised this stone to say,
You followed still where honour led the way :
And by this tribute, which his pity pays,
Twines his own virtues with his soldiers' praise.
Now Brandon's cliffs my wandering gazes meet,
Whose craggy surface mocks the lingering feet ;
Queen Bess's gift, (so ancient legends say)
To Bristol's fair ; where to the sun's warm ray 40
On the rough bush the linen white they spread,
Or deck with russet leaves the mossy bed.

 Here as I musing take my pensive stand,
Whilst evening shadows lengthen o'er the land,
O'er the wide landscape cast the circling eye,
How ardent memory prompts the fervid sigh.
O'er the historic page my fancy runs,
Of Britain's fortunes—of her valiant sons.
Yon castle, erst of Saxon standards proud,
Its neighbouring meadows dyed with Danish blood. 50
Then of its later fate a view I take :
Here the sad monarch lost his hope's last stake ;
When Rupert bold, of well-achieved renown,
Stained all the fame his former prowess won.
But for its ancient use no more employed,
Its walls are mouldered and its gates destroyed ;

In history's roll it still a shade retains,
Though of the fortress scarce a stone remains.
Eager at length I strain each aching limb,
And breathless now the mountain's summit climb. 60
Here does attention her fixed gaze renew,
And of the city takes a nearer view.
The yellow Avon, creeping at my side,
In sullen billows rolls a muddy tide ;
No sportive naiads on her streams are seen,
No cheerful pastimes deck the gloomy scene ;
Fixed in a stupor by the cheerless plain,
For fairy flights the fancy toils in vain :
For though her waves, by commerce richly blest,
Roll to her shores the treasures of the west, 70
Though her broad banks trade's busy aspect wears,
She seems unconscious of the wealth she bears.
Near to her banks, and under Brandon's hill,
There wanders Jacob's ever-murmuring rill,
That, pouring forth a never-failing stream,
To the dim eye restores the steady beam.
Here too (alas ! though tottering now with age)
Stands our deserted, solitary stage,
Where oft our Powel, Nature's genuine son,
With tragic tones the fixed attention won : 80
Fierce from his lips his angry accents fly,
Fierce as the blast that tears the northern sky ;
Like snows that trickle down hot Ætna's steep,
His passion melts the soul, and makes us weep :
But oh ! how soft his tender accents move—
Soft as the cooings of the turtle's love—
Soft as the breath of morn in bloom of spring,
Dropping a lucid tear on zephyr's wing !
O'er Shakespeare's varied scenes he wandered wide,
In Macbeth's form all human power defied ; 90

In shapeless Richard's dark and fierce disguise,
In dreams he saw the murdered train arise;
Then what convulsions shook his trembling breast,
And strewed with pointed thorns his bed of rest!
But fate has snatched thee—early was thy doom,
How soon enclosed within the silent tomb!
No more our raptured eyes shall meet thy form,
No more thy melting tones our bosoms warm.
Without thy powerful aid, the languid stage
No more can please at once and mend the age.   100
Yes, thou art gone! and thy beloved remains
Yon sacred old cathedral wall contains;
There does the muffled bell our grief reveal,
And solemn organs swell the mournful peal,
Whilst hallowed dirges fill the holy shrine,
Deservèd tribute to such worth as thine.
No more at Clifton's scenes my strains o'erflow,
For the muse, drooping at this tale of woe,
Slackens the strings of her enamoured lyre,
The flood of gushing grief puts out her fire;   110
Else would she sing the deeds of other times,
Of saints and heroes sung in monkish rhymes;
Else would her soaring fancy burn to stray,
And through the cloistered aisle would take her way,
Where sleep (ah! mingling with the common dust)
The sacred bodies of the brave and just.
But vain the attempt to scan that holy lore,
These softening sighs forbid the muse to soar.
So treading back the steps I just now trod,
Mournful and sad I seek my lone abode.   120

THE COPERNICAN SYSTEM

The sun revolving on his axis turns,
And with creative fire intensely burns;
Impelled the forcive air, our earth supreme
Rolls with the planets round the solar gleam.
First Mercury completes his transient year,
Glowing, refulgent, with reflected glare;
Bright Venus occupies a wider way,
The early harbinger of night and day;
More distant still, our globe terraqueous turns,
Nor chills intense, nor fiercely heated burns;   10
Around her rolls the lunar orb of light,
Trailing her silver glories through the night.
On the earth's orbit see the various signs,
Mark where the sun, our year completing, shines;
First the bright Ram his languid ray improves;
Next glaring watery, through the Bull he moves;
The amorous Twins admit his genial ray;
Now burning, through the Crab he takes his way;
The Lion flaming, bears the solar power;
The Virgin faints beneath the sultry shower.   20
Now the just Balance weighs his equal force,
The slimy Serpent swelters in his course;
The sabled Archer clouds his languid face;
The Goat, with tempests, urges on his race;
Now in the Waterer his faint beams appear,
And the cold Fishes end the circling year.
Beyond our globe, the sanguine Mars displays
A strong reflection of primæval rays;
Next belted Jupiter far distant gleams,
Scarcely enlightened with the solar beams;   30

With four unfixed receptacles of light,
He tours majestic through the spacious height ;
But farther yet the tardy Saturn lags,
And five attendant luminaries drags ;
Investing with a double ring his pace,
He circles through immensity of space.

 These are Thy wondrous works, first Source of God.
Now more admired in being understood.
D. B.

 Bristol, 23rd *December* [1769]

HORATIUS : Lib. I. Carm. V.

WHAT gentle youth, my lovely fair one, say,
 With sweets perfumed, now courts thee to the bower,
Where glows with lustre red the rose of May,
 To form thy couch in love's enchanting hour?

By zephyrs waved, why does thy loose hair sweep
 In simple curls around thy polished brow?
The wretch that loves thee now too soon shall weep
 Thy faithless beauty and thy broken vow.

Though soft the beams of thy delusive eyes
 As the smooth surface of the untroubled stream ; 10
Yet, ah! too soon the ecstatic vision flies,
 Flies like the fairy paintings of a dream.

Unhappy youth, oh, shun the warm embrace,
 Nor trust too much affection's flattering smile :
Dark poison lurks beneath that charming face,
 Those melting eyes but languish to beguile.

Thank heaven, I've broke the sweet but galling chain,
Worse than the horrors of the stormy main !
D. B.

HORATIUS: Lib. I. Carm. XIX.

Yes! I am caught, my melting soul
To Venus bends without control,
   I pour the impassioned sigh.
Ye gods! what throbs my bosom move,
Responsive to the glance of love,
   That beams from Stella's eye.

Oh, how divinely fair that face,
And what a sweet resistless grace
   On every feature dwells!
And on those features all the while
The softness of each frequent smile
   Her sweet good-nature tells.

O love! I'm thine, no more I sing
Heroic deeds, the sounding string
   Forgets its wonted strains;
For aught but love the lyre's unstrung,
Love melts and trembles on my tongue,
   And thrills in every vein.

Invoking the propitious skies,
The green-sod altar let us rise,
   Let holy incense smoke.
And, if we pour the sparkling wine,
Sweet, gentle peace may still be mine,
   This dreadful chain be broke.   D. B.

AN EPITAPH ON AN OLD MAID

Here lies, her debt of nature paid,
A handsome, proud, and ancient maid,
Who used (you'll think it strangely odd)
This as a plea to cheat her God:
That few are blest who fondly wed,
So rare the joys of marriage-bed;
Thus broke the law that first was given
By the kind hand of parent Heaven.
Be wise, ye fair, and this apply—
God orders you to multiply. 10

SUNDAY: A FRAGMENT

Hervenis, harping on the hackneyed text,
By disquisitions is so sore perplexed,
He stammers—instantaneously is drawn
A bordered piece of inspiration lawn,
Which being thrice unto his nose applied,
Into his pineal gland the vapours glide;
And now again we hear the doctor roar
On subjects he dissected thrice before.
I own at church I very seldom pray,
For vicars, strangers to devotion, bray. 10
Sermons, though flowing from the sacred lawn,
Are flimsy wires from reason's ingot drawn;
And, to confess the truth, another cause
My every prayer and adoration draws;
In all the glaring tinctures of the bow,
The ladies front me in celestial row.

SUNDAY

(Though, when black melancholy damps my joys,
I call them nature's trifles, airy toys;
Yet when the goddess reason guides the strain,
I think them, what they are, a heavenly train.) 20
The amorous rolling, the black sparkling eye,
The gentle hazel, and the optic sly;
The easy shape, the panting semi-globes,
The frankness which each latent charm disrobes;
The melting passions, and the sweet severe,
The easy amble, the majestic air;
The tapering waist, the silver-mantled arms,
All is one vast variety of charms.
Say, who but sages stretched beyond their span,
Italian singers, or an unmanned man, 30
Can see Elysium spread upon their brow,
And to a drowsy curate's sermon bow?

If (but 'tis seldom) no fair female face
Attracts my notice by some glowing grace,
Around the monuments I cast my eyes,
And see absurdities and nonsense rise.
Here rueful-visaged angels seem to tell,
With weeping eyes, a soul is gone to hell;
There a child's head, supported by duck's wings,
With toothless mouth a hallelujah sings; 40
In funeral pile eternal marble burns,
And a good Christian seems to sleep in urns.
A self-drawn curtain bids the reader see
An honourable Welchman's pedigree;
A rock of porphyry darkens half the place,
And virtues blubber with no awkward grace;
Yet, strange to tell, in all the dreary gloom
That makes the sacred honours of the tomb,
No quartered coats above the bel appear,
No battered arms, or golden corsets there. 50

* * * * *

SUICIDE

Since we can die but once, what matters it,
If rope or garter, poison, pistol, sword,
Slow-wasting sickness, or the sudden burst
Of valve arterial in the noble parts,
Curtail the miseries of human life?
Though varied is the cause, the effect's the same:
All to one common dissolution tends.

THE RESIGNATION

O God, Whose thunder shakes the sky,
    Whose eye this atom globe surveys,
To Thee, my only rock, I fly,
    Thy mercy in Thy justice praise.

The mystic mazes of Thy will,
    The shadows of celestial light,
Are past the power of human skill,—
    But what the Eternal acts is right.

O teach me in the trying hour,
    When anguish swells the dewy tear,
To still my sorrows, own Thy power,
    Thy goodness love, Thy justice fear.

If in this bosom aught but Thee
    Encroaching sought a boundless sway,
Omniscience could the danger see,
    And mercy look the cause away.

Then why, my soul, dost thou complain?
    Why drooping seek the dark recess?
Shake off the melancholy chain,
    For God created all to bless.

But ah! my breast is human still;
  The rising sigh, the falling tear,
My languid vitals' feeble rill,
  The sickness of my soul declare.

But yet, with fortitude resigned,
  I'll thank the inflictor of the blow;
Forbid the sigh, compose my mind,
  Nor let the gush of misery flow.

The gloomy mantle of the night,
  Which on my sinking spirit steals,   30
Will vanish at the morning light
  Which God, my East, my Sun, reveals.

ON THE IMMORTALITY OF THE SOUL

SAY, O my soul, if not allowed to be
Immortal, whence the mystery we see
Day after day, and hour after hour,
But to proclaim its never-ceasing power?
If *not* immortal, then our thoughts of thee
Are visions but of non-futurity.
Why do we live to feel of pain on pain,
If, in the midst of hope, we hope in vain?
Perish the thought in night's eternal shade:
To *live*, then *die*, man was not *only* made.   10
There's yet an awful something else remains,
Either to lessen or increase our pains.
Whate'er it be, whate'er man's future fate,
Nature proclaims there *is* another state
Of woe, or bliss. But who is he can tell?
None but the good, and they that have done well.

Oh! may that happiness be ours, my friend!
The little we have now will shortly end;
When joy and bliss more lasting will appear,
Or all our hopes translated into fear.   20
Oh! may our portion in that world above,
Eternal Fountain of Eternal Love,
Be crowned with peace that bids the sinner *live*;
With praise to Him who only can forgive—
Blot out the stains and errors of our youth;
Whose smile is mercy, and whose word is truth.

ENQUIRY AFTER HAPPINESS

[Written on a blank leaf in a copy of Lucas's "Enquiry after Happiness."]

THOUGH happiness be each man's darling aim,
Yet folly too, too often plays the game;
To that one centre all our wishes tend,
We fly the means yet still pursue the end.
No wonder then we find our hopes were vain;
The wretch who shuns his cure must still complain.
In labyrinths of crooked error lost,
Or on life's sea with raging tempest tossed,
We by no compass steer, but blindly stray,
And, knowing we are wrong, ne'er ask the way.   10
'How hard, how very hard to walk', they cry,
'In thorny roads while flowery meads are nigh!'
But know, deluded mortals, virtue's race
Is run in paths of pleasantness and peace;
Though narrow, yet sufficient for the few
Who have this pearl of price alone in view.
'But how', they ask, 'can we this gem obtain?'
Be that thy task, O Lucas, to explain.

As Milton, eyeless bard, has sweetly sung
The fatal course whence all our woes first sprung,
So he has taught, though not in measured phrase,
A lesson which deserves full greater praise ;
How man (as once in Eden) may be blest,
And paradise be found in every breast.
O ! may you find it there, may you obtain
The bliss which too much knowledge rendered vain,
By tasting boldly the fair fruit again.

Lucas like Milton, wondrous bard, was blind,
Like Milton too, illumined was his mind :
Then ask thy Guide, for he who seeks shall find.
                                                    D. B.

LAST VERSES

FAREWELL, Bristolia's dingy piles of brick,
Lovers of mammon, worshippers of trick !
Ye spurned the boy who gave you antique lays,
And paid for learning with your empty praise.
Farewell, ye guzzling aldermanic fools,
By nature fitted for corruption's tools !
I go to where celestial anthems swell ;
But you, when you depart, will sink to hell.
Farewell, my mother !—cease, my anguished soul,
Nor let distraction's billows o'er me roll !
Have mercy, Heaven ! when here I cease to live,
And this last act of wretchedness forgive.   T. C.

24th August 1770

THE
COMPLETE
POETICAL WORKS
of
THOMAS CHATTERTON

VOLUME II

CONTENTS

VOLUME II

THE ROWLEY POEMS

The Execution of Sir Charles Bawdin	1
Ælla:—	
Epistle to Mastre Canynge on Ælla	15
Letter to the digne Mastre Canynge	16
Introduction	18
Ælla	19
Prologue to Goddwyn	71
Goddwyn	72
English Metamorphosis	80
An Excelente Balade of Charitie	84
To Johne Ladgate	87
Songe to Ælla	88
Lines by John Ladgate	89
The Tournament	90
Battle of Hastings (No. 1)	98
Battle of Hastings (No. 2)	115
The Romaunte of the Cnyghte	139
The Romance of the Knight, modernised by Chatterton	140
Eclogues:—	
1. Robert and Raufe	142
2. Nigel	144
3. A man, a woman, Sir Roger	147
4. Elinoure and Juga	150
The Storie of William Canynge	152
On Our Lady's Church	157
On the same	158

On the Dedication of Our Lady's Church	159
The Parlyamente of Sprytes	160
On the Minster	169
Fragment on Richard I.	170
The Warre	171
The World	172
The Unknown Knight	174
The Broder of Orderys Whyte	178
Dialogue between Master Philpot and Walworth	179
The Merrie Trickes of Lamyngetowne	180
Songe of Seyncte Baldwynne	184
Songe of Seyncte Warburghe	185
On Oure Ladyes Chirch	186
A Chronycalle of Brystowe	188
On Happienesse	189
The Gouler's Requiem	190
Onn Johne a Dalbenie	191
Heraudyn	191
Epitaph on Robert Canynge	191
The Accounte of W. Canynge's Feast	192
Fragment, attributed to Elmar, Bishop of Selseie	192
Fragment, attributed to Ecca, Bishop of Hereford	193
NOTES	194
GLOSSARY	208
INDEX OF FIRST LINES (Vols. i. and ii.)	219

THE ROWLEY POEMS

THE EXECUTION OF SIR CHARLES BAWDIN

The feathered songster chanticleer
   Has wound his bugle horn,
And told the early villager
   The coming of the morn:

King Edward saw the ruddy streaks
   Of light eclipse the gray;
And heard the raven's croaking throat
   Proclaim the fated day.

'Thou'rt right', quoth he, 'for, by the God
   That sits enthroned on high!   10
Charles Bawdin, and his fellows twain,
   To-day shall surely die'.

Then with a jug of nappy ale
   His knights did on him wait;
'Go tell the traitor, that to-day
   He leaves this mortal state'.

Sir Canterlone then bended low,
   With heart brim full of woe;
He journeyed to the castle gate,
   And to Sir Charles did go.   20

But when he came, his children twain,
    And eke his loving wife,
With briny tears did wet the floor,
    For good Sir Charles's life.

'O good Sir Charles!' said Canterlone,
    'Bad tidings I do bring'.
'Speak boldly, man', said brave Sir Charles,
    'What says thy traitor king?'

'I grieve to tell, before yon sun
    Does from the welkin fly,   30
He hath upon his honour sworn,
    That thou shalt surely die'.

'We all must die', quoth brave Sir Charles,
    'Of that I'm not afeared;
What boots to live a little space?
    Thank Jesu, I'm prepared;

But tell thy king, for mine he's not,
    I'd sooner die to-day
Than live his slave, as many are,
    Tho' I should live for aye'.   40

Then Canterlone he did go out,
    To tell the mayor straight
To get all things in readiness
    For good Sir Charles's fate.

Then Master Canynge sought the king,
    And fell down on his knee;
'I'm come', quoth he, 'unto your grace
    To move your clemency'.

Then quoth the king, 'Your tale speak out,
    You have been much our friend;   50
Whatever your request may be,
    We will to it attend'.

'My noble liege ! all my request
  Is for a noble knight,
Who tho' mayhap he has done wrong,
  He thought it still was right :
He has a spouse and children twain,
  All ruined are for aye ;
If that you are resolved to let
  Charles Bawdin die to-day'.   60
'Speak not of such a traitor vile',
  The king in fury said ;
'Before the evening star shall shine,
  Bawdin shall lose his head :
Justice does loudly for him call,
  And he shall have his meed :
Speak, Master Canynge ! What thing else
  At present do you need ?'
'My noble liege', good Canynge said,
  'Leave justice to our God,   70
And lay the iron rule aside ;
  Be thine the olive rod.
Was God to search our hearts and reins,
  The best were sinners great ;
Christ's vicar only knows no sin,
  In all this mortal state.
Let mercy rule thine infant reign,
  'Twill fast thy crown full sure ;
From race to race thy family
  All sovereigns shall endure :   80
But if with blood and slaughter thou
  Begin thy infant reign,
Thy crown upon thy children's brows
  Will never long remain'.

THE EXECUTION OF

'Canynge, away! this traitor vile
  Has scorned my power and me;
How canst thou then for such a man
  Entreat my clemency?'

'My noble liege! the truly brave
  Will valorous actions prize;   90
Respect a brave and noble mind
  Although in enemies'.

'Canynge, away! By God in heaven
  That did me being give,
I will not taste a bit of bread
  Whilst this Sir Charles doth live.

By Mary, and all saints in heaven,
  This sun shall be his last'.
Then Canynge dropped a briny tear,
  And from the presence past.   100

With heart brim full of gnawing grief,
  He to Sir Charles did go,
And sat him down upon a stool,
  And tears began to flow.

'We all must die', quoth brave Sir Charles;
  'What boots it how or when;
Death is the sure, the certain fate
  Of all we mortal men.

Say why, my friend, thy honest soul
  Runs over at thine eye;   110
Is it for my most welcome doom
  That thou dost child-like cry?'

Quoth godly Canynge, 'I do weep,
  That thou so soon must die,
And leave thy helpless sons behind;
  'Tis this that wets mine eye'.

'Then dry the tears that out thine eye
  From godly fountains spring;
Death I despise, and all the power
  Of Edward, traitor king.   120

When through the tyrant's welcome means
  I shall resign my life,
The God I serve will soon provide
  For both my sons and wife.

Before I saw the lightsome sun,
  This was appointed me;
Shall mortal man repine and grudge
  What God ordains to be?

How oft in battle have I stood,
  When thousands died around;   130
When smoking streams of crimson blood
  Imbrued the fattened ground?

How did I know that every dart,
  That cut the airy way,
Might not find passage to my heart,
  And close mine eyes for aye?

And shall I now, for fear of death,
  Look wan and be dismayed?
Nay! from my heart fly childish fear,
  Be all the man displayed.   140

Ah, godlike Henry! God forfend,
  And guard thee and thy son,
If 'tis His will; but if 'tis not,
  Why then, His will be done.

My honest friend, my fault has been
  To serve God and my prince;
And that I no time-server am,
  My death will soon convince.

In London city was I born,
    Of parents of great note;   150
My father did a noble arms
    Emblazon on his coat.

I make no doubt but he is gone
    Where soon I hope to go;
Where we for ever blest shall be,
    From out the reach of woe.

He taught me justice and the laws
    With pity to unite;
And eke he taught me how to know
    The wrong cause from the right.   160

He taught me with a prudent hand
    To feed the hungry poor;
Nor let my servants drive away
    The hungry from my door.

And none can say but all my life
    I have his wordès kept;
And summed the actions of the day
    Each night before I slept.

I have a spouse, go ask of her,
    If I defiled her bed?   170
I have a king, and none can lay
    Black treason on my head.

In Lent, and on the holy eve,
    From flesh I did refrain;
Why should I then appear dismayed
    To leave this world of pain?

No, hapless Henry! I rejoice,
    I shall not see thy death;
Most willingly in thy just cause
    Do I resign my breath.   180

Oh, fickle people, ruined land !
  Thou wilt know peace no moe ;
While Richard's sons exalt themselves,
  Thy brooks with blood will flow.

Say, were ye tired of godly peace,
  And godly Henry's reign,
That you did chop your easy days
  For those of blood and pain?

What tho' I on a sled be drawn,
  And mangled by a hind, 190
I do defy the traitor's power,
  He can not hurt my mind ;

What tho', uphoisted on a pole,
  My limbs shall rot in air,
And no rich monument of brass
  Charles Bawdin's name shall bear ;

Yet in the holy book above,
  Which time can't eat away,
There with the servants of the Lord
  My name shall live for aye. 200

Then welcome death ! for life eterne
  I leave this mortal life ;
Farewell, vain world, and all that's dear,
  My sons and loving wife !

Now death as welcome to me comes,
  As e'er the month of May ;
Nor would I even wish to live,
  With my dear wife to stay'.

Quoth Canynge, ' 'Tis a goodly thing
  To be prepared to die ; 210
And from this place of care and pain
  To God in heaven to fly'.

THE EXECUTION OF

And now the bell began to toll,
    And clarions to sound;
Sir Charles he heard the horses' feet
    A-prancing on the ground:

And, just before the officers,
    His loving wife came in,
Weeping unfeigned tears of woe,
    With loud and dismal din.   220

'Sweet Florence! now I pray forbear,
    In quiet let me die;
Pray God that every christian soul
    May look on death as I.

Sweet Florence! why these briny tears?
    They wash my soul away,
And almost make me wish for life,
    With thee, sweet dame, to stay.

'Tis but a journey I shall go
    Unto the land of bliss;   230
Now, as a proof of husband's love,
    Receive this holy kiss'.

Then Florence, faltering in her say,
    Trembling these wordès spoke,
'Ah, cruel Edward, bloody king!
    My heart is well nigh broke:

Ah, sweet Sir Charles! why wilt thou go,
    Without thy loving wife?
The cruel axe that cuts thy neck,
    It eke shall end my life'.   240

And now the officers came in
    To bring Sir Charles away,
Who turnèd to his loving wife,
    And thus to her did say:

'I go to life, and not to death;
 Trust thou in God above,
And teach thy sons to fear the Lord,
 And in their hearts Him love:

Teach them to run the noble race
 That I their father run;
Florence, did death thee take—adieu!
 Ye officers, lead on'.

Then Florence rav'd as any mad,
 And did her tresses tear;
'Oh stay, my husband, lord, and life!'—
 Sir Charles then dropped a tear.

Till, tirèd out with raving loud,
 She fell upon the floor;
Sir Charles exerted all his might,
 And march'd from out the door.

Upon a sled he mounted then
 With looks full brave and sweet;
Looks, that enshone no more concern
 Than any in the street.

Before him went the council-men,
 In scarlet robes and gold,
And tassels spangling in the sun,
 Much glorious to behold.

The friars of Saint Augustine next
 Appearèd to the sight,
All clad in homely russet weeds
 Of godly monkish plight.

In different parts a godly psalm
 Most sweetly they did chant;
Behind their backs six minstrels came,
 Who tuned the strung bataunt.

Then five-and-twenty archers came;
　Each one the bow did bend,
From rescue of king Henry's friends
　Sir Charles for to defend.　　　　　　280

Bold as a lion came Sir Charles,
　Drawn, on a cloth-laid sled,
By two black steeds in trappings white,
　With plumes upon their head.

Behind him five-and-twenty more
　Of archers strong and stout,
With bended bow each one in hand,
　Marchèd in goodly rout.

Saint James's friars marchèd next,
　Each one his part did chant;　　　　290
Behind their backs six minstrels came,
　Who tuned the strung bataunt.

Then came the mayor and aldermen,
　In cloth of scarlet deck't;
And their attending men, each one
　Like eastern princes trick't.

And after them a multitude
　Of citizens did throng;
The windows were all full of heads,
　As he did pass along.　　　　　　　300

And when he came to the high cross,
　Sir Charles did turn and say,
'O Thou, that savest man from sin,
　Wash my soul clean this day!'

At the great minster window sat
　The king in mickle state,
To see Charles Bawdin go along
　To his most welcome fate.

SIR CHARLES BAWDIN

Soon as the sled drew nigh enough,
   That Edward he might hear,   310
The brave Sir Charles he did stand up
   And thus his words declare:

'Thou seest me, Edward, traitor vile!
   Exposed to infamy;
But be assured, disloyal man!
   I'm greater now than thee.

By foul proceedings, murder, blood,
   Thou wearest now a crown;
And hast appointed me to die,
   By power not thy own.   320

Thou thinkest I shall die to-day;
   I have been dead till now,
And soon shall live to wear for aye
   A crown upon my brow;

Whilst thou, perhaps, for some few years,
   Shalt rule this fickle land,
To let them know how wide the rule
   'Twixt king and tyrant hand:

Thy power unjust, thou traitor slave!
   Shall fall on thy own head'—   330
From out of hearing of the king
   Departed then the sled.

King Edward's soul rushed to his face,
   He turned his head away,
And to his brother Gloucester
   He thus did speak and say:

'To him that so-much-dreaded death
   No ghastly fears can bring,
Behold the man! he spoke the truth,
   He's greater than a king!'   340

'So let him die!' duke Richard said;
'And may each one our foes
Bend down their necks to bloody axe,
And feed the carrion crows'.

And now the horses gently drew
Sir Charles up the high hill;
The axe did glister in the sun,
His precious blood to spill.

Sir Charles did up the scaffold go,
As up a gilded car 350
Of victory, by valorous chiefs
Gained in the bloody war:

And to the people he did say,
'Behold, you see me die
For serving loyally my king,
My king most rightfully.

As long as Edward rules this land,
No quiet you will know;
Your sons and husbands shall be slain,
And brooks with blood shall flow. 360

You leave your good and lawful king
When in adversity;
Like me, unto the true cause stick,
And for the true cause die'.

Then he, with priests, upon his knees,
A prayer to God did make,
Beseeching Him unto Himself
His parting soul to take.

Then, kneeling down, he laid his head
Most seemly on the block; 370
Which from his body fair at once
The able headsman struck.

And out the blood began to flow,
  And round the scaffold twine;
And tears, enough to wash't away,
  Did flow from each man's eyne.

The bloody axe his body fair
  Into four parties cut;
And every part, and eke his head,
  Upon a pole was put.   380.

One part did rot on Kynwulph hill,
  One on the minster tower,
And one from off the castle gate
  The crowen did devour;

The other on Saint Paul's good gate,
  A dreary spectacle;
His head was placed on the high cross,
  In High-street most nobile.

Thus was the end of Bawdin's fate.
  God prosper long our king,   390.
And grant he may, with Bawdin's soul,
  In heaven God's mercy sing!

ÆLLA:

A TRAGYCAL ENTERLUDE, OR DISCOOR-SEYNGE TRAGEDIE, WROTENN BIE THOMAS ROWLEIE;

PLAIEDD BEFORE MASTRE CANYNGE, ATTE HYS HOWSE NEMPTE THE RODDE LODGE;

ALSOE BEFORE THE DUKE OF NORFOLCK, JOHAN HOWARD.

EPISTLE TO MASTRE CANYNGE ON ÆLLA

'TIS sung by minstrels, that in ancient time,
  When reason hid herself in clouds of night,
The priest delivered all the law in rhyme,
  Like painted tilting-spears to please the sight,
The which in its fell use do make much dere;
So did their ancient lay deftly delight the ear.

Perchance in virtue's cause rhyme might be then,
  But oft now flieth to the other side;
In holy priest appears the ribald's pen,
  In humble monk appears the baron's pride; 10
But rhyme with some, as adder without teeth,
Makes pleasure to the sense, but may do little scath.

Sir John, a knight, who hath a barn of lore,
  Knows Latin at first sight from French or Greek;
Tortureth his knowledge ten years or more,
  To rynge upon the Latin word to speak.
Whoever speaketh English is despised,
The English, him to please, must first be Latinized.

Vivian, a monk, a good requiem sings,
  Can preach so well, each hind his meaning knows; 20
Albeit these good gifts away he flings,
  Being as bad in verse as good in prose.
He sings of saints who dièd for their God,
And every winter night afresh he sheds their blood.

To maidens, housewives, and unlearned dames,
  He reads his tales of merriment and woe.
Laugh loudly soundeth from the dolt adrames;
  He swells in praise of fools, tho' knows them so;

Sometimes at tragedy they laugh and sing,
At merry jesting tale some hard-drained water bring. 30
   Yet Vivian is no fool, beyond his lines.
     Geoffrey makes verse, as handycrafts their ware;
   Words without sense full foolishly he twines,
     Cutting his story off as with a shear;
Waits months on nothing, and (his story done)
No more you from it know than if you ne'er begun.

   Enough of others; of myself to write,
     Requiring what I do not now possess,
   To you I leave the task; I know your might
     Will make my faults, my many faults, be less. 40
'Ælla' with this I send, and hope that you
Will from it cast away what lines may be untrue.

   Plays made from holy tales I hold unmeet,
     Let some great story of a man be sung;
   When as a man we God and Jesus treat,
     In my poor mind, we do the Godhead wrong.
But let no words, which modesty might not hear,
Be placèd in the same. Adieu until anere.

LETTER TO THE DIGNE MASTRE CANYNGE

   Strange doom it is, that, in these days of ours,
     Naught but a bare recital can have place;
   Now shapely poesy hath lost its powers
     And meagre history is only grace;
   They pick up loathsome weeds instead of flowers,
     And families, instead of wit, they trace:
Now poesy can meet with no regrate,
Whilst prose and heraldry rise in estate.

ÆLLA

Let kings and rulers, when they gain a throne,
  Shew what their grandsires and great-grandsires
    bore, 10
Emarschalled arms that, not before their own,
  Now ranged with what their fathers had before;
Let trades and town-folk let such things alone,
  Nor fight for sable in a field of ore;
Seldom or never are arms virtue's meed,
She nillynge to take mickle aye doth heed.

A man askance upon a piece may look,
  And shake his head to stir his rede about;
Quoth he, if I askaunted o'er this book,
  Should find therein that truth is left without; 20
Eke if unto a view perchance I took
  The long bede-roll of all the writing rout,
Asserius, Ingulphus, Turgot, Bede,
Throughout them all naught like it I could read.

Pardon, ye graybeards, if I say, unwise
  Ye are to stick so close and bysmarelie
To history; you do it too much prize,
  Which amenusèd thoughts of poesy;
Some drybblette share you should to that alyse,
  Not making everything be history; 30
Instead of mounting on a wingèd horse,
You on a cart-horse drive in doleful course.

Canynge and I from common course dissent,
  We ride the steed, but give to him the rein,
Nor will between crazed mouldering books be pent,
  But soar on high, and in the sunbeams' sheen;
And where we know some broken flowers besprent,
  We take it, and from old rust do it clean;
We will not chainèd to one pasture be,
But sometimes soar 'bove truth of history. 40

Say, Canynge, what was verse in days of yore?
　Fine thoughts, and couplets fetyvelie bewryen,
Not such as do annoy this age so sore,
　A keppened poyntelle resting at each line.
Verse may be good, but poesy wants more,
　A boundless subject, and a song adygne;
According to the rule I have this wrought,
If it please Canynge, I care not a groat.

The thing itself must be its own defence,
　Some metre may not please a woman's ear.　50
Canynge looks not for poesy, but sense;
　And digne and wordie thoughts is all his care.
Canynge, adieu! I do you greet from hence;
　Full soon I hope to taste of your good cheer;
Good Bishop Carpenter did bid me say
He wish'd you health and happiness for aye.
T. ROWLEIE.

INTRODUCTION

SOME cherisaunei 'tis to gentle mind,
　When they have chevyced their land from bane,
When they are dead, they leave their name behind,
　And their good deeds do on the earth remain;
　Down in the grave we bury every stain,
Whilst all their gentleness is made to sheene,
Like fetive baubles rarely to be seen.

Ælla, the warden of this castle-stead,
　Whilst Saxons did the English sceptre sway,
Who made whole troops of Dacian men to bleed,　10

Then closed his eyes, and closed his eyes for aye,
We rouse him up, before the Judgment Day,
to say what he, as clergyond, can ken,
And how he sojourned in the vale of men.

ÆLLA

Scene, BRISTOL

Enter CELMONDE

Cel. Before yon ruddy sun has drove his wain
    Through half his journey, dight in robes of gold,
  Me, hapless me, he will a wretch behold,
    Myself, and all that's mine, bound in mischance's chain.

  Ah! Bertha, why did nature frame thee fair?
    Why art thou all that poyntelle can bewreene?
  Why art thou not as coarse as others are?
    But then—thy soul would through thy visage sheene,
  That shimmers on thy comely semlykeene,
    Like nutbrown clouds, when by the sun made red,   10
  Or scarlet, with choice linen cloth ywreene;
    Such would thy sprite upon thy visage spread.
This day brave Ælla doth thine hand and heart
Claim as his own to be, which ne'er from his must part.

  And can I live to see her with anere?
    It cannot, must not, nay, it shall not be!
  This night I'll put strong poison in the beer,
    And him, her, and myself, at once will sle.

Assist me, hell! let devils round me 'tend,
To slay myself, my love, and eke my doughty friend. [*Exit.* 20

Enter ÆLLA *and* BERTHA

Æl. Not when the holy priest did make me knight,
Blessing the weapon, telling future deed,
How by my hand the hardy Dane should bleed,
How I should often be, and often win, in fight;

Not when I first beheld thy beauteous hue,
Which struck my mind, and roused my softer soul;
Not, when from the barbèd horse in fight did view
The flying Dacians o'er the wide plain roll,
When all the troops of Denmark made great dole,
Did I feel joy with such reddour as now, 30
When holy priest, the lechemanne of the soul,
Did knit us both in an enforcing vow;
Now hailie Ælla's happiness is great,
Fate haveth now y-made his woes for to emmate.

Ber. My lord and husband, such a joy is mine;
But maiden modesty must not so say,
Albeit thou mayest read it in mine eyne,
Or in my heart, where thou shalt be for aye;
In sooth, I have but meeded out thy faie;
For twelve times twelve the moon hath been yblent, 40
As many times hath vied the god of day,
And on the grass her rays of silver sent,

ÆLLA

Since thou didst choose me for thy sweet to be,
Enacting in the same most faithfully to me.
  Oft have I seen thee at the noon-day feast,
    When daisèd by thyself, for want of peers,
  Awhile thy merrymen did laugh and jest,
    On me thou seem'st all eyes, to me all ears.
  Thou wardest me as if in hundred fears
    Lest a disdainful look to thee be sent,   50
  And offerings made me, more than thy compeers,
    Of scarfs of scarlet, and fine parament;
  All thy intent to please was lyssed to me,
  I say it, I must strive that you rewarded be.

Æl. My little kindnesses which I did do
    Thy gentleness doth corven them so great,
  Like bawsyn elephants my gnats do shew;
    Thou dost my thoughts of paying love amate.
  But had my actions stretched the roll of fate,
    Plucked thee from hell, or brought heaven down to thee,   60
  Laid the whole world a footstool at thy feet,
    One smile would be sufficient meed for me.
  I am love's borrower, and can never pay,
  But be his borrower still, and thine, my sweet, for aye.

Ber. Love, do not rate your services so small,
    As I to you, such love unto me bear;
  For nothing past will Bertha ever call,
    Nor on a food from heaven think to cheer.
  As far as this frail brittle flesh will spare,
    Such, and no further, I expect of you;   70
  Be not too slack in love, nor over-dear;
    A small fire than a loud flame proves more true.

Æl. Thy gentle wordès do thy volunde ken
     To be more clergionde than is in most of men.

Enter CELMONDE *and* MINSTRELS

Cel. All blessings shower on gentle Ælla's head!
     Oft may the moon, in silver shining light,
     In varied changes varied blessings shed,
     Scattering far abroad mischance's night;
     And thou, fair Bertha! thou, fair dame, so bright,
     Long mayest thou with Ælla find much peace,   80
     With happiness, as with a robe, bedight,
     With every changing moon new joys increase!
     I, as a token of my love to speak,
     Have brought you jugs of ale, at night your brain to break.

All. When supper's past we'll drink your ale so strong,
     'Tide life, 'tide death.

Cel.   Ye minstrels, chant your song.

Minstrels' Song, by a man and woman

Man. Turn thee to thy shepherd swain,
         Bright sun has not drunk the dew
         From the flowers of yellow hue;
         Turn thee, Alice, back again.   90

Wom. No, deceiver, I will go,
         Softly tripping o'er the mees,
         Like the silver-footed doe,
         Seeking shelter in green trees.

Man. See the moss-grown daisied bank,
    Peering in the stream below;
    Here we'll sit, on dewy dank,
    Turn thee, Alice, do not go.

Wom. I've heard erste my grandame say,
    Young damoiselles should not be   100
    In the swotie month of May,
    With young men by the greenwood tree.

Man. Sit thee, Alice, sit and hark,
    How the blackbird chants his note,
    The chelandree, gray morn lark,
    Chanting from their little throat.

Wom. I heard them from each greenwood tree,
    Chanting forth so blatantly,
    Telling lecturnyes to me,
    Mischief is when you are nigh.   110

Man. See along the mees so green
    Pièd daisies, kingcups swote;
    All we see, by none be seen,
    Naught but sheep sets here a fote.

Wom. Shepherd swain, you tear my gratche,
    Out upon you! let me go;
    Leave me swythe, or I'll alatche.
    Robin, this your dame shall know.

Man. See the crooking bryony
    Round the poplar twist his spray;   120
    Round the oak the green ivy
    Flourisheth and liveth aye.

  Let us seat us by this tree,
   Laugh, and sing to loving airs;
  Come, and do not coyen be,
   Nature made all things by pairs.

  Courted cats will after kind;
   Gentle doves will kiss and coo.
Wom. But man, he must be ywrynde
   Till sir priest make one of two.   130

  Tempt me not to the foul thing,
   I will no man's leman be;
  Till sir priest his song doth sing,
   Thou shalt ne'er find aught of me.

Man. By Our Lady her Yborne,
   To-morrow, soon as it is day,
  I'll make thee wife, nor be forsworn,
   So 'tide me life or death for aye.

Wom. What doth lettè, but that now
   We at once, thus hand in hand,   140
  Unto divinistre may go,
   And be linked in wedlock's band?

Man. I agree, and thus I plight
   Hand and heart, and all that's mine;
  Good sir Roger, do us right,
   Make us one at Cuthbert's shrine.

Both. We will in a cottage live,
   Happy, though of no estate;
  Every clocke more love shall give,
   We in goodness will be great.   150

Æl. I like this song, I like it mickle well;
  And there is money for your singing now.
  But have you none that marriage-blessings tell?
Cel.   In marriage, blessings are but few, I trow.

Minst. Loverde, we have; and, if you please, will sing,
    As well as our chough-voices will permit.
Æl. Come then, and see you sweetly tune the string,
    And stretch and torture all the human wit,
    To please my dame.
Minst.   We'll strain our wit and sing.

Minstrels' Song

First M. The budding flowerets blushes at the light,   160
    The mees be sprinkled with the yellow hue;
    In daisied mantles is the mountain dight,
        The nesh young cowslip bendeth with the dew;
    The trees enleafèd, unto heaven straught,
    When gentle winds do blow, to whistling din is brought.

    The evening comes, and brings the dew along;
    The ruddy welkin shineth to the eyne;
    Around the ale-stake minstrels sing the song,
    Young ivy round the doorpost do entwine;
I lay me on the grass; yet, to my will,   170
Albeit all is fair, there lacketh something still.

Second M. So Adam thoughten when, in Paradise,
    All heaven and earth did homage to his mind;
    In woman only mannes pleasure lies,
        As instruments of joy were made the kind.

Go, take a wife unto thine arms, and see
Winter, and barren hills, will have a charm
    for thee.

Third M. When Autumn bleak and sunburnt do appear,
    With his gold hand gilding the falling leaf,
    Bringing up Winter to fulfil the year,   180
    Bearing upon his back the ripèd sheaf,
When all the hills with woody seed is white,
When lightning-fires and lemes do meet from far the sight;

    When the fair apple, red as even sky,
      Do bend the tree unto the fruitful ground,
    When juicy pears, and berries of black dye,
      Do dance in air, and call the eyes around;
    Then, be the even foul, or even fair,
    Methinks my hartys joy is steyncèd with some care.

Second M. Angels be wrought to be of neither kind,   190
    Angels alone from hot desire be free,
    There is a somewhat ever in the mind,
      That, without woman, cannot stillèd be
    No saint in cell, but, having blood and tere,
    Do find the sprite to joy on sight of woman fair.

Women be made, not for themselves, but man,
  Bone of his bone, and child of his desire;
From an ynutyle member first began,
  Y-wrought with much of water, little fire;
Therefore they seek the fire of love, to heat   200
The milkiness of kind, and make themselves complete.

Albeit, without women, men were peers
  To savage kind, and would but live to slay;
But woman oft the sprite of peace so cheers,
  Tochelod in angels' joy they angels be.
Go, take thee quickly to thy bed a wife,
  Be bannèd, or blessèd hie, in proving marriage life.

Another Minstrel's Song, by
SYR THYBBOT GORGES

As Elinor by the green lesselle was sitting,
  As from the sun's hetè she hurried,
She said, as her white hands white hosen was knitting,   210
  'What pleasure it is to be married!

My husband, Lord Thomas, a forester bold,
  As ever clove pin or the basket,
Does no cherysauncys from Elinor hold,
  I have it as soon as I ask it.

When I lived with my father in merry Cloud-dell,
  Tho' 'twas at my liefe to mind spinning ;
I still wanted something, but what ne'er could tell ;
  My lord father's barbed hall had naught winning.

Each morning I rise, do I set my maidens,   220
  Some to spin, some to curdle, some bleaching ;
If any new entered do ask for my aidens,
  Then quickly you find me a-teaching.

Lord Walter, my father, he lovèd me well,
  And nothing unto me was needing ;
But, should I again go to merry Cloud-dell,
  In sooth it would be without redeynge'.

She said, and Lord Thomas came over the lea,
  As he the fat deerkins was chasing,
She put up her knitting, and to him went she ;   230
  So we leave them both kindly embracing.

Æl. I like eke this ; go in unto the feast,
  We will permit you antecedent be ;
  There sweetly sing each carol, and yaped jest,
  And there is money, that you merry be.
Come, gentle love, we will to spouse-feast go,
And there in ale and wine be drownèd every woe.

Enter MESSENGER

Mess. Ælla, the Danes are thundering on our coast,
  Like shoals of locusts, cast up by the sea ;
Magnus and Hurra, with a doughty host,   240
  Are raging, to be stilled by none but thee ;

  Haste, swift as lightning, to these rovers flee,
   Thy dogs alone can tame this raging bull.
  Haste quickly, for anigh the town they be,
   And Wedëcester's roll of doom be full.
  Haste, haste, O Ælla, to the battle fly,
  For in a moment's space ten thousand men may
   die.

Æl. Beshrew thee for thy news! I must be gone,
   Was ever luckless doom so hard as mine?
  Thus from dysportysment to war to run,   250
   To change the silk vest for the gaberdine.
Ber. O! like an adder, let me round thee twine,
   And hide thy body from the shafts of war.
  Thou shalt not, must not, from thy Bertha ryne,
   But ken the din of clarions from afar.
Æl. O love, was this thy joy, to shew the treat,
  Then, groffyshe, to forbid thy hungered guests
   to eat?

  O my upswelling heart, what words can say
   The pains, that passeth in my soul ybrent?
  Thus to be torn upon my spousal day,   260
   O! 'tis a pain beyond entendëment.
  Ye mighty gods, and is your favours sent,
   As thus, fast dented to a load of pain?
  Must we aye hold in chase the shade content,
   And, for a bodykyn, a swarthe obtain?
  O! why, ye saints, oppress ye thus my soul?
  How shall I speak my woe, my freme, my
   dreary dole?

Cel. Sometimes the wisest lacketh poor man's rede.
   Reason and cunning wit oft flees away.
  Then, loverde, let me say, with homaged
   dread,   270
  (Beneath your feet y-lain), my counsel say.

If thus we let the matter lethlen lay,
　　The foemen, every honde-poyncte, getteth foot.
My loverde, let the spearmen, dight for fray,
　　And all the sabbataners go about.
I speak, my loverde, only to uprise
Your wit from marvel, and the warrior to alyse.

Æl. Ah! now thou puttest arrows in my heart,
　　My soul doth now begin to see hersel',
　　I will uprise my might, and do my part　　280
　　　To slay the foemen in my fury fell.
　　But how can tongue my ramping fury tell,
　　　Which riseth from my love to Bertha fair?
　　Nor could the queed, and all the might of hell,
　　　Found out impleasaunce of so black a geare.
Yet I will be myself, and rouse my sprite
To act with glory, and go meet the bloody fight.

Ber. No, thou shalt never leave thy Bertha's side,
　　Nor shall the wind upon us blow alleyne;
　　I, like an adder, will untò thee bide,　　290
　　　'Tide life, 'tide death, it shall behold us twain.
　　I have my part of dreary dole and pain,
　　　It bursteth from me at the holtred eyne;
　　In tides of tears my swarthynge soul will drain;
　　　If dreary dole is thine, 'tis two times mine.
Go not, O Ælla; with thy Bertha stay,
For, with thy countenance, my soul will go away.

Æl. Oh! 'tis for thee, for thee alone I feel;
　　Yet I must be myself; with valour's gear
　　I'll dight my heart, and knot my limbs in steel,　　300
　　And shake the bloody sword and stainèd spear.

Ber. Can Ælla from his breast his Bertha tear?
Is she so rough and ugsomme to his sight?
Intriguing wight, is deadly war so dear?
Thou prizest me below the joys of fight.
Thou shalt not leave me, albeit the earth
Hung pendant by thy sword, and cravèd for
thy morthe.

Æl. Didst thou know how my woes, as stars ybrent,
Headed by these wordès, do on me fall,
Thou wouldest strive to give my heart content, 310
Waking my sleeping mind to honour's call.
Of happiness, I prize thee more than all
Heaven can me send, or cunning wit acquire;
Yet I will leave thee, on the foe to fall,
Returning to thy eyen with double fire.

Ber. Must Bertha boon request, and be denied?
Receive at once a dart, in happiness and pride?

Æl. Do stay, at least, till morrow's sun appears.
Thou knowest well the Dacians' mighty power;
With them a minute worketh bane for years; 320
They undo realms within a single hour.
Rouse all thy honour, Bertha; look attoure
Thy bleeding country, which for hasty deed
Calls, for the rodeynge of some doughty power,
To royn its royners, make its foemen bleed.

Ber. Rouse all thy love, false and intriguing wight,
Nor leave thy Bertha thus upon pretence of fight.
Thou needst not go, until thou hast command
Under the signet of our lord the king.

Æl. And wouldst thou make me then a recreand? 330
Holy Saint Mary, keep me from the thing!

        Here, Bertha, thou hast put a double sting,
          One for thy love, another for thy mind.
Ber.   Offended Ælla, thine upbraiding blynge;
          'Twas love of thee that foul intent ywrynde.
        Yet hear me supplicate, to me attend,
        Hear from my groted heart the lover and the friend.

        Let Celmonde in thine armour-brace be dight,
          And in thy stead unto the battle go.
        Thy name alone will put the Danes to flight,   340
          The air that bears it would press down the foe.
Æl.   Bertha, in vain thou wouldst me recreand do;
          I must, I will, fight for my country's weal,
        And leave thee for it. Celmonde, swiftly go,
          Tell my Brystowans to dight in steel;
        Tell them I scorn to know them from afar,
        But leave the virgin bridal bed for bed of war.
          [*Exeunt* CELMONDE *and* Messenger.

Ber.   And thou wilt go? Oh! my agroted heart!
Æl.   My country waits my march, I must away;
          Albeit I should go to meet the dart   350
        Of certain death, yet here I would not stay.
        But thus to leave thee, Bertha, doth asswaie
          More torturing pains than can be said by tyngue.
        Yet rouse thy honour up, and wait the day,
          When round about me song of war they sing.
        O Bertha, strive my torture to accaie,
        And joyous see my arms, dight out in war array.

Ber. Difficile is the penance, yet I'll strive
    To keep my woe behyltren in my breast.
  Albeit naught may to me pleasure give,   360
    Like thee, I'll strive to set my mind at rest.
  Yet oh! forgive if I have thee distressed;
    Love, doughty love, will bear no other sway.
  Just as I was with Ælla to be blest,
    Fate foully thus hath snatchèd him away.
  It was a tene too weighty to be born,
  Without an ounde of fears and breast with sighs y-torn.

Æl. Thy mind is now thyself; why wilt thou be
    All pure, all kingly, all so wise in mind,
    Only to let poor wretched Ælla see   370
    What wondrous jewels he now must leave behind?
  O Bertha fair, ward every coming wind,
    On every wind I will a token send;
  On my long shield ycorne thy name thou'lt find;
    But here comes Celmonde, wordie knight and friend.

Cel. Thy Bristol knights for thy forthcoming lynge;
  Each one athwart his back his long war-shield doth sling.

Æl. Bertha, adieu; but yet I cannot go.
Ber.   Life of my soul, my gentle Ælla, stay;
  Torture me not with such a dreary woe.   380
Æl. I must; I will; 'tis honour calls away.
Ber. Oh! my agroted heart, braste, braste in twaie.
  Ælla, for honour, flies away from me!
Æl. Bertha, adieu; I may not here obaie.
  I'm flying from myself in flying thee. [*Exit.*

Ber. O Ælla, husband, friend, and loverde, stay;
   He's gone, he's gone, alas! perchance he's gone
      for aye.   [*Exit.*

Cel. Hope, holy sister, sweeping through the sky,
   In crown of gold, and robe of lily white,
   Which far abroad in gentle air do fly,   390
     Meeting from distance the enjoyous sight,
     Albeit oft thou takest thy high flight
     Hecket in a mist, and with thine eyes yblent,
   Now comest thou to me with starry light;
   Unto thy vest the red sun is adente;
The summer tide, the month of May appear
Depycte with skilléd hand upon thy wide aumere.

   I from a night of hopelen am adawed,
     Astonished at the festiveness of day;
   Ælla, by naught more than his myndbruche
     awed,   400
     Is gone, and I must follow to the fray;
   Celmonde can ne'er from any battle stay.
     Doth war begin? there's Celmonde in the
       place;
   But when the war is done, I'll haste away.
     The rest from 'neath time's mask must shew
       its face.
I see unnumbered joys around me rise,
Blake standeth future doom, and joy doth me
   alyse.

   Oh honour, honour, what is by thee hanne?
     Happy the robber and the bordelyer,
   Who knows not thee, or is to thee bestanne, 410
     And nothing does thy mickle ghastness
       fear;

Fain would I from my bosom all thee tear.
Thou there dysperpellest thy lightning-
brand;
Whilst my soul's forwyned, thou art the gare;
Slain is my comfort by thy fiery hand;
As some tall hill, when winds do shake the
ground,
It carveth all abroad, by bursting hidden wound.

Honour! what be it? 'tis a shadow's shade,
A thing of wychencref, or idle dream,
One of the fonnis which the clerche have
made,   420
Men without souls and women for to fleme.
Knights, who oft know the loud din of the
beme,
Should be forgard to such enfeebling ways,
Make every act, alyche their souls, be breme,
And for their chivalry alone have praise.
Oh thou, whate'er thy name, or Zabalus or
Queed,
Come, steel my sable sprite for strange and dole-
ful deed!   [*Exit*.

Scene, near WATCHET

Enter MAGNUS, HURRA, *and* HIGH PRIEST, *with
the* ARMY

Mag. Quick, let the offerings to the gods begin,
To know of them the issue of the fight.
Put the blood-stainèd sword and pavyes in, 430
Spread quickly all around the holy light.

ÆLLA

HIGH PRIEST *singeth*

Ye, who high in murky air
Dealeth seasons foul or fair,
Ye, who, when ye were agguylte,
The moon in bloody mantles hylte,
Moved the stars, and did unbind
Every barrier to the wind;
When the oundynge waves distressed
Stroven to be overest,
Sucking in the spire-girt town,   440
Swallowing whole nations down,
Sending death, on plagues astrodde,
Moving like the earthès God,
To me send your hest divine,
Light enlighten all mine eyne,
That I may now undevise
All the actions of the emprise.
    [*Falls down and afterwards riseth.*

Thus say the gods; 'Go, issue to the plain,
For there shall meynte of mighty men be slain'.

Mag. Why, so there ever was, when Magnus fought,   450
  Oft have I treynted noyance through the host;
  Athorowe swords, alyche the queed distraught,
    Have Magnus pressing wrought his foemen loaste.
  As when a tempest vexeth sore the coast,
    The sounding wave the sandy strand do tear,
  So did I in the war the javelin tossed,
    Full many a champion's breast received my spear.

My shield, like summer morie gronfer droke,
My deadly spear, alyche a lightning-melted oak.

Hur. Thy words are great, full high of sound, and eke 460
  Like thunder, to the which doth come no rain.
It lacketh not a doughty hand to speak;
  The cock sayeth least, yet armed is he alleyne.
Certès thy wordès maie thou might'st have sayne
Of me, and many more, who eke can fight,
Who haveth trodden down the adventayle,
  And torn the helms from heads of mickle might.
Since then such might is placèd in thy hand,
Let blows thine actions speak, and by thy courage stand.

Mag. Thou art a warrior, Hurra, that I ken, 470
And mickle famèd for thy handy deed.
Thou fightest against maidens, and not men,
  Nor aye thou makest armèd hearts to bleed.
Oft I, caparisoned on bloody steed,
  Haveth thee seen beneath me in the fight,
With corpses I investing every mead,
  And thou aston, and wondering at my might.
Then wouldest thou come in for my renome,
Albeit thou wouldst run away from bloody doom.

Hur. How! but be bourne, my rage — I know aright 480
  Both thee and thine may not be worthy peene;
Eftsoon I hope we shall engage in fight,
  Then to the soldiers all thou wilt bewreene.

  I'll prove my courage on the armèd green,
  'Tis there alone I'll tell thee what I be.
  If I wield not the deadly spear adeene,
   Then let my name be full as low as thee.
  This my fastened shield, this my war-spear
  Shall tell the falling foe if Hurra's heart can fear.

Mag. Magnus would speak, but that his noble sprite   490
  Doth so enrage, he knows not what to say.
  He'd speak in blows, in drops of blood he'd write,
   And on thy heasod paint his might for aye.
  If thou against a wolfin's rage wouldst stay,
   'Tis here to meet it; but if not, be goe,
  Lest I in fury should my arms display,
   Which to thy body will work mickle woe.
  Oh! I be mad, distraught with burning rage,
  No seas of smoking gore will my chafed heart assuage.

Hur. I know thee, Magnus, well; a wight thou art,   500
  That dost aslee along in doled distress,
  Strong bull in body, lyoncelle in heart,
   I almost wish thy prowess were made less!
  When Ælla (name dressed up in ugsomness
   To thee and cowards) thundered on the plain,
  How didst thou thorowe first of fliers press!
   Swifter than feathered arrow didst thou reyne.
  A running prize on saint day to ordain,
  Magnus, and none but he, the running prize will gain.

Mag. Eternal plagues devour thy banèd tongue ! 510
Myriads of adders prey upon thy sprite !
Mayest thou feel all the pains of age whilst young,
Unmanned, uneyed, excluded aye the light,
Thy senses, like thyself, enwrapped in night,
A scoff to foemen, and to beasts a peer.
May forkèd lightning on thy head alight,
May on thee fall the fury of the unweere,
Fen-vapours blast thy every manly power,
May thy bante body quick the loathsome pains devour !
Fain would I curse thee further, but my tyngue 520
Denies my heart the favour so to do.
Hur. Now by the Dacian gods, and heaven's king,
With fury, as thou didst begin, pursue ;
Call on my head all tortures that be rou,
Bane on, till thy own tongue thy curses feel ;
Send on my head the blighting lightning blue,
The thunder loud, the swelling azure rele.
Thy words be high of din, but naught beside,
Bane on, good chieftain, fight with words of mickle pride ;
But do not waste thy breath, lest Ælla come. 530
Mag. Ælla and thee together sink to hell !
Be your names blasted from the roll of doom !
I fear not Ælla, that thou knowest well.
Unlydgefulle traitor, wilt thou now rebel ?
'Tis knowèn, that thy men be linked to mine,
Both sent, as troops of wolves to slaughter fell ;
But now thou lackest them to be all thine.

Now, by the gods that rule the Dacian state,
Speak thou in rage once more, I will thee dysregate.

Hur. I prize thy threats just as I do thy banes, 540
The seed of malice and recendize all.
Thou art a stain unto the name of Danes;
Thou only to thy tongue for proof canst call.
Thou beest a worm so grossile and so small,
I with thy blood would scorn to foul my sword,
But with thy weapons would upon thee fall,
Alyche thy own fear, slay thee with a word.
I Hurra am myself, and aye will be
As great in valorous acts and in command as thee.

Enter a Messenger

Mes. Cease your contentions, chiefs; for, as I stood 550
Upon my watch, I spied an army coming,
Not like a handful of a frighted foe,
But black with armour, moving terribly,
Like a black full cloud, that doth go along
To drop in hail, and help the thunder-storm.
Mag. Are there many of them?
Mes. Thick as the ant-flies in a summer's noon,
Seeming as though they sting as persante too.

Hur. What matters that? let's set our war-array.
Go, sound the beme, let champions prepare, 560
Not doubting, we will sting as fast as they.
What, dost forgard thy blood; is it for fear?

   Wouldest thou gain the town and castle-
    stere,
    And yet not battle with the soldier-guard?
   Go, hide thee in my tent, aneath the lere,
    I of thy body will keep watch and ward.
Mag. Our gods of Denmark know my heart is good—
Hur. For naught upon the earth, but to be
    choughen's food!

    Enter a second Messenger

Second M. As from my tower I kende the coming
    foe,
    I spied the crossèd shield and bloody
     sword,   570
   The furious Ælla's banner; within ken
   The army is. Disorder through our host
   Is flying, borne on wings of Ælla's name;
   Stir, stir, my lords.
Mag.   What, Ælla! and so near!
   Then Denmark's ruined. Oh! my rising fear!

Hur. What dost thou mean? This Ælla's but a man.
   Now by my sword, thou art a very berne.
   Of late I did thy coward valour scan,
    When thou didst boast so much of action
     derne.   580
   But I to war my doings must atturne,
    To cheer the sabbataneres to deere deed.
Mag. I to the knights on every side will burn,
    Telling them all to make their foemen
    bleed.
   Such shame or death on either side will be,
   My heart I will uprise, and in the battle slea.
            [*Exeunt.*

ÆLLA

Scene, near WATCHET

Enter ÆLLA, CELMONDE, *and* ARMY

Æl. Now, having done our matins and our vows,
　　Let us for the intended fight be boune ;
　　And every champion put the joyous crown
　　Of certain mastership upon his glist'ring
　　　　brows.　　　　　　　　　　　　　590
　　　As for my heart, I own it is, as e'er
　　　It has been in the summer-shine of fate,
　　　Unknowèn to the ugsomme garb of fear ;
　　　My blood embollen, with mastery elate
　　　Boils in my veins, and rolls in rapid state ;
　　　Impatient for to meet the piercing steel,
　　　And tell the world that Ælla died as great
　　　　As any knight who fought for England's
　　　　　weal.
　　Friends, kin, and soldiers, in black armour
　　　drear,
　　My actions imitate, my present counsel hear.　600
　　　There is no house, athrow this fate-scourged
　　　　isle,
　　　That has not lost a kin in these fell fights ;
　　　Fat blood has surfeited the hungered soil,
　　　And towns enlowèd lemèd up the nights.
　　　In gyte of fire our holy church they dyghtes ;
　　　Our sons lie storven in their smoking gore ;
　　　Up by the roots our tree of life they pyghtes,
　　　　Vexing our coast, as billows do the shore.
　　Ye men, if ye are men, display your name,
　　　Y-brende their troops, alyche the roaring
　　　　tempest flame.　　　　　　　　　　610

ÆLLA

Ye Christians, do as worthy of the name,
    These royners of our holy houses slea ;
Burst like a cloud from whence doth come the flame,
    Like torrents, gushing down the mountains, be.
And when along the green their champions flee,
    Swift as the red for-weltrynge lightning-brand
That haunts the flying murderer o'er the lea,
    So fly upon these royners of the land.
Let those that are unto their battayles fled
Take sleep eterne upon a fiery flaming bed.   620

Let coward London see her town on fire,
    And strive with gold to stay the royner's hand ;
Ælla and Bristol haveth thoughts that's higher,
    We fight not for ourselves, but all the land.
As Severn's hyger layeth banks of sand,
    Pressing it down beneath the running stream,
With dreary din enswolters the high strand,
    Bearing the rocks along in fury breme,
So will we bear the Dacian army down,
And through a storm of blood will reach the champion's crown.   630

If in this battle luck ne wayte our gare,
    To Bristol they will turn their fury dire ;
Bristol, and all her joys, will sink to air,
    Burning perforce with unaccustomed fire.

Then let our safety doubly move our ire,
  Like wolfins, roving for the evening prey,
Seeing the lamb and shepherd near the briar,
  Doth the one for safety, the one for hunger slay.
Then when the raven croaks upon the plain,
Oh! let it be the knell to mighty Dacians slain! 640

  Like a red meteor shall my anlace shine,
    Like a strong lyoncelle I'll be in fight,
  Like falling leaves the Dacians shall be slain,
    Like a loud dinning stream shall be my might.
  Ye men, who would deserve the name of knight,
    Let bloody tears by all your paves be wept;
  To coming times no poyntelle shall ywrite,
    'When England had her foemen, Bristol slept'.
Yourselves, your children, and your fellows cry,
'Go, fight in honour's cause, be brave, and win or die'. 650

    I say no more; your spryte the rest will say,
      Your spryte will wrynne that Bristol is your place;
    To honour's house I need not mark the way,
      In your own hearts you may the foot-path trace.
    'Twixt fate and us there is but little space;
      The time is now to prove yourselves be men;
    Draw forth the burnished bill with fetyve grace,
      Rouse, like a wolfynne rousing from his den.

ÆLLA

Thus I enrone my anlace. Go, thou sheath!
I'll put it not in place, till it is sick with death. 660

On, Ælla, on; we long for bloody fray,
 We long to hear the raven sing in vain;
On, Ælla, on; we, certès, gain the day,
 When thou dost lead us to the deadly plain.
Cel. Thy speech, O loverde, fireth the whole train;
 They pant for war, as hunted wolves for breath.
Go, and sit crowned on corpses of the slain,
 Go and ywielde the massy sword of death.
From thee, O Ælla, all our courage reigns,
Each one in phantasy do lead the Danes in chains. 670

Æl. My countrymen, my friends, your noble sprites
 Speak in your eyes, and do your master tell,
Swift as the rain-storm to the earth alights,
 So will we fall upon these royners fell.
Our mowing swords shall plunge them down to hell,
 Their thronging corpses shall onlyghte the stars:
The barrows bursting with the slain shall swell,
 Brynnynge to coming times our famous wars;

ÆLLA

In every eye I see the flame of might
Shining abroad, alyche a hill-fire in the night. 680

When poyntelles of our famous fight shall say,
Each one will marvel at the dernie deed;
Each one will wissen he had seen the day,
And bravely helped to make the foemen bleed.
But for their help our battle will not need,
Our force is force enough to stay their hand.
We will return unto this greenèd mead,
O'er corses of the foemen of the land,
Now to the war let all the clarions sound,
The Dacian troops appear on yonder rising ground. 690

Chiefs, head your bands, and lead. [*Exeunt.*

Scene, near WATCHET

Enter DANES *flying*

1 *Dane.* Fly, fly, ye Danes! Magnus, the chief, is slain,
The Saxons come with Ælla at their head;
Let's strive to get away to yonder green,
Fly, fly; this is the kingdom of the dead.
2 *Dane.* O gods! have thousands by my anlace bled,
And must I now for safety fly away?
See! far besprengèd all our troops are spread,
Yet I will singly dare the bloody fray.
But no! I'll fly, and murder in retreat, 700
Death, blood, and fire shall mark the going of my feet.

ÆLLA

Dane. Enthoghteynge for to 'scape the brondeynge foe,
  As near unto the billowed beach I came,
  Far off I spied a sight of mickle woe,
    Our towering battayles wrapped in sails of flame;
  The armèd Dacians, who were in the same,
    From side to side fled the pursuit of death,
  The swelling fire their courage do inflame,
    They leap into the sea, and bubbling yield their breath;
Whilst those that be upon the bloody plain, 710
Be death-doomed captivest ta'en, or in the battle slain.

Hur. Now by the gods, Magnus, discourteous knight,
  By coward 'haviour haveth done our woe,
  Dyspendynge all the tall men in the fight
    And placing valorous men where dross might go.
  Sythence our fortune haveth turnèd so,
    Gather the soldiers left to future shappe;
  To some new place for safety we will go;
    In future day we will have better hap.
Sound the loud clarion for a quick forloyne, 720
Let all the Dacians swythe unto our banner join.

  Through hamlets we will sprenge sad death and dole,
    Bathe in hot gore, and wash ourselves therein;
  Gods! here the Saxons, like a billow, roll,
    I hear the anlaces' detested din!
Away, away, ye Danes, to yonder penne,
We now will make retreat, in time to fight again.   [*Exeunt.*

Enter CELMONDE

Cel. Oh for a spryte all fire ! to tell the day,
   The day which shall astound the hearer's rede,
   Making our foemen's envying hearts to bleed, 730
   Ybereynge through the world our rennomde name for aye.

   Bright sun had in his ruddy robes been dight,
      From the red east he flitted with his train,
   The hoürs drew away the robe of night,
      Her sable tapestry was rent in twain.
   The dancing streaks bedeckèd heaven's plain,
      And on the dew did smile with shimmering eye,
   Like drops of blood which do black armour stain,
      Shining upon the borne which standeth by.
The soldiers stood upon the hillis side, 740
Like young enleafèd trees which in a forest bide.

   Ælla rose like the tree beset with briars,
      His tall spear shining as the stars at night,
   His eyes enseeming as a flame of fire ;
      When he encheerèd every man to fight,
   His gentle words did move each valourous knight.
      It moveth them, as hunters lyoncelle ;
   In trebled armour is their courage dight,
      Each warring heart for praise and glory swells ;
   Like slowly sounding of the croucheynge stream, 750
   Such did the murmuring sound of the whole army seem.

He leads them on to fight. Oh! then to say
 How Ælla looked, and looking did encheere,
Moving alyche a mountain in affraie,
 When a loud whirlwind do its bosom tear.
To tell how every look would banish fear
 Would ask an angel's poyntelle or his tongue.
Like a tall rock that riseth heaven-were,
 Like a young wolfynne furious and strong,
So did he go, and mighty warriors head ;   760
With gore-depicted wings mastery around him fled.

The battle joined ; swords upon swords did ring ;
 Ælla was chafed, as lions madded be ;
Like falling stars, he did the javelin fling,
 His mighty anlace mighty men did slea ;
Where he did come, the frighted foe did flee,
 Or fell beneath his hand, as falling rain ;
With such a fury he did on them dree,
 Hills of their bowkes did rise upon the plain.
Ælla, thou art—but stay, my tongue, say nee ;   770
How great I him may make, still greater he will be.

Nor did his soldiers see his acts in vain ;
 Here a stout Dane upon his compheere fell,
Here lord and hyndlette sank upon the plain,
 Here son and father trembled into hell,

Chief Magnus sought his way, and, shame to
    tell!
  He sought his way for flight; but Ælla's
    spear
  Upon the flying Dacian's shoulder fell
    Quite through his body, and his heart it
      tare ;
He groaned, and sank upon the gory green, 780
And with his corse encreased the piles of
  Dacians sleen.

  Spent with the fight, the Danish champions
    stand,
    Like bulls whose strength and wondrous
      might is fled ;
  Ælla, a javelin gripped in either hand,
    Flies to the throng, and dooms two Dacians
      dead.
  After his act, the army all yspedde ;
    From every one unmissing javelins flew ;
  They stretched their doughty swords, the
      foemen bled ;
    Full three of four of mighty Danes they
      slew.
The Danes, with terror ruling at their head, 790
Threw down their banner tall, and like a raven
  fled.

  The soldiers followed with a mighty cry,
    Cries that well might the stoutest hearts
      affray.
  Swift as their ships, the vanquished Dacians
    fly ;
    Swift as the rain upon an April day,

ÆLLA

Pressing behind, the English soldiers slay;
   But half the tithes of Danish men remain.
Ælla commands they should the slaughter stay,
   But bind them prisoners on the bloody plain.
The fighting being done, I came away,   800
In other fields to fight a more unequal fray.

Enter a Squire

My servant squire, prepare a flying horse,
   Whose feet are wings, whose pace is like the wind,
Who will outstrip the morning light in course,
   Leaving the mantles of the night behind;
   Some secret matters do my presence find.
   Give out to all that I was slain in fight;
If in this cause thou dost my order mind,
   When I return, thou shalt be made a knight.
Fly, fly, be gone! an hour is a day,   810
Quick dight my best of steeds, and bring him here; away!   [*Exit* Squire.

Ælla is wounded sore, and in the town
   He waiteth, till his wounds be brought to ethe.
And shall I from his brows pluck off the crown,
   Making the victor in his victory blethe?
Oh no! full sooner should my heart's blood smethe,
   Full sooner would I tortured be to death!
But—Bertha is the prize; ah! it were ethe
   To gain so gain a prize with loss of breath.

But then renown eterne—it is but air, 820
Bred in the phantasy, and only living there.

 Albeit everything in life conspire
  To tell me of the fault I now should do,
 Yet would I battentlie assuage my fire,
  And the same means, as I shall now, pursue.
 The qualities I from my parents drew
  Were blood and murder, mastery and war;
 These I will hold to now, and heed no moe
  A wound in honour than a body-scar.
Now, Ælla, now I'm planting of a thorn, 830
By which thy peace, thy love, thy glory shall be torn.   [*Exit.*

Scene, BRISTOL

Enter BERTHA *and* EGWINA

Ber. Gentle Egwina, do not preach me joy;
  I cannot joy in anything but weere.
 Oh! that aught should our happiness destroy,
  Flooding the face with woe and briny tear!
Egw. You must, you must endeavour for to cheer
  Your heart unto some comfortable rest.
 Your loverde from the battle will appear,
  In honour and a greater love be dressed;
 But I will call the minstrels' roundelay, 840
 Perchance the swotie sound may chase your grief away. [*Enter* Minstrels.

ÆLLA

Minstrel's Song

Oh ! sing unto my roundelay ;
  Oh ! drop the briny tear with me ;
Dance no more at holiday ;
  Like a running river be.
    My love is dead,
    Gone to his death-bed,
    All under the willow-tree.

Black his hair as the winter night,
  White his rode as the summer snow,
Red his face as the morning light ;
  Cold he lies in the grave below.
    My love is dead,
    Gone to his death-bed,
    All under the willow-tree.

Sweet his tongue as the throstle's note,
  Quick in dance as thought can be,
Deft his tabour, cudgel stout ;
  Oh ! he lies by the willow-tree.
    My love is dead,
    Gone to his death-bed,
    All under the willow-tree.

Hark ! the raven flaps his wing,
  In the briared dell below ;
Hark ! the death-owl loud doth sing
  To the night-mares, as they go.
    My love is dead,
    Gone to his death-bed,
    All under the willow-tree.

See ! the white moon shines on high,
  Whiter is my true love's shroud,
Whiter than the morning sky,
  Whiter than the evening cloud.

My love is dead,
  Gone to his death-bed,
  All under the willow-tree.

Here, upon my true love's grave,
  Shall the barren flowers be laid;
Not one holy saint to save
  All the celness of a maid.
    My love is dead,
    Gone to his death-bed,
    All under the willow-tree.

With my hands I'll dente the briars,
  Round his holy corse to gre,
Elfin fairy, light your fires,
  Here my body still shall be.
    My love is dead,
    Gone to his death-bed,
    All under the willow-tree.

Come, with acorn-cup and thorn,
  Drain my hartys blood away;
Life and all its good I scorn,
  Dance by night, or feast by day.
    My love is dead,
    Gone to his death-bed,
    All under the willow-tree.

Water-witches, crowned with reytes,
  Bear me to your lethal tide.
I die! I come! my true love waits;—
  Thus the damsel spake and died.

Ber. This singing haveth what could make it please,
  But my uncourtly fate bereaves me of all ease.
                [*Exeunt.*

ÆLLA

Scene, WATCHET

Enter ÆLLA

Æl. Curse on my tardy wounds! bring me a steed!
  I will away to Bertha by this night;
Albeit from my wounds my soul do bleed,
  I will away, and die within her sight.
Bring me a steed, with eagle-wings for flight;
  Swift as my wish, and, as my love is, strong.
The Danes have wrought me mickle woe in fight,   910
  In keeping me from Bertha's arms so long.
Oh! what a doom was mine, sythe mastery
Can give no pleasure, nor my land's good light mine eye!
Ye gods, how is a lover's temper formed!
  Sometimes the same thing will both bane and bless;
One time encalede, then by the same thing warmed,
  Estroughted forth and then ybrogten less.
'Tis Bertha's loss which do my thoughts possess.
  I will, I must away; why stays my steed?
My servants, hither haste; prepare a dress   920
  Which couriers in hasty journies need.
Oh heavens! I must away to Bertha's eyne,
For in her looks I find my being do entwine.
          [*Exit.*

Scene, BRISTOL

Enter CELMONDE

Cel. The world is dark with night; the winds are still;
  Faintly the moon her pallid light makes gleam;
The risen sprites the silent churchyard fill,
  With elfin fairies joining in the dream;

The forest shineth with the silver leme.
Now may my love be sated in its treat;
Upon the bank of some swift running stream, 930
At the sweet banquet I will sweetly eat.
This is the house; ye hinds quickly appear.

Enter a Servant

Go tell to Bertha straight, a stranger waiteth here. [*Exit* Servant.

Enter BERTHA

Ber. Celmonde! ye saints! I hope thou hast good news.
Cel. The hope is lost; for heavy news prepare.
Ber. Is Ælla well?
Cel. He lives; and still may use
The promised blessings of a future year.
Ber. What heavy tidings then have I to fear?
Of what mischance didst thou so lately say?
Cel. For heavy tidings quickly now prepare; 940
Ælla sore wounded is, in battle's fray;
In Wedëcester's wallèd town he lies.
Ber. O my agroted breast!
Cel. Without your sight, he dies.
Ber. Will Bertha's presence ease her Ælla's pain?
I fly; new wings do from my shoulders spring.
Cel. My steed without will deftly bear us twain.
Ber. Oh! I will fly as wind, and noway lynge;
Swiftly caparisons for riding bring.
I have a mind winged with the lightning plume.
O Ælla! Ælla! didst thou know the sting, 950
The which doth canker in my hartys room

ÆLLA

Thou wouldst see plain thyself the cause to be;
Arise, upon thy love, and fly to meeten me.

Cel. The steed on which I came is swift as air,
    My servitors do wait me near the wood;
Quickly with me unto the place repair,
    To Ælla I will give you conduct good.
Your eyes, alyche a balm, will staunch his blood,
    Heal up his wounds, and give his heart all cheer.
Upon your eyes he holds his livelihood;   960
    You do his sprite and all his pleasure bear.
Come, let's away, albeit it is moke,
Yet love will be a torch to turn to fire night's smoke.

Ber. Albeit tempests did the welkin rend,
    Rain, alyche falling rivers, did fierce be,
Earth with the air enchafèd did contend,
    Everychone breath of wind with plagues did sle,
Yet I to Ælla's eyes eftsoon would flee.
Albeit hawthorns did my flesh enseam,
Owlets, with shrieking, shaking every tree,   970
And water-adders wriggling in each stream,
Yet would I fly, nor under covert stay,
But seek my Ælla out; brave Celmonde, lead the way.   [*Exeunt.*

    Scene, A WOOD
    Enter HURRA *and* DANES

Hur. Here in this forest let us watch for prey,
    Revenging on our foemen our ill war;
Whatever shall be English we will slay,
    Spreading our ugsomme rennome to afar.

Ye Dacian men, if Dacian men ye are,
   Let naught but blood sufficient for ye be;
On every breast in gory letters scar,   980
   What sprites you have, and how those sprites may dree.
And if ye get away to Denmark's shore,
Eftsoons we will return, and vanquished be no more.

   The battle lost a battle was indeed;
      Not queedes themselves could stand so hard a fray;
   Our very armour and our helms did bleed,
      The Dacian's sprites, like dew-drops, fled away.
   It was an Ælla did command the day;
      In spite of foemen, I must say his might.
   But we in hynd-lettes' blood the loss will pay,   990
      Shewing that we know how to win in fight.
We will, like wolves enloosed from chains, destroy,—
Our armours winter night, shut out the day of joy.

   When swift-foot time do roll the day along,
      Some hamlet shall unto our fiery brend;
   Bursting alyche a rock, or mountain strong,
      The tall church-spire upon the green shall bend;
   We will the walls and ancient turrets rend,
      Pete every tree with golden fruit do bear.
   Down to the gods the owners thereof send,   1000
      Besprengynge all abroad sad war and bloody weere.

But first to yonder oak-tree we will fly,
And thence will issue out on all that cometh
by.   [*Exeunt.*

Scene, ANOTHER PART OF THE WOOD
Enter CELMONDE *and* BERTHA

Ber. This darkness do affray my woman's breast;
How sable is the spreading sky arrayed!
Happy the cottager, who lives to rest,
Nor is at nightys flemynge hue dismayed.
The stars do scantily the sable brayde;
Wide is the silver rays of comfort wove.
Speak, Celmonde, does it make thee not
afraid?   1010
Cel. Darker the night, the fitter tide for love.
Ber. Sayest thou for love? ah! love is far away.
Fain would I see once more the ruddy lights
of day.

Cel. Love may be nigh, would Bertha call it here.
Ber. How, Celmonde, doth thou mean?
This Celmonde means:
Cel. No gleam, no eyes, nor mortal man appear,
Nor light, an act of love for to bewreenc;
Naught in this forest but this torch doth
sheen,
The which, put out, do leave the whole in
night.
See! how the branching trees do here
entwine,   1020
Making this bower so pleasing to the sight;
This was for love first made, and here it
stands,
That herein lovers may enlink in true love's
bonds.

Ber. Celmonde, speak what thou meanest, or else my
  thoughts
  Perchance may rob thy honesty so fair.
Cel. Then hear, and know, hereto I have you
  brought,
  My long-hid love unto you to make clear.
Ber. Oh heaven and earth! what is it I do hear?
  Am I betrayed? Where is my Ælla, say?
Cel. Oh do not now to Ælla such love bear,   1030
  But geven some on Celmonde's head.
Ber.   Away!
 I will begone, and grope my passage out,
 Albeit adder's stings my legs do twine about.

Cel. Now, by the saints, I will not let thee go,
  Until thou dost my burning love amate.
  Those eyes have causèd Celmonde mickle
   woe,
  Then let their smile first take him in regrate.
  O! didst thou see my breastis troublous
   state,
   There love doth harrow up my joy and
    ethe!
  I wretched be, beyond the help of fate,   1040
   If Bertha still will make my heart-veins
    blethe.
 Soft as the summer flowerets, Bertha, look,
 Full ill I can thy frowns and hard displeasure
  brook.

Ber. Thy love is foul; I would be deaf for aye,
  Rather than hear such deslavatie said;
  Quickly fly from me, and no further say,
   Rather than hear thy love, I would be dead.

Ye saints! and shall I wrong my Ælla's bed?
And wouldst thou, Celmonde, tempt me to the thing?
Let me be gone—all curses on thy head! 1050
Was it for this thou didst a message bring?
Let me be gone, thou man of sable heart,
Or heaven and her stars will take a maiden's part.

Cel. Sythence you will not let my suit avail,
My love will have its joy, although with guilt;
Your limbs shall bend, albeit strong as steel,
The gloomy season will your blushes hylte.
Ber. Help, help, ye saints! Oh that my blood was spilt!
Cel. The saints at distance stand in time of need.
Strive not to go; thou canst not, if thou wilt. 1060
Unto my wish be kind, and naught else heed.
Ber. No, foul deceiver! I will rend the air,
Till death doth stay my din, or some kind traveller hear,

Help, help, oh God!

Enter HURRA *and* DANES

Hur. Ah! that's a woman cries.
I know them; say, who are you, that be there?
Cel. Ye hinds, away! or by this sword ye dies.
Hur. Thy words will ne'er my hartys seat affear.

Ber. Save me! oh save me from this royner here!
Hur. Stand thou by me; now say thy name and land,
Or quickly shall my sword thy body tear. 1070
Cel. Both I will shew thee by my furious hand.
Hur. Beset him round, ye Danes.
Cel. Come on, and see
If my strong anlace may bewryen what I be.

Fight all against CELMONDE; *many Danes he slayeth, and falleth to* HURRA

Cel. Oh! I forslagen be! Ye Danes, now ken
I am that Celmonde, second in the fight,
Who did, at Watchet, so forslege your men.
I feel mine eyes to swim in eterne night:—
To her be kind. [*Dieth.*
Hur. Then fell a worthy knight.
Say, who be you?
Ber. I am great Ælla's wife.
Hur. Ah!
Ber. If against him you harbour foul despite, 1080
Now with the deadly anlace take my life.
My thanks I ever on you will bestow,
From ewbryce you me plucked, the worst of mortal woe.

Hur. I will; it shall be so; ye Dacians, hear:
This Ælla, haveth been our foe for aye;
Thorowe the battle he did furious tear,
Being the life and head of every fray;
From every Dacian power he won the day,
Forslagen Magnus, all our ships ybrente;
By his fell arm we now are made to stray, 1090
The spear of Dacia he in pieces shente.

ÆLLA

<blockquote>
When hantoned barks unto our land did come,
Ælla the cause they said, and wished him bitter doom.
</blockquote>

Ber. Mercy!

Hur.   Be still.
<blockquote>
But yet he is a foeman good and fair,
  When we are spent, he soundeth the forloyne;
The captive's chain he tosseth in the air,
  Cheerèd the wounded both with bread and wine.
Has he not unto some of you been digne?
  You would have smoked on Wedëcestrian field,
But he behylte the clarion for to cleyne,   1100
  Throwing on his wide back his wider-spreading shield.
When you, as caytysned, in field did be,
He oathed you to be still, and straight did set you free.
</blockquote>

<blockquote>
Shall we forslege his wife, because he's brave?
  Because he fighteth for his country's gare?
Will he, who haveth been this Ælla's slave,
  Rob him of what perchance he holdeth dear?
Or shall we men of manly sprites appear,
  Doing him favour for his favour done,
Swift to his palace this damoiselle bear,   1110
  Declare our case, and to our way be gone?
The last you do approve; so let it be.
Damoiselle, come away; you safe shall be with me.
</blockquote>

Ber. All blessings may the saints unto ye give!
<blockquote>
All pleasure may your lengthened livings be!
Ælla, when knowing that by you I live,
  Will think too small a gift the land and sea.
</blockquote>

O Celmonde ! I may deftly read by thee,
What ill betideth the enfoulèd kind.
May not thy cross-stone of thy crime bewree! 1120
May all men know thy valour, few thy mind !
Soldier ! for such thou art in noble fray,
I will thy goings 'tend, and do thou lead the way.

Hur. The morning 'gins along the east to sheene ;
Darkling the light do on the waters play ;
The faint red light slow creepeth o'er the green,
To chase the murkiness of night away ;
Swift flies the hours that will bring out the day ;
The soft dew falleth on the growing grass ;
The shepherd-maiden, dighting her array, 1130
Scarce sees her visage in the wavy glass.
By the full daylight we shall Ælla see,
Or Bristol's wallèd town ; damoiselle, follow me.
[*Exeunt.*

Scene, BRISTOL

Enter ÆLLA *and* Servants

Æl. 'Tis now full morn. I thoughten by last night
To have been here ; my steed hath not my love.
This is my palace ; let my hinds alight,
Whilst I go up, and wake my sleeping dove.
Stay here, my hyndlettes ; I shall go above.
Now, Bertha, will thy look enheal my sprite,
Thy smiles unto my wounds a balm will prove, 1140
My leaden body will be set aright.

Egwina, haste, and ope the portal door,
That I on Bertha's breast may think of war no
more.

Enter EGWINA

Egw. Oh, Ælla!

Æl. Ah! that countenance to me
Speaketh a legendary tale of woe.

Egw. Bertha is—

Æl. What? where? how? say, what of she?

Egw. Gone—

Æl. Gone! ye gods!

Egw. Alas! it is too true.
Ye saints, he dies away with mickle woe!
Ælla! what? Ælla! Oh! he lives again!

Æl. Call me not Ælla; I am him no moe.   1150
Where is she gone away? ah! speak!
how? when?

Egw. I will.

Æl. Caparison a score of steeds; fly! fly!
Where is she? quickly speak, or instant thou
shalt die.

Egw. Still thy loud rage, and hear thou what I
know.

Æl. Oh! speak.

Egw. Like primrose, drooping with the
heavy rain,
Last night I left her, drooping with her weere,
Her love the cause that gave her heart
such pain.

Æl. Her love! to whom?

Egw. To thee, her spouse alleyne.
As is my hentylle every morn to go,
I went, and oped her chamber door in
twain,   1160
But found her not, as I was wont to do.

       Then all around the palace I did seere,
       But could (to my heart's woe) not find her any where.

Æl. Thou liest, foul hag! thou liest! thou art her aid
       To cheer her lust :—but no; it cannot be.

Egw. If truth appear not in what I have said,
       Draw forth thine anlace, quickly then me slea.

Æl. But yet it must, it must be so; I see,
       She with some lusty paramour is gone.
       It must be so.—Oh! how it racketh me! 1170
       My race of love, my race of life, is run.
       Now rage, and furious storm, and tempest come!
       Naught living upon earth can now enswote my doom.

Enter a Servant

Ser. Loverde! I am about the truth to say.
       Last night, full late I did return to rest.
       As to my chamber I did bend my way,
       To Bertha one his name and place addressed;
       Down to him came she, but thereof the rest
       I know no matter; so, my homage made—

Æl. Oh! speak no more; my heart flames in its hest. 1180
       I once was Ælla, now be not its shade.
       Had all the fury of misfortune's will
       Fallen on my bennèd head, I had been Ælla still.

       This only was unarmed, of all my sprite :
       My honour, honour, frowned on the soft wind
       That steekèd on it; now with rage I'm pyghte;
       A furious tempest is my tortured mind.

My honour yet some drybblet joy may find,
To the Dane's wounds I will another give.
When thus my glory and my peace is rynde, 1190
It were a cowardice to think to live.
My servants, unto every asker tell,
If nobly Ælla lived, as nobly Ælla fell.
[*Stabbeth his breast.*

Ser. Ælla is slain; the flower of England's marred!
Æl. Be still; quick let the churches ring my knell.
Call hither brave Coërnyke; he, as ward
Of this my Bristol castle, will do well.
[*Knell rings.*

Enter COËRNYKE

Æl. (to Coër.) Thee I ordain the ward; so all may tell.
I have but little time to drag this life;
My deadly tale, alyche a deadly bell, 1200
Sound in the ears of her I wished my wife.
But ah! she may be fair.
Egw. That she must be.
Æl. Ah! say not so; that word would Ælla doubly slea.

Enter BERTHA *and* HURRA

Æl. Ah! Bertha here!
Ber. What sound is this? What means this deadly knell?
Where is my Ælla? speak; where? how is he?
Oh Ælla! art thou then alive and well?
Æl. I live indeed; but do not live for thee.

Ber. What means my Ælla?
Æl. Here my meaning see.
Thy foulness urged my hand to give this
wound;
It me unsprites.
Ber. It hath unsprited me. 1210
Æl. Ah heavens! my Bertha falleth to the
ground!
But yet I am a man, and so will be.
Hur. Ælla! I am a Dane, but yet a friend to thee.

This damoiselle I found within a wood,
Striving full hard against an armèd swain.
I sent him miring in my comrades' blood.
Celmonde his name, chief of thy warring
train.
This damoiselle sought to be here again,
The which, albeit foemen, we did will;
So here we brought her with you to
remain. 1220
Coïr. Ye noble Danes! with gold I will you fill.
Æl. Bertha, my life! my love! Oh, she is fair.
What faults could Bertha have? What faults
could Ælla fear?

Ber. Am I then thine? I cannot blame thy fear,
But do rest me upon my Ælla's breast.
I will to thee declare the woeful gare.
Celmonde did come to me at time of rest,
Wordeynge for me to fly, at your request,
To Watchet town, where you deceasing lay.
I with him fled; through a dark wood we
pressed, 1230
Where he foul love unto my ears did say;

The Danes—
Æl.   Oh! I die content.— [*Dieth.*
Ber. Oh! is my Ælla dead?
      Oh! I will make his grave my virgin spousal bed.   [BERTHA *fainteth.*
Coër. What? Ælla dead? and Bertha dying too?
      So falls the fairest flowerets of the plain.
      Who can explain the wurchys heaven can do,
      Or who untwist the roll of fate in twain?
      Ælla, thy glory was thy only gain,
      For that, thy pleasure and thy joy was lost.
      Thy countrymen shall rear thee, on the plain,   1240
      A pile of carnes, as any grave can boast.
      Further, a just reward to thee to be,
      In heaven thou sing of God, on earth we'll sing of thee.

GODDWYN
A TRAGEDIE

By THOMAS ROWLIE

PROLOGUE

MADE BY MAISTRE WILLIAM CANYNGE

  WHILOM by writers much ungentle name
    Have upon Godwin, earl of Kent, been laid,
  Thereby bereaving him of faith and fame;
    Unliart divinistres haveth said,
That he was knowen to no holy wurch;
But this was all his fault, he gifted not the church.

  The author of the piece which we enact,
    Although a clergyman, truth will write;
  In drawing of his men, no wit is lacked,
    Even a king might be full pleased to-night.   10
Attend, and mark the parts now to be done,
We, better for to do, do challenge any one.

GODDWYN

Enter GODDWYN *and* HAROLDE

God. Harold!
Har. My loverde!
God.   O! I weep to think
What foemen riseth to devour the land.
They fatten on her flesh, her heart's blood drink,
And all is granted from the royal hand.
Har. Let not thy grievance cease, nor idly stand.
Be I to weep? I weep in tears of gore.
Am I deceived? So should my angry bronde
Display the wrongs on him from whom I bore.
God. I know thy sprite full well; gentle thou art,
Strong, terrible, grim, as smoking armies seem; 10
Yet oft, I fear, thy heat's too great a part,
And that thy rede be oft born down by breme.
What tidings from the king?
Har. His Normans know;
I make no compheeres of the shimmering train.
God. Ah Harold! 'tis a sight of mickle woe,
To know these Normans every glory gain.
What tiding with the folk?
Har. Still murmuring at their fate, still to the king
They roll their troubles, like a surgy sea.
Hath England then a tongue, but not a sting? 20
Doth all complain, yet none will righted be?

God. Await the time, when God will send us aid.
Har. No; we must strive to aid ourselves with power.
 When God will send us aid ! 'tis nobly prayed !
 Must we thus cast away the livelong hour?
 Thus cross our arms, and not to live dareygne,
 Unarmed, inactive, unespryte?
 Far from my heart be fled such thought of pain,
 I'll free my country, or I'll die in fight.

God. But let us wait until some season fit.   30
 My Kentishmen, thy Summertons shall rise;
 Adented prowess to the robe of wit,
 Again the argent horse shall dance in skies.
 Oh Harold, here distracting wanhope lies.
 England, Oh England ! 'tis for thee I blethe.
 Whilst Edward to thy sons will naught alyse,
 Should any of thy sons feel aught of ethe?
 Upon the throne I set thee, held thy crown;
 But oh ! 'twere homage now to pluck thee down.

 Thou art all priest and nothing of the king,   40
 Thou art all Norman, nothing of my blood.
 Know, it becomes thee not a mass to sing;
 Serving thy liege-folk, thou art serving God.

Har. Then I'll do heaven a service. To the skies
 The daily contekes of the land ascend.
 The widow, fatherless, and bondsmen's cries
 Acheke the murky air and heaven astende.
 On us, the rulers, do the folk depend.
 Cut off from earth these Norman slaves shall be.
 Like a loud-roaring flame, my sword shall brend,   50
 Like falling soft raindrops, I will them slea.

We wait too long; our purpose will defayte,
Aboune the high emprise, and rouse the champions straight.

God. Thy sister—
Har. Aye, I know, she is his queen;
Albeit, did she speak her foemen fair,
I would destroy her comely seemlykeene,
And fold my bloody anlace in her hair.
God. Thy fury cease—
Har. No, bid the deadly mere,
Swollen with hidden winds and cause unken'd,
Command it to be still; so 'twill appear, 60
Ere Harold hide his name, his country's friend.
The red-stained brigandine, the aventayle,
The fiery anlace broad shall make my cause prevail.

God. Harold, what wouldest do?
Har. Bethink thee what.
Here lieth England, all her rights unfree,
Here lieth Normans cutting her by lot,
Forbidding every native plant to gre,
What would I do? I furious would them slea,
Tear out their sable heart by rightful breme.
Their death a means unto my life should be, 70
My sprite should revel in their heart-blood stream.
Eftsoons I will declare my rageful ire,
And Goddìs anlace wield in fury dire.

GODDWYN

God. What wouldst thou with the king?
Har. Take off his crown;
    The ruler of some minster him ordain,
    Set up some worthier than I have plucked
        down,
    And peace in England should be brayd again.
God. No, let the super-holy saint-king reign,
    And some more reded rule the untentyff
        realm;
    King Edward, in his courtesy, will deign   80
    To yield the spoils, and only wear the helm.
But from my heart be every thought of gain,
Not any of my kin I wish him to ordain.

Har. Tell me the means, and I will 'bout it straight;
    Bid me to slay myself, it shall be done.
God. To thee I will quickly the means unplayte,
    By which thou, Harold, shalt be proved my
        son.
    I have long seen what pains were under-
        gone,
    What grievances branch out from the general
        tree.
    The time is coming when the mollock
        gron   90
    Drainèd of all its swelling waves shall be.
My remedy is good; our men shall rise,
Eftsoon the Normans and our grievance flies.

Har. I will to the west, and gemote all my knights,
    With bills that pant for blood, and shields as
        brede
    As the y-brochèd moon, when white she
        dights
    The woodland ground or water-mantled
        mead;

With hands whose might can make the doughtiest bleed,
Who oft have knelt upon forslagen foes,
Who with their feet o'er set a castle-stede,   100
Who dare on kings for to revenge their woes.
Now will the men of England hail the day,
When Goddwyn leads them to the rightful fray.

God. But first we'll call the loverdes of the west,
The earls of Mercia, Coventry, and all.
The more we gain, the cause will prosper best,
With such a number we can never fall.

Har. True, so we shall do best to link the chain,
And all at once the spreading kingdom bind.
No crossèd champion with a heart more fain   110
Did issue out the holy sword to find,
Than I now strive to rid my land of pain.
Goddwyn, what thanks our labours will enheap!
I'll rouse my friends unto the bloody plain;
I'll wake the honour that is now asleep.
When will the chiefs meet at thy festive hall,
That I with voice aloud may there upon them call?

God. Next eve, my son.
Har.   Now, England, is the time,
When thee or thy fell foeman's cause must die.
Thy geason wrongs be run into their prime;   120
Now will thy sons unto thy succour fly;

GODDWYN

    Alyche a storm assembling in the sky,
      'Tis full, and bursteth on the barren ground,
    So shall my fury on the Normans fly,
      And all their mighty men be slain around.
    Now, now will Harold or oppression fall,
    No more the Englishmen in vain for help shall call.   [*Exeunt.*

    Enter King EDWARD *and his* Queen

Queen.   But, loverde, why so many Normans here?
      Me thinketh, we be not in English land,
      These browded strangers alway do appear,   130
      They part your throne, and sit at your right hand.
King.   Go to, go to, you do not understand.
      They gave me life, and did my person keep;
      They did me feast, and did embower me grand;
      To treat them ill would let my kindness sleep.
Queen.   Mancas you have in store, and to them part;
      Your liege-folk make much dole, you have their worth asterte.
King.   I ask no rede of you. I know my friends.
      Holy are they, full ready me to hele.
      Their volundes are y-storven to self ends,   140
      No denwere in my breast I of them feel.
      I must to prayers; go in, and you do well;
      I must not lose the duty of the day;
      Go in, go in, and view the azure rele,
      Full well I wot you have no mind to pray.
Queen.   I leave you to do homage heaven-were;
      To serve your liege-folk too, is doing homage there.   [*Exit* Queen.

Enter Sir HUGH

King. My friend, Sir Hugh, what tidings brings thee here?

Hugh. There are no mancas in my loverde's ente;
The house expenses unpaid do appear, 150
The last receivure is eftsoon dispent.

King. Then guylde the west.

Hugh. My loverde, I did speak
Unto the mitte earl Harold of the thing;
He raised his hand, and smote me on the cheek,
Saying, 'Go, bear that message to the king'.

King. Divest him of his power; by Goddis word,
No more that Harold shall y-wield the erlies sword.

Hugh. At season fit, my loverde, let it be,
But now the folk do so embrace his name,
In striving to slea him, ourselves we slea: 160
Such is the doughtiness of his great fame.

King. Hugh, I bethink, thy rede is not to blame.
But thou mayest find full store of marks in Kent.

Hugh. My noble loverde, Goddwyn is the same;
He swears he will not swell the Norman's ente.

King. Ah traitor! but my rage I will command;
Thou art a Norman, Hugh, a stranger to the land.
Thou knowest how these English earls do bear
Such firmness in the ill and evil thing,
But at the good they hover in denwere, 170
Onknowlachynge if thereunto to cling.

Hugh. Unworthy such a marvel of a king!
Oh Edward! thou deservest purer leege,
To thee they shoulden all their mancas bring,
Thy nod should save men, and thy frown forslege.
I am no flatterer, I lack no wite,
I speak what be the truth, and what all see is right.

King. Thou art a holy man, I do thee prize.
Come, come, and hear, and help me in my prayers,
Full twenty mancas I will thee alyse, 180
And twain of hamlets to thee and thy heirs.
So shall all Normans from my land be fed,
They only have such love as to acquire their bread. [*Exeunt.*

Chorus

When freedom, dressed in bloodstained vest,
To every knight her warsong sung,
pon her head wild weeds were spread,
A gory anlace by her hung.
She dancèd on the heath,
She heard the voice of death.

Pale-eyed affright, his heart of silver hue, 190
In vain assayled her bosom to acale.
She heard, onflemed, the shrieking voice of woe,
And sadness in the owlet shake the dale.
She shook the armed spear,
On high she raised her shield,
Her foemen all appear,
And fly along the field.

Power, with his heasod straught into the skies,
  His spear a sunbeam, and his shield a star;
Alyche two flaming meteors rolls his eyes,   200
  Stamps with his iron feet, and sounds to war.
    She sits upon a rock,
      She bends before his spear,
    She rises from the shock,
      Wielding her own in air.
Hard as the thunder doth she drive it on,
  Wit, closely mantled, guides it to his crown;
His long sharp spear, his spreading shield is gone,
  He falls, and falling, rolleth thousands down.
War, gore-faced war, by envy armed, arist,   210
  His fiery helmet nodding to the air,
Ten bloody arrows in his straining fist—

    *   *   *   *   *

ENGLISH METAMORPHOSIS
By T. Rowleie

When Scythians, savage as the wolves they chased,
  Painted in horrowe forms by nature dight,
Wrappèd in beast-skins, slept upon the waste,
  And with the morning roused the wolf to fight.
Swift as descending rays of ruddy light
  Plunged to the hidden bed of laving seas,
Rent the black mountain-oaks, in pieces twight,
  And ran in thought along the azure mees,
Whose eyes did fiery shine, like blue-haired defs,
That dreary hang upon Dover's emblanched cliffs.   10

  Soft-bounding over swelling azure reles,
    The savage natives saw a ship appear.
  An unknown tremor to their bosom steals,
    Their might is fastened in the frost of fear.

ENGLISH METAMORPHOSIS

The headed javelin boundeth here and there;
  They stand, they run, they look with eager eyne.
The ship's sail, swelling with the kindly air,
  Runneth to harbour from the beating brine.
They drive away aghast, when to the strand
An armèd Trojan leaps, with morglaien sword in hand. 20

Him followed eftsoon his compheeres, whose swords
  Glistered like livid stars in frosty neet,
Hailing their captain in chirckynge words
  King of the land, whereon they set their feet.
The great king Brutus then they did him greet,
  Prepared for battle, marshallèd the fight.
They urged the war, the natives fled as fleet
  As flying clouds that swim before the sight;
Till tired with battles, for to cease the fray,
They uncted Brutus king, and gave the Trojans sway. 30

Twain of twelve years have lighted up the minds,
  Alloyed the savage unthewes of their breast,
Improved in mystic war, and lymed their kinds,
  When Brute from Britons sank to eterne rest.
Eftsoon the gentle Locrine was possessed
  Of sway, and vested in the parament;
Haleeld the warring Huns, who did infest
  His waking kingdom with a foul intent;
As his broad sword o'er Humber's head was hung,
He turned to river wide, and roaring rolled along. 40

He wedded Gwendoline of royal seed,
  Upon whose countenance red health was spread;
Blushing alyche the scarlet of her weed,
  She sank to pleasure on the marriage-bed.

Eftsoon her peaceful joy of mind was fled ;
  Elstrid ametten with the king Locrine.
Unnumbered beauties were upon her shed,
  Much fine, much fairer, than was Gwendoline ;
The morning tinge, the rose, the lily flower,
In ever-running race, on her did paint their power. 50

The gentle suit of Locrine gained her love,
  They lived soft moments to a swotie age,
Oft wandering in the coppice, dell, and grove,
  Where no one eyes might their disport engage ;
There did they tell the merry loving fage,
  Crop the primrosen flower to deck their head.
The fiery Gwendoline, in woman-rage,
  Assembled warriors to revenge her bed.
They rose ; in battle was great Locrine sleen ;
The fair Elstrida fled from the enragèd queen. 60

A tie of love, a daughter fair she hanne,
  Whose budding morning shewèd a fair day,
Her father Locrine, once a happy man.
  With the fair daughter did she haste away,
To where the western mighty piles of clay
  Arise into the clouds, and do them bear ;
There did Elstrida and Sabrina stay,
  The first tricked out awhile in warrior's gratch and gear,
Vincent was she y-clept, but full soon fate
Sent death to tell the dame she was not in regrate. 70

The queen Gwendoline sent a giant knight,
  Whose doughty head swept the emmertleynge skies,
To slay her wheresoe'er she should be pyghte,
  Eke every one who should her help emprise.

Swift as the roaring winds the giant flies,
  Stayed the loud winds, and shaded realms in night,
Stepped over cities, on meint acres lies,
  Meeting the herehaughtes of morning light;
Till, moving to the west, mischance his gye,
Ie thorowe warrior's gratch fair Elstrid did espy.   80

He tore a ragged mountain from the ground,
  Harried up nodding forests to the sky,
Then with a fury, might the earth astound,
  To middle air he let the mountain fly;
The flying wolfins sent a yelling cry;
  On Vincent and Sabrina fell the mount;
To live eternal did they eftsoon die.
  Thorowe the sandy grave boiled up the purple fount,
)n a broad grassy plain was laid the hill,
itaying the running course of many a glassy rill.   90

The gods, who knew the actions of the wight,
  To lessen the sad hap of twain so fair,
Hollow did make the mountain by their might;
  Forth from Sabrina ran a river clear,
Roaring and rolling on in course bysmare;
  From female Vincent shot a ridge of stones,
Each side the river rising heaven-were;
  Sabrina's flood was held in Elstrid's bones.
o are they clepèd; gentle and the hind
an tell that Severn's stream by Vincent's rock's y-wrynde.   100

The bawsyn giant, he who did them slea,
  To tell Gwendoline quickly was y-spedde;
When, as he strode along the shaking lea,
  The ruddy lightning glistered on his head;

Into his heart the azure vapours spread;
   He writhed around in dreary cruel pain;
   When from his life-blood the red flames were fed,
     He fell an heap of ashes on the plain;
Still does his ashes shoot into the light,
A wondrous mountain high, and Snowdon is it hyghte.   110

AN EXCELENTE BALADE OF CHARITIE

(AS WROTEN BIE THE GODE PRIEST,
THOMAS ROWLEY, 1464)

In Virginè the sweltry sun 'gan sheene,
   And hot upon the mees did cast his ray;
The apple ripened from its paly green,
   And the soft pear did bend the leafy spray;
   The pied chelàndre sung the livelong day;
'Twas now the pride, the manhood of the year,
And eke the ground was dressed in its most neat aumere.

The sun was gleaming in the midst of day,
   Dead-still the air, and eke the welkin blue,
When from the sea arose in drear array   10
   A heap of clouds of sable sullen hue,
   The which full fast unto the woodland drew,
Hiding at once the sunnìs beauteous face,
And the black tempest swelled, and gathered up apace.

Beneath a holm, fast by a pathway-side,
   Which did unto Saint Godwin's convent led,
A hapless pilgrim moaning did abide,
   Poor in his view, ungentle in his weed,
   Long fillèd with the miseries of need.

A BALADE OF CHARITIE

Where from the hailstone could the beggar fly? 20
He had no houses there, nor any convent nigh.

    Look in his clouded face, his sprite there scan;
       How woe-begone, how withered, sapless, dead!
    Haste to thy church-glebe-house, accursèd man!
    Haste to thy kiste, thy only sleeping bed.
    Cold as the clay which will grow on thy head
Is charity and love among high elves;
Knightis and barons live for pleasure and themselves.

    The gathered storm is ripe; the big drops fall,
       The sun-burnt meadows smoke, and drink the rain; 30
    The coming ghastness do the cattle 'pall,
       And the full flocks are driving o'er the plain;
    Dashed from the clouds, the waters fly again;
The welkin opes; the yellow lightning flies,
And the hot fiery steam in the wide lowings dies.

    List! now the thunder's rattling noisy sound
       Moves slowly on, and then embollen clangs,
    Shakes the high spire, and lost, expended, drowned,
    Still on the frighted ear of terror hangs;
    The winds are up; the lofty elmen swangs; 40
Again the lightning and the thunder pours,
And the full clouds are burst at once in stony showers.

    . Spurring his palfrey o'er the watery plain,
       The Abbot of Saint Godwin's convent came;
    His chapournette was drentèd with the rain,
       And his pencte girdle met with mickle shame;
    He backwards told his bede-roll at the same
The storm increases, and he drew aside,
With the poor alms-craver near to the holm to bide.

A BALADE OF CHARITIE

His cloak was all of Lincoln cloth so fine, 55
  With a gold button fastened near his chin,
His autremete was edged with golden twine,
  And his shoe's peak a loverde's might have been
  Full well it shewn he thoughten cost no sin.
The trammels of his palfrey pleased his sight,
For the horse-milliner his head with roses dight.

  'An alms, sir priest!' the drooping pilgrim said,
    'Oh! let me wait within your convent-door,
  Till the sun shineth high above our head,
    And the loud tempest of the air is o'er. 60
  Helpless and old am I, alas! and poor.
No house, no friend, no money in my pouch,
All that I call my own is this my silver crouche'.

  'Varlet!' replied the Abbot, 'cease your din;
    This is no season alms and prayers to give,
  My porter never lets a beggar in;
    None touch my ring who not in honour live'.
  And now the sun with the black clouds did strive,
And shedding on the ground his glaring ray;
The abbot spurred his steed, and eftsoon rode away. 70

  Once more the sky was black, the thunder rolled,
    Fast running o'er the plain a priest was seen;
  Not dight full proud, not buttoned up in gold,
    His cope and jape were grey, and eke were clean;
    A limitour he was of order seen;
  And from the pathway-side then turnèd he,
Where the poor beggar lay beneath the elmen tree.

  'An alms, sir priest!' the drooping pilgrim said,
    'For sweet Saint Mary and your order sake'.
  The limitour then loosened his pouch-thread, 80
    And did thereout a groat of silver take:
    The needly pilgrim did for halline shake,

'Here, take this silver, it may ease thy care,
We are God's stewards all, naught of our own we
　　bear.
　But ah ! unhappy pilgrim, learn of me.
　　Scathe any give a rent-roll to their Lord ;
　Here, take my semi-cope, thou'rt bare, I see,
　　'Tis thine ; the saints will give me my reward '.
　　He left the pilgrim, and his way aborde.
Virgin and holy saint, who sit in gloure,　　　　90
Or give the mighty will, or give the good man power.

TO JOHNE LADGATE

SENT WITH THE FOLLOWING 'SONGE TO ÆLLA')

Well, then, good John, since it must needs be so,
　That thou and I a bouting-match must have,
Let it not breaking of old friendship do,
　This is the only all-a-boone I crave.

Remember Stowe, the Bristol Carmelite,
　Who, when John Clarkynge, one of mickle lore,
Did throw his gauntlet-pen, with him to fight,
　He shewed small wit, and shewed his weak-
　　ness more.

This is my 'formance, which I now have writ,
The best performance of my little wit.　　　10

SONGE TO ÆLLA,

LORD OF THE CASTLE OF BRISTOL IN DAYS OF YORE

OH thou, or what remains of thee,
    Ælla, the darling of futurity,
Let this my song bold as thy courage be,
    As everlasting to posterity.
When Dacia's sons, whose hairs of blood-red hue,
Like king-cups bursting with the morning dew,
      Arranged in drear array,
      Upon the deadly day,
Spread far and wide on Watchet's shore;
    Then didst thou furious stand,   10
    And by thy valiant hand
Besprenged all the mees with gore.

      Drawn by thine anlace fell,
      Down to the depths of hell
          Thousands of Dacians went;
      Brystowans, men of might,
      Y-dared the bloody fight,
          And acted deeds full quent.

    Oh thou, where'er (thy bones at rest)
    Thy sprite to haunt delighteth best,   20
Whether upon the blood-embruèd plain,
      Or where thou know'st from far
      The dismal cry of war,
Or seest some mountain made of corse of slain;

      Or seest the hatchèd steed
      Y-prancing o'er the mead,
And neigh to be among the pointed spears;
      Or, in black armour stalk around
      Embattled Bristol, once thy ground,
And glow, ardurous, on the castle-stairs;   30

Or fiery round the minster glare,
  Let Bristol still be made thy care;
Guard it from foemen and consuming fire.
  Like Avon's stream, ensyrke it round,
  Nor let a flame enharm the ground,
Till in one flame all the whole world expire.

THE UNDERWRITTEN LINES WERE COMPOSED BY JOHN LADGATE, A PRIEST IN LONDON, AND SENT TO ROWLIE, AS AN ANSWER TO THE PRECEDING 'SONGE TO ÆLLA'.

HAVING with much attention read
  What you did to me send,
Admire the verses much I did,
  And thus an answer lend.

Among the Greecès Homer was
  A poet much renowned,
Among the Latins Virgilius
  Was best of poets found.

The British Merlin often hanne
  The gift of inspiration,
And Alfred to the Saxon men
  Did sing with elocation.

In Norman times, Turgotus and
  Good Chaucer did excel,
Then Stowe, the Bristol Carmelite
  Did bear away the bell.

Now Rowlie in these mokie days
  Lends out his shining lights,
And Turgotus and Chaucer lives
  In every line he writes.

THE TOURNAMENT

AN INTERLUDE

Enter a Herald

Herald. The tournament begins; the hammers sound;
 The coursers lysse about the measured field;
The shimmering armour throws the sheen around,
 Quaintissèd fons depicted on each shield.
The fiery helmets, with the wreaths amield,
 Supports the romping lyoncelle or bear,
With strange depyctures nature may not yield,
 Unseemly to all order do appear,
Yet that to men, who think and have a sprite,
Makes knowen that the phantasy's unright. 10

 I, son of honour, 'spenser of her joys,
  Must quickly go to give the spears around;
 With adventayle and borne I meynte employ,
  Who without me would fall unto the ground.
 So the tall oak the ivy twisteth round,
  So the nesh flower grows in the woodland shade.
 The world by difference is in order found,
  Without unlikeness nothing could be made;
 As in the bowke naught only can be done,
 So in the weal of kind all things are parts of one. 20

THE TOURNAMENT

Enter Sir SIMON DE BOURTONNE

Bour. Herald, by heaven, these tilters stay too long,
 My phantasy is dying for the fight;
 The minstrels have begun the third war-song,
 Yet not a spear of them hath greet my sight.
I fear there be no man worthy my might.
 I lack a Guid, a William to entilt.
To run against a feeble-bodied knight,
 It gets no glory if his blood be spilt.
By heaven and Mary, it is time they're here.
I like not useless thus to wield the spear.   30

Her. Methinks I hear their clarion's sound from far.
Bour. Ah! quickly my shield and tilting-lance be bound;
 Eftsoon command my squire to the war.
 I fly before to claim a challenge-ground.
          [*Exit.*
Her. Thy valorous acts would meynte of men astound,
 Hard be their fate encountering thee in fight;
Against all men, thou bearest to the ground,
 Like the hard hail doth the tall rushes pyghte.
As when the morning sun y-dronks the dew,
 So doth thy valorous acts drink each knight's hue.   40

The Lists. Enter the KING, Sir SIMON DE BOURTONNE, Sir HUGO FERRARIS, Sir RANULPH NEVILLE, Sir LODOVICK DE CLYNTON, Sir JOHAN DE BERGHAMME, *and other Knights, Heralds, Minstrels, and Servitors.*

King. The barganette! ye minstrels, tune the string,
Some action dire of ancient kings now sing.

Minst. William, the Norman's flower, but England's thorn,
The man whose might activity had knit,
Bent up his long strung bow and shield aborne,
Commanding all his hommageres to fight.
Go, rouse the lion from his hidden den,
Let thy floes drink the blood of anything but men.

In the treed forest do the knights appear,
William with might his bow en-ironed plies; 50
Loud sounds the arrow in the wolfin's ear;
He riseth, loudly roars, he pants, he dies;
Forslagen at thy feet let wolfins be,
Let thy floes drink their blood, but do not brethren slea.

Through the dark shade of twisting trees he rides;
The frighted owlet flaps her eve-specked wing;
The lordynge toad in all his passes bides;
The berten adders at him dart the sting.
Still, still he passes on, his steed astrodde,
Nor heeds the dangerous way if leading unto blood. 60

The lyoncelle, from sultry countries brought,
Couching beneath the shelter of the briar,
At coming sound doth raise himself distraught,
He looketh with an eye of flames of fire.

Go, stick the lion to his hidden den,
Let thy floes drink the blood of anything
    but men.

  With passent step the lion moveth along ;
  William his iron-woven bow he bends,
  With might alyche the rolling thunder strong,
  The lion in a roar his sprite forth sends. 70
Go, slay the lion in his blood-stained den,
But be thine arrow dry from blood of other
    men.

  Swift from the thicket starts the stag away,
  The couraciers as swift do after fly.
  He leapeth high, he stands, he keeps at bay,
  But meets the arrow, and eftsoon doth die.
Forslagen at thy foot let wild beasts be,
Let thy floes drink their blood, yet do not
    brethren slea.

  With murder tired, he slings his bow alyne.
    The stag is ouched with crowns of lily
      flowers.   80
  Around their helms they green vert do
      entwine,
    Joying and rev'lous in the greenwood
      bowers.
Forslagen with thy floe let wild beasts be,
·Feast thee upon their flesh, do not thy
    brethren slea.

King. Now, to the tourney ; who will first affray ?
Her.   Neville, a baron, be that honour thine.
Bour. I claim the passage.
Nev.   I dispute thy way.
Bour. Then there's my gauntlet on my gaberdine,

Her.   A lawful challenge, knights and champions
              digne,
                 A lawful challenge! Let the clarion
                     sound,   90
                     [Sir SIMON *and* NEVILLE *tilt.*
                 Neville is going, man and horse, to
                     ground.
                                        [NEVILLE *falls.*
              Loverdes, how doughtily the tilters join!
              Ye champions, here Simon de Bourtonne fights,
              One he hath quaced; oppose him, ye knights.

Ferraris. I will against him go; my squire, my shield,
              Or one or other will do mickle scethe;
              Before I do depart the listed field,
              Myself or Bourtonne hereupon will blethe.
              My shield!
Bour.   Come on, and fit thy tilt-lance
                     cthe.
              When Bourtonne fights, he meets a
                  doughty foe.   100
                         [*They tilt.* FERRARIS *falls.*
              He falleth; now, by heaven, thy wounds
                  do smethe;
              I fear me, I have wrought thee mickle woe.
Her.   Bourtonne his second beareth to the field.
              Come on, ye knights, and win the honoured
                  shield.

Bergh. I take the challenge; squire, my lance and
                  steed.
              I, Bourtonne, take the gauntlet; for me
                  stay.
              But, if thou fightest me, thou shalt have
                  meed.
              Some other I will champion to affray;

THE TOURNAMENT

    Perchance from them I may possess the day,
      Then I shall be a foeman for thy spear. 110
    Herald, to the banks of knightès say,
      De Berghamme waiteth for a foeman here.

Clinton. But long thou shalt not wait. I do thee 'fy;
    Like forreying lightning shall my tilt-lance fly.
        [BERGHAMME *and* CLINTON *tilt.*
          CLINTON *falls.*

Bergh. Now, now, sir knight, attoure thy beavered eyne,
    I have borne down, and eft do gauntlet thee.
    Quickly begin, and wyrnne thy fate or mine,
      If thou discomfit, it will doubly be.
        [BOURTONNE *and* BERGHAMME *tilt.*
          BERGHAMME *falls.*

Her. Simon de Bourtonne haveth borne down three,
    And by the third hath honour of a fourth. 120
    Let him be set aside, till he doth see
      A tilting for a knight of gentle worth.
    Here cometh strange knightés; if courteous they,
    It well becomes to give them right of fray.

1st Kn. Strangers we be, and humbly do we claim
    The honour in this tourney for to tilt;
    Thereby to prove from cravens our good name,
      Declaring that we gentle blood have spilt.

Her. Ye knights, of courtesy these strangers say,
    Be you full willing for to give them fray? 130
      [Five Knights *tilt with the strange* Knight,
        and are every one overthrown.

Bour. Now, by Saint Mary, if on all the field
    Y-crased spears and helmets be besprent,
  If every knight did hold a piercèd shield,
    If all the field with champions' blood be stent,
  Yet to encounter him I be content.
    Another lance, marshal, another lance.
  Albeit he with flames of fire y-brent,
    Yet Bourtonne would against his helm advance.
  Five haveth fallen down beneath his spear,
  But he shall be the next that falleth here.   140

    By thee, Saint Mary, and thy Son I swear,
      That in what place yon doughty knight shall fall
    Beneath the strong push of my stretched-out spear,
    There shall arise a holy church's wall,
    The which in honour, I will Mary call,
      With pillars large, and spire full high and round,
    And this I faithfully will stand to all,
      If yonder stranger falleth to the ground.
  Stranger, be boune; I champion you to war;
  Sound, sound the clarions, to be heard from far.   150
        [BOURTONNE *and the* Stranger *tilt.*
        Stranger *falls.*

King. The morning tilts now cease.
Her.   Bourtonne is king.
  Display the English banner on the tent.
  Round him, ye minstrels, songs of achments sing.
  Ye heralds, gather up the spears besprent;

THE TOURNAMENT

To king of tourney-tilt be all knees bent.
  Dames fair and gentle, for your loves he fought;
For you the long tilt-lance, the sword he shente;
  He jousted, only having you in thought.
Come, minstrels, sound the string, go on each side,
Whilst he unto the king in state do ride.   160

Minst. When battle, smoking with new quickened gore,
  Bending with spoils, and bloody dropping head,
Did the dark wood of ease and rest explore,
  Seeking to lie on pleasure's downy bed,
    Pleasure, dancing from her wood,
      Wreathed with flowers of eglantine,
    From his visage washed the blood,
      Hid his sword and gaberdine.

With such an eye she sweetly him did view,
  Did so y-corven every shape to joy,   170
His sprite did change unto another hue,
  His arms, nor spoils, might any thoughts employ.
    All delightsome and content,
      Fire enshooting from his eyne,
    In his arms he did her hent,
      Like the night-shade do entwine.

So, if thou lovest pleasure and her train,
  Onknowlachynge in what place her to find,
This rule y-spende, and in thy mind retain;
  Seek honour first, and pleasure lies behind.   180

BATTLE OF HASTINGS
(No. 1)

OH Christ, it is a grief for me to tell
   How many a noble earl and valorous knight
In fighting for king Harold nobly fell,
   All slain in Hastings field in bloody fight.
O sea, our teeming donor! had thy flood
   Had any fructuous entendèment,
Thou wouldst have rose and sunk with tides of blood,
   Before duke William's knights had hither went;
Whose coward arrows many earlès slain,
And 'brued the field with blood, as season-rain.   10

   And of his knights did eke full many die,
      All passing high, of mickle might each one,
   Whose poignant arrows, tipped with destiny,
      Caused many widows to make mickle moan.
   Lordings, avaunt! that chicken-hearted are,
      From out of hearing quickly now depart;
   Full well, I wot, to sing of bloody war
      Will grieve your tenderly and maiden heart.
Go, do the weakly woman in man's gear,
And scond your mansion if grim war come there.   20

   Soon as the early matin-bell was tolled,
      And sun was come to bid us all good day,
   Both armies on the field, both brave and bold,
      Prepared for fight in champion array.
   As when two bulls, destined for Hocktide fight,
      Are yokèd by the neck within a spar,
   They rend the earth, and travellers affright,
      Lackynge to gage the sportive bloody war;
So lackèd Harold's men to come to blows,
The Normans lackèd for to wield their bows.   30

BATTLE OF HASTINGS (I)

King Harold turning to his liegemen spake:
' My merry men, be not cast down in mind;
Your only lode for aye to mar or make,
Before yon sun has done his welke, you'll find.
Your loving wives, who erst did rid the land
Of lurdanes, and the treasure that you hanne,
Will fall into the Norman robber's hand,
Unless with hand and heart you play the man.
Cheer up your hearts, chase sorrow far away,
"God and Saint Cuthbert" be the word to-day'. 40

And then duke William to his knights did say:
' My merry men, be bravely everiche;
If I do gain the honour of the day,
Each one of you I will make mickle rich.
Bear you in mind, we for a kingdom fight;
Lordships and honours each one shall possess;
Be this the word to-day, "God and my right";
Nor doubt but God will oür true cause bless'.
The clarions then sounded sharp and shrill;
Death-doing blades were out, intent to kill. 50

And brave king Harold had now done his say,
He threw with might amain his short horse-spear,
The noise it made the duke to turn away,
And hit his knight, De Beque, upon the ear.
His crested beaver did him small abound,
The cruel spear went thórough all his head;
The purple blood came gushing to the ground,
And at duke William's feet he tumbled dead:
So fell the mighty tower of Standrip, when
It felt the fury of the Danish men. 60

O Afflem, son of Cuthbert, holy Saint!
Come, aid thy friend, and shew duke William's pain;
Take up thy pencil, all his features paint;
Thy colouring excels a singer's strain.

Duke William saw his friend slain piteously,
  His loving friend whom he much honourèd,
For he had loved him from puerilitie,
  And they together both had been y-bred :
O ! in duke William's heart it raised a flame,
To which the rage of empty wolves is tame.   70
  He took a brazen cross-bow in his hand,
    And drew it hard with all his might amain,
  Not doubting but the bravest in the land
    Had by his sounding arrow-head been slain.
  Alured's steed, the finest steed alive,
    By comely form knowlachèd from the rest ;
  But now his destined hoür did arrive,
    The arrow hit upon his milk-white breast ;
So have I seen a lady-smock so white,
Blown in the morning, and mowed down at night. 80
  With such a force it did his body gore,
    That in his tender guts it enterèd,
  In verity, a full cloth-yard or more,
    And down with flaiten noise he sunken dead.
  Brave Alured, beneath his faithful horse,
    Was smeared all over with the gory dust,
  And on him lay the racer's lukewarm corse,
    That Alured could not himself aluste.
The standing Normans drew their bow each one,
And brought full many English champions down. 90
  The Normans kept aloof, at distance still,
    The English naught but short horse-spears could wield ;
  The English many death-sure darts did kill,
    And many arrows twanged upon the shield.
  King Harold's knights desired for handy stroke,
    And marchèd furious o'er the bloody plain,
  In body close, and made the plain to smoke ;
    Their shields rebounded arrows back again.

BATTLE OF HASTINGS (1)

The Normans stood aloof, nor heed the same,
Their arrows would do death, tho' from far off they
    came.

    Duke William drew again his arrow-string,
        An arrow with a silver head drew he:
    The arrow dancing in the air did sing,
        And hit the horse [of] Tosslyn on the knee.
At this brave Tosslyn threw his short horse-spear,
    Duke William stoopèd to avoid the blow;
The iron weapon hummèd in his ear,
    And hit Sir Doullie Naibor on the prow,
Upon his helm so furious was the stroke,
It split his beaver, and the rivets broke.

    Down fell the beaver, by Tosslyn split in twain,
        And on his head exposed a puny wound,
    But on Destoutville's shoulder came amain,
        And felled the champion to the bloody ground.
    Then Doullie mightily his bow-string drew,
        And thought to give brave Tosslyn bloody wound,
    But Harold's asenglave stopped it as it flew,
        And it fell bootless on the bloody ground.
Sir Doullie, when he saw his 'venge thus broke,
Death-doing blade from out the scabbard took.

    And now the battle closed on every side,
        And face to face appeared the knights full brave;
    They lifted up their bills with mickle pride,
        And many wounds unto the Normans gave.
    So have I seen two weirs at once give ground,
        White-foaming high, to roaring combat run;
    In roaring din and heaven-breaking sound,
        Burst waves on waves, and spangle in the sun;
And when their might in bursting waves is fled,
Like cowards, steal along their oozy bed.

Young Egelrede, a knight of comely mien,
   Affynd unto the king of Dynefarre,
At every tilt and tourney he was seen,
   And loved to be among the bloody war;
He couched his lance, and ran with mickle might
   Against the breast of Sieur de Bonoboe;
He groaned and sunken on the place of fight,
   O Christ! to feel his wound, his heart was woe.
Ten thousand thoughts pushed in upon his mind,
Not for himself, but those he left behind.   140
   He died and leffèd wife and children twain,
      Whom he with cherishment did dearly love:
   In England's court, in good king Edward's reign,
      He won the tilt, and wore her crimson glove.
   And thence unto the place where he was born,
      Together with his wealth and better wife,
   To Normandy he did, perdie, return,
      In peace and quietness to lead his life,
And now with sovereign William he came,
To die in battle, or get wealth and fame.   150
   Then, swift as lightning, Egelredus set
      Against Du Barlie of the mountain-head;
   In his dear heart's blood his long lance was wet,
      And from his courser down he tumbled dead.
   So have I seen a mountain-oak, that long
      Has cast his shadow to the mountain-side,
   Brave all the winds, though ever they so strong,
      And view the briars below with self-taught pride.
But, when thrown down by mighty thunder-stroke,
He'd rather be a briar than an oak.   160
   Then Egelred did, in a declynie,
      His lance uprear with all his might amain,
   And struck Fitzport upon the dexter eye,
      And at his poll the spear came out again.

But as he drew it forth, an arrow fled
   With mickle might sent from De Tracy's bow,
And at his side the arrow enterèd,
   And out the crimson stream of blood 'gan flow;
In purple streaks it did his armour stain,
And smoked in puddles on the dusty plain.   170

But Egelred, before he sunken down,
   With all his might amain his spear besped,
It hit Bertrammil Manne upon the crown,
   And both together quickly sunken dead.
So have I seen a rock o'er others hang,
   Who, strongly placed, laughed at his slippery state;
But, when he falls with heaven-piercing bang,
   That he the sleave unravels all their fate,
And, broken on the beach, this lesson speak,
The strong and firm should not defame the weak.   180

Howel ap Jevah came from Matraval,
   Where he by chance had slain a noble's son,
And now was come to fight at Harold's call,
   And in the battle he much good had done;
Unto king Harold he fought mickle near,
   For he was yeoman of the body-guard;
And with a target and a fighting-spear
   He of his body had kept watch and ward.
True as a shadow to a substant thing,
So true he guarded Harold, his good king.   190

But when Egélred tumbled to the ground,
   He from king Harold quickly did advance,
And struck De Tracy such a cruel wound,
   His heart and liver came out on the lance:
And then retreated, for to guard his king.
   On dented lance he bore the heart away;
An arrow came from Auffroie Griel's string
   Into his heel, beneath his iron stay;

BATTLE OF HASTINGS (I)

The grey-goose pinion, that thereon was set,
Eftsoon with smoking crimson blood was wet.   200

   His blood at this was waxen flaming hot,
   Without ado, he turnèd once again,
   And hit De Grïel such a blow, God wot,
   Maugre his helm, he split his head in twain.
This Auffroie was a man of mickle pride,
   Whose featliest beauty ladden in his face;
His chance in war he ne'er before had tried,
   But lived in love and Rosalind's embrace;
And, like a useless weed among the hay,
Among the slain warrïors Grïel lay.   210

   King Harold then he put his yeomen by,
   And fiercely rode into the bloody fight;
Earl Ethelwolf, and Goodrick, and Alfie,
   Cuthbert, and Goddard, mickle men of might,
Ethelwin, Ethelbert, and Egwin too,
   Effred the famous, and earl Ethelwarde,
King Harold's liegemen, earlès high and true,
   Rode after him, his body for to guard;
The rest of earlès, fighting other-wheres,
Stainèd with Norman blood their fighting-spears.   220

   As when some river, with the season-rains
   White foaming high, doth break the bridges oft,
O'erturns the hamlet and all [it] contains,
   And layeth o'er the hills a muddy soft,
So Harold ran upon his Norman foes,
   And laid the great and small upon the ground,
And dealt among them such a store of blows,
   Full many a Norman fell by him, dead-wound;
So who he be that elfin fairies strike,
Their souls will wander to king Offa's dyke.   230

BATTLE OF HASTINGS (I)

Fitz Salnarville, duke William's favourite knight,
  To noble Edelwarde his life did yield;
With his tilt-lance he struck with such a might,
  The Norman's bowels steamed upon the field.
Old Salnarville beheld his son lie dead,
  Against earl Edelwarde his bow-string drew;
But Harold at one blow made twain his head;
  He died before the poignant arrow flew.
So was the hope of all the issue gone,
And in one battle fell the sire and son.   240

D' Aubigny rode fiercely thro' the fight,
  To where the body of Salnarville lay;
Quoth he, 'And art thou dead, thou man of might?
  I'll be revenged, or die for thee this day'.
'Die then thou shalt', earl Ethelwarde he said;
  'I am a cunning earl, and that can tell';
Then drew his sword, and ghastly cut his head,
  And on his friend eftsoon he lifeless fell,
Stretched on the bloody plain; great God forfend,
It be the fate of no such trusty friend!   250

Then Egwin Sieur Pikeny did attack,
  He turned about and vilely sought to fly;
But Egwin cut so deep into his back,
  He rollèd on the ground and soon did die.
His distant son, Sire Romara de Biere,
  Sought to revenge his fallen kinsman's lot,
But soon earl Cuthbert's dented fighting-spear
  Stuck in his heart, and stayed his speed, God wot.
He tumbled down close by his kinsman's side,
(Mingle their streams of purple blood), and died.   260

And now an arrow from a bow unwot
  Into earl Cuthbert's heart eftsoon did flee ;
Who, dying, said, 'Ah me ! how hard my lot !
  Now slain, mayhap, of one of low degree'.
So have I seen a leafy elm of yore
  Have been the pride and glory of the plain ;
But, when the spending landlord is grown poor,
  It falls beneath the axe of some rude swain ;
And like the oak, the sovereign of the wood,
Its fallen body tells you how it stood.   270

When Edelwarde perceived earl Cuthbert die,
  On Hubert, strongest of the Norman crew,
As wolves, when hungered, on the cattle fly,
  So Edelwarde amain upon him flew.
With such a force he hit him to the ground,
  And was demasing how to take his life,
When he behind received a ghastly wound
  Given by De Torcie, with a stabbing knife ;
Base treacherous Normans, if such acts you do,
The conquered may claim victory of you.   280

The earlè felt De Torcie's treacherous knife
  Had made his crimson blood and spirits flow ;
And knowlaching he soon must quit this life,
  Resolvèd Hubert should too with him go.
He held his trusty sword against his breast,
  And down he fell, and pierced him to the heart ;
And both together then did take their rest,
  Their souls from corpses unaknelled depart :
And both together sought the unknown shore,
Where we shall go, where many's gone before.   290

King Harold Torcie's treachery did spy,
  And high aloft his tempered sword did wield,
Cut off his arm, and made the blood to fly,
  His proof-steel armour did him little shield ;

BATTLE OF HASTINGS (I)

And not content, he split his head in twain,
  And down he tumbled on the bloody ground.
Meanwhile the other earlés on the plain
  Gave and receivèd many a bloody wound,
Such as the arts in war had learnt with care ;
But many knights were women in men's gear.   300

Hcrewald, born on Sarum's spreading plain,
  Where Thor's famed temple many ages stood ;
Where Druids, ancient priests, did rites ordain,
  And in the middle shed the victim's blood ;
Where ancient Bardi did their verses sing,
  Of Cæsar conquered, and his mighty host,
And how old Tynyan, necromancing king,
  Wrecked all his shipping on the British coast,
And made him in his tattered barks to fly,
'Till Tynyan's death and opportunity.   310

To make it more renownèd than before,
  (I, though a Saxon, yet the truth will tell),
The Saxons stained the place with British gore,
  Where naught but blood of sacrifices fell.
Though Christians, still they thought much of the pile,
  And here they met when causes did it need.
'Twas here the ancient elders of the isle
  Did by the treachery of Hengist bleed ;
O Hengist ! had thy cause been good and true,
Thou wouldst such murderous acts as these eschew.   320

The earlè was a man of high degree,
  And had that day full many Normans slain,
Three Norman champīons of high degree
  He left to smoke upon the bloody plain :

BATTLE OF HASTINGS (I)

The Sieur Fitzbotevilleine did then advance,
And with his bow he smote the earlès head
Who eftsoons gored him with his tilting-lance,
And at his horse's feet he tumbled dead :
His parting spirit hovered o'er the flood
Of sudden-rushing much-loved purple blood.   330
De Viponte then, a squire of low degree,
An arrow drew with all his might amain ;
The arrow grazed upon the earlès knee,
A puny wound, that caused but little pain.
So have I seen a dolthead place a stone,
In thought to stay a driving river's course ;
But better had it been to let alone,
It only drives it on with mickle force ;
The earlè, wounded by so base a hind,
Raised furious doings in his noble mind.   340
The Sieur Chatillion, younger of that name,
Advancèd next before the earlès sight ;
His father was a man of mickle fame,
And he renowned and valorous in fight.
Chatillion his trusty sword forth drew,
The earl draws his, men both of mickle might ;
And at each other vengefully they flew,
As mastiff-dogs at Hocktide set to fight ;
Both scorned to yield, and both abhorred to fly,
Resolved to vanquish, or resolved to die.   350
Chatillion hit the earlè on the head.
That split eftsoon his crested helm in twain ;
Which he, perforce, with target coverèd,
And to the battle went with might amain.
The earlè hit Chatillion such a blow
Upon his breast, his heart was plain to see ;
He tumbled at the horses' feet also,
And in death-pangs he seized the racer's knee.

Fast as the ivy round the oak doth climb,
So fast he, dying, gripped the racer's limb.   360
   The racer then began to fling and kick,
     And tossed the earlè far off to the ground
   The earlès squire then a sword did stick
     Into his heart, a deadly ghastly wound;
   And down he fell upon the crimson plain,
     Upon Chatillion's soulless corse of clay;
   A puddly stream of blood flowed out amain;
     Stretched out at length, besmeared with gore, he lay;
As some tall oak, felled from the greeny plain,
To live a second time upon the main.   370
   The earlè now a horse and beaver hanne,
     And now again appearèd on the field;
   And many a mickle knight and mighty man
     To his death-doing sword his life did yield.
   When Sieur de Broque an arrow long let fly,
     Intending Herewaldus to have slain;
   It missed; but hit Edardus on the eye,
     And at his poll came out with horrid pain.
Edardus fell upon the bloody ground,
His noble soul came rushing from the wound.   380
   This Herewald perceived, and full of ire
     He on the Sieur de Broque with fury came;
   Quoth he, 'Thou'st slaughtered my belovèd squire,
     But I will be revengèd for the same'.
   Into his bowels then his lance he thrust,
     And drew thereout a steamy, dreary load;
   Quoth he, 'These offals are for ever cursed,
     Shall serve the choughs and rooks and daws for food'.
Then on the plain the steamy load he throwed,
Smoking with life, and dyed with crimson blood.   390

BATTLE OF HASTINGS (I)

 Fitz Broque, who saw his father killèd lie,
 'Ah me!' said he; 'what woeful sight I see!
But now I must do something more than sigh';
And then an arrow from the bow drew he.
Beneath the earlès navel came the dart:
 Fitz Broque on foot had drawn it from the bow;
And upwards went into the earlès heart,
And out the crimson stream of blood 'gan flow,
As from a hatch, drawn with a vehement geer,
White rush the bursting waves, and roar along the weir. 400
 The earl with one hand grasped the racer's mane,
 And with the other he his lance besped;
And then fell bleeding on the bloody plain.
His lance it hit Fitz Broque upon the head;
Upon his head it made a wound full slight,
But pierced his shoulder, ghastly wound inferne;
Before his optics danced a shade of night,
Which soon were closèd in a sleep eterne.
The noble earlè then, without a groan,
Took flight, to find the regiöns unknown. 410

 Brave Alured from beneath his noble horse
 Was gotten on his legs, with blood all smore;
And now, alighted on another horse,
Eftsoon he with his lance did many gore.
The coward Norman knights before him fled,
 And from a distance sent their arrows keen;
But no such destiny awaits his head,
As to be slayèn by a wight so mean.
Though oft the oak falls by the peasant's shock,
'Tis more than hinds can do, to move the rock. 420

 Upon Du Chatelet he fiercely set,
 And pierced his body with a force full great;
The asenglave of his tilt-lance was wet,
 The rolling blood along the lance did fleet.

Advancing, as a mastiff at a bull,
   He ran his lance into Fitz Warren's heart;
From Partaie's bow, a wight unmerciful,
   Within his own he felt a cruel dart;
Close by the Norman champions he had slain,
He fell; and mixed his blood with theirs upon the plain.   430

Earl Ethelbert then hove, with clinie just,
   A lance, that struck Partaie upon the thigh,
And pinned him down unto the gory dust;
   'Cruel', quoth he, 'thou cruelly shalt die'.
With that his lance he entered at his throat;
   He shrieked and screamed in melancholy mood;
And at his back eftsoon came out, God wot,
   And after it a crimson stream of blood.
In agony and pain he there did lie,
While life and death strove for the mastery.   440

He gripèd hard the bloody murdering lance,
   And in a groan he left this mortal life.
Behind the earlè, Fiscampe did advance,
   Bethought to kill him with a stabbing knife;
But Egward, who perceived his foul intent,
   Eftsoon his trusty sword he forthwith drew,
And such a cruel blow to Fiscampe sent,
   That soul and body's blood at one gate flew.
Such deeds do all deserve, whose deeds so foul
Will black their earthly name, if not their soul.   450

When lo! an arrow from Walleris' hand,
   Wingèd with fate and death, dancèd along;
And slew the noble flower of Powisland,
   Howel ap Jevah, who y-clept the strong.

When he the first mischance receivèd hanne,
   With horseman's haste he from the army rode;
And did repair unto the cunning man,
   Who sang a charm, that did it mickle good;
Then prayed St Cuthbert and our holy Dame
To bless his labour, and to heal the same: 460
   Then drew the arrow, and the wound did seck,
      And put the taint of holy herbès on;
   And put a row of blood-stones round his neck;
      And then did say: 'Go, champion, get agone!'
   And now was coming Harold to defend,
      And metten with Walleris' cruel dart;
   His shield of wolf-skin did him not attend,
      The arrow pierced into his noble heart;
As some tall oak, hewn from the mountain-head,
Falls to the plain, so fell the warrior dead.   470
   His countryman, brave Mervyn ap Teudor,
      Who, love of him, had from his country gone,
   When he perceived his friend lie in his gore,
      As furious as a mountain-wolf he ran.
   As elfin fairies, when the moon shines bright,
      In little circles dance upon the green,
   All living creatures fly far from their sight,
      Nor by the race of destiny be seen;
For what he be that elfin fairies strike,
Their souls will wander to king Offa's dyke.   480
   So from the face of Mervyn Tewdor brave
      The Normans eftsoon fled away aghast;
   And left behind their bow and asenglave,
      For fear of him, in such a coward haste.
   His garb sufficient were to move affright;
      A wolf-skin girded round his middle was;
   A bear-skin, from Norwegians won in fight,
      Was tightened round his shoulders by the claws.

BATTLE OF HASTINGS (*I*)

So Hercules, 'tis sung, much like to him,
Upon his shoulder wore a lion's skin.   490

    Upon his thighs and hart-swift legs he wore
      A hugè goat-skin, all of one great piece;
    A boar-skin shield on his bare arms he bore;
      His gauntlets were the skin of hart of grease.
    They fled; he followed close upon their heels,
      Vowing vengeance for his dear countryman;
    And Sieur de Sancelotte his vengeance feels;
      He pierced his back, and out the blood it ran;
His blood went down the sword unto his arm,
In springing rivulet, alive and warm.   500

    His sword was short, and broad, and mickle keen,
      And no man's bone could stand to stop its way;
    The Norman's heart in partès two cut clean,
      He closed his eyes, and closed his eyes for aye.
    Then with his sword he set on Fitz du Valle,
      A knight much famous for to run at tilt;
    With such a fury on him he did fall,
      Into his neck he ran the sword and hilt;
As mighty lightning often has been found
To drive an oak into unfallowed ground.   510

    And with the sword, that in his neck yet stuck,
      The Norman fell unto the bloody ground;
    And with the fall ap Tewdor's sword he broke,
      And blood afresh came trickling from the wound.
    As when the hinds, before a mountain wolf,
      Fly from his paws, and angry visage grim;
    But when he falls into the pitty gulf,
      They dare him to his beard, and batten him;
And 'cause he frighted them so much before,
Like coward hinds, they batten him the more.   520

So when they saw ap Tewdor was bereft
Of his keen sword, that wrought such great dismay;
They turned about, eftsoon upon him leapt,
And full a score engagèd in the fray.
Mervyn ap Tewdor, raging as a bear,
Seized on the beaver of the Sieur de Laque,
And wrung his head with such a vehement geer,
His visage was turned round unto his back.
Back to his heart retired the useless gore,
And fell upon the plain, to rise no more. 530

Then on the mighty Sieur Fitz Pierce he flew,
And broke his helm and seized him by the throat:
Then many Norman knights their arrows drew,
That entered into Mervyn's heart, God wot.
In dying pang he griped his throat more strong,
And from their sockets started out his eyes;
And from his mouth came out his blameless tongue,
And both in pain and anguish eftsoon dies.
As some rude rock, torn from his bed of clay,
Stretched on the plain the brave ap Teudor lay. 540

And now earl Ethelbert and Egward came,
Brave Mervyn from the Normans to assist;
A mighty sire, Fitz Chatulet by name,
An arrow drew that did them little list.
Earl Egward points his lance at Chatulet,
And Ethelbert at Walleris set his;
And Egwald did the sire a hard blow hit,
But Ethelbert by a mischance did miss:
Fear laid Walleris flat upon the strand,
He ne'er deserved a death from earlès hand. 550

Betwixt the ribs of Sire Fitz Chatulet
The pointed lance of Egward did y-pass:
The distant side thereof was ruddy wet,
And he fell breathless on the bloody grass.

As coward Walleris lay on the ground,
  The dreaded weapon hummèd o'er his head,
And hit the squire such a deadly wound,
  Upon his fallen lord he tumbled dead:
Oh shame to Norman arms! a lord a slave,
A captive villein than a lord more brave!   560

From Chatulet his lance earl Egward drew,
  And hit Walleris on the dexter cheek,
Pierced to his brain, and cut his tongue in two:
  'There, knight', quoth he, 'let that thy actions speak'.

*   *   *   *   *

BATTLE OF HASTINGS

(No. II)

Oh truth! immortal daughter of the skies,
  Too little known to writers of these days,
Teach me, fair saint! thy passing worth to prize,
  To blame a friend and give a foeman praise.
The fickle moon, bedecked with silver rays,
  Leading a train of stars of feeble light,
With look adigne the world below surveys,
  The world, that wotted not it could be night;
With armour donned, with human gore y-dyed,
She sees king Harold stand, fair England's curse and
    pride.   10

With ale and vernage drunk, his soldiers lay;
  Here was a hind, anigh an earlè spread,
Sad keeping of their leader's natal day!
  This even in drink, to-morrow with the dead!

Through every troop disorder reared her head ;
  Dancing and heideignes was the only theme.
Sad doom was theirs who left this easy bed,
  And waked in torments from so sweet a dream.
Duke William's men, of coming death afraid,
All night to the great God for succour asked and prayed. 20

Thus Harold to his wights that stood around :
  'Go, Gurth and Eilward, take bills half-a-score,
And search how far our foeman's camp doth bound ;
  Yourself have rede, I need to say no more.
My brother best beloved of any ore,
  My Leöfwinus, go to every wight,
Tell them to range the battle to the grore,
  And waiten till I send the hest for fight '.
He said ; the loyal brothers left the place,
Success and cheerfulness depicted on each face. 30

Slowly brave Gurth and Eilward did advance,
  And marked with care the army's distant side ;
When the dire clattering of the shield and lance
  Made them to be by Hugh Fitzhugh espied.
He lifted up his voice, and loudly cried :
  Like wolves in winter did the Norman yell.
Gurth drew his sword, and cut his burlèd hide ;
  The proto-slain man of the field, he fell.
Out streamed the blood, and ran in smoking curls,
Reflected by the moon, seemed rubies mixed with pearls. 40

A troop of Normans from the mass-song came,
  Roused from their prayèrs by the flotting cry.
Though Gurth and Eilwardus perceived the same,
  Not once they stood abashed or thought to fly.

BATTLE OF HASTINGS (II)

He seized a bill, to conquer or to die;
  Fierce as a clevis from a rock y-torn,
That makes a valley wheresoe'er it lie,
  Fierce as a river bursting from the borne,
So fiercely Gurth hit Fitz du Gore a blow,
And on the verdant plain he laid the champion low. 50

Tancarville thus: 'All peace, in William's name;
  Let none y-draw his arcublaster bow'.
Gurth cased his weapon, as he heard the same,
  And 'venging Normans stayed the flying floe.
The sire went on: 'Ye men, what mean ye so,
  Thus unprovoked to court a bloody fight?'
Quoth Gurth: 'Our meaning we now care to shew,
  Nor dread thy duke with all his men of might;
Here single, only these, to all thy crew
Shall shew what English hands and hearts can do'. 60

'Seek not for blood', Tancarville calm replied,
  'Nor joy in death, like madmen most distraught;
In peace and mercy is a Christian's pride,
  He that doth contests prize is in a fault'.
And now the news was to duke William brought,
  That men of Harold's army taken were;
For their good cheer all caties were enthought,
  And Gurth and Eilwardus enjoyed good cheer.
Quoth William: 'Thus shall William be found,
A friend to every man that treads on English ground'. 70

Earl Leöfwinus through the camp y-passed,
  And saw both men and earlès on the ground;
They slept, as though they would have slept their last,
  And had already felt their fatal wound.

He started back, and was with shame astound,
  Looked wan with anger, and he shook with rage,
When through the hollow tents these words did sound,
  'Rouse from your sleep, detractors of the age!
Was it for this the stout Norwegian bled?
Awake, ye house-carles, now, or waken with the dead!' So

As when the shepherd in the shady bower
  In gentle slumbers chase the heat of day,
Hears doubling echo wind the wolfin's roar,
  That near his flock is watching for a prey;
He, trembling for his sheep, drives dream away,
  Grips fast his burlèd crook, and, sore adradde,
With fleeting strides he hastens to the fray;
  And rage and prowess fires the coistrel lad;
With trusty talbots to the battle flies,
And yell of men and dogs and wolfins tear the skies.   90

Such was the dire confusion of each wight,
  That rose from sleep and loathsome power of wine;
They thought the foe by treachery in the night
  Had broke their camp and gotten past the line;
Now here, now there, the burnished shields and bill-spear shine;
  Throughout the camp a wild confusion spread;
Each braced his armlace siker ne desygne;
  The crested helmet nodded on the head;
Some caught a clarion, and an onset wound,
King Harold heard the charge, and wondered at the sound.   100

BATTLE OF HASTINGS (II)

Thus Leöfwine : ' O women, cased in steel !
Was it for this Norwegia's stubborn seed
Through the black armour did the anlace feel,
And ribs of solid brass were made to bleed,
Whilst yet the world was wondering at the deed?
You soldiers, that should stand with bill in hand,
Get full of wine, devoid of any rede.
Oh, shame ! Oh, dire dishonour to the land ! '
He said, and shame on every visage spread ;
None saw the earlès face, but, wakened, hung their head.   110

Thus he : ' Rouse ye, and form the body tight,
The Kentishmen in front, for strength renowned,
Next, the Bristolians dare the bloody fight,
And last, the numerous crew shall press the ground.
I and my king be with the Kenters found,
Bythric and Alfwold head the Bristol band,
And Bertram's son, the man of glorious wound,
Led in the rear the mengèd of the land ;
And let the Londoners and Sussers ply
By Hereward's memuine, and the light skirts annoy '.   120

He said ; and as a pack of hounds belent,
When that the tracking of the hare is gone,
If one perchance shall hit upon the scent,
With twice redoubled fire the alans run ;
So stirred the valiant Saxons every one ;
Soon, linkèd man to man, the champions stood.
To 'tone for their bewrate so soon 'twas done,
And lifted bills appeared an iron wood.
Here glorious Alfwold towered above the wights,
And seemed to brave the fire of twice ten thousand fights.   130

Thus Leöfwine: 'To-day will England's doom
  Be fixed for aye, for good or evil state,
  This sun's aunture be felt for years to come;
  Then bravely fight, and live till death of date.
Think of brave Ælfridus, y-clept "the Great";
  From port to port the red-haired Dane he chased,
  The Danes, with whom not lyoneelles could mate,
  Who made of peopled realms a barren waste;
Think how at onee by you Norwegia bled,
Whilst death and victory for mastery bested.   140

  Meanwhile did Gurth unto king Harold ride,
  And told how he did with duke William fare.
Brave Harold looked askance, and thus replied;
  'And ean thy faith be bought with drunken cheer?'
Gurth waxèd hot; fire in his eyes did glare,
  And thus he said—'Oh! brother, friend, and king,
  Have I deserved this fremèd speech to hear?
  By God's high halidome, ne'er thought the thing.
When Tostus sent me gold and silver store,
I scorned his present vile, and scorned his treason more'.   150

  'Forgive me, Gurth', the brave king Harold cried;
    'Who ean I trust, if brothers are not true?
  Think thou of Tostus, once my joy and pride'.
  Gurth said, with look adigne, 'My lord, I do.
  But what our foemen are', quoth Gurth, 'I'll shew.
  By God's high halidome, they priestès are'.
'Do not', quoth Harold, 'Gurth mistell them so,
  For they are every one brave men at war'.

BATTLE OF HASTINGS (II)

Quoth Gurth, 'Why will ye then provoke their hate?'
Quoth Harold, 'Great the foe, so is the glory great'. 160
And now duke William marshallèd his band,
   And stretched his army out, a goodly row.
First did a rank of arcublastries stand,
   Next those on horseback drew the ascending floe ;
Brave champions, each well learnèd in the bow,
   Their asenglave across their horses tied ;
Or with their loverds squires behind did go,
   Or waited, squire-like, at the horse's side.
When thus duke William to a monk did say,
'Prepare thyself with speed, to Harold haste away. 170
Tell him from me one of these three to take :
   That he to me do homage for this land,
Or me his heir, when he deceaseth, make,
   Or to the judgment of Christ's vicar stand'.
He said ; the monk departed out of hand,
   And to king Harold did this message bear,
Who said, 'Tell thou the duke, at his likand,
   If he can get the crown, he may it wear'.
He said, and drove the monk out of his sight,
And with his brothers roused each man to bloody fight. 180
A standard made of silk and jewels rare,
   Wherein all colours, wrought about in bighes,
An armèd knight was seen death-doing there,
   Under this motto—'He conquers or he dies'.
This standard rich, endazzling mortal eyes,
   Was borne near Harold at the Kenters' head,
Who charged his brothers for the great emprise,
   That straight the hest for battle should be spread.

To every earl and knight the word is given,
And cries '*A guerre!*' and clarions shake the vaulted
    heaven.   190
  As when the earth, torn by convulsions dire,
    In realms of darkness hid from human sight;
  The warring force of water, air, and fire,
    Burst from the regions of eternal night,
  Through the dark caverns seek the realms of light;
    Some lofty mountain, by its fury torn,
  Dreadfully moves, and causes great affright;
    Now here, now there, majestic nods the bourne,
And awful shakes, moved by the almighty force;
Whole woods and forests nod, and rivers change their
    course.   200
  So did the men of war at once advance,
    Linked man to man, appeared one body light;
Above, a wood, y-formed of bill and lance,
    That nodded in the air, most strange to sight;
Hard as the iron were the men of might,
    No need of clarions to enrouse their mind;
Each shooting spear y-readen for the fight,
    More fierce than falling rocks, more swift than
    wind;
With solemn step, by echo made more dire,
One single body all, they marched, their eyes on
    fire.   210
  And now the grey-eyed morn with violets dressed,
    Shaking the dewdrops on the flowery meads,
  Fled with her rosy radiance to the west.
    Forth from the eastern gate the fiery steeds
  Of the bright sun awaiting spirits leads.
    The sun, in fiery pomp enthroned on high,
  Swifter than thought along his journey gledes,
    And scatters night's remains from out the sky.

He saw the armies make for bloody fray,
And stopped his driving steeds, and hid his lightsome
    ray.   220
  King Harold high in air majestic raised
    His mighty arm, decked with a manchyn rare;
  With even hand a mighty javelin poised,
    Then furious sent it whistling through the air.
  It struck the helmet of the Sieur de Beer.
    In vain did brass or iron stop its way;
  Above his eyes it came, the bones did tear,
    Piercing quite through, before it did allay.
He tumbled, screeching with his horrid pain,
His hollow cuishes rang upon the bloody plain. 230

  This William saw, and, sounding Roland's song,
    He bent his iron interwoven bow,
  Making both ends to meet with might full strong;
    From out of mortal's sight shot up the floe.
  Then, swift as falling stars to earth below,
    It slanted down on Alfwold's painted shield,
  Quite through the silver-bordured cross did go,
    Nor lost its force, but stuck into the field;
The Normans, like their sovereign, did prepare,
And shot ten thousand floes uprising in the air. 240

  As when a flight of cranes, that takes their way
    In household armies through the flanchèd sky,
  Alike the cause, or company or prey,
    If that perchance some boggy fen is nigh,
  Soon as the muddy nation they espy,
    In one black cloud they to the earth descend;
  Fierce as the falling thunderbolt they fly,
    In vain do reeds the speckled folk defend;
So prone to heavy blow the arrows fell,
And pierced through brass, and sent many to heaven
    or hell.   250

BATTLE OF HASTINGS (II)

Ælan Adelfred, of the stowe of Leigh,
Felt a dire arrow burning in his breast;
Before he died, he sent his spear away,
Then sunk to glory and eternal rest.
Neville, a Norman of all Normans best,
Through the joint cuishè did the javelin feel,
As he on horseback for the fight addressed,
And saw his blood come smoking o'er the steel;
He sent the avenging floe into the air,
And turned his horse's head, and did to lecch
    repair.   260

And now the javelins, barbed with death his wings,
Hurled from the English hands by force aderne,
Whizz drear along, and songs of terror sings,
Such songs as always closed in life eterne.
Hurled by such strength along the air they burn,
Not to be quenchèd but in Normans' blood.
Where'er they came, they were of life forlorn,
And always followed by a purple flood.
Like clouds the Norman arrows did descend,
Like clouds of carnage full, in purple drops did
    end.   270

Nor, Leöfwinus, didst thou still y-stand;
Full soon thy pheon glittered in the air;
The force of none but thine and Harold's hand
Could hurl a javelin with such deadly geer.
It whizzed a ghastly din in Norman's ear,
Then, thundering, did upon his greave alight,
Pierce to his heart, and did his bowels tear;
He closed his eyes in everlasting night.
Ah! what availed the lions on his crest,
His hatchments rare with him upon the ground were
    pressed.   280

William again y-made his bow-ends meet,
    And high in air the arrow winged his way;
Descending like a shaft of thunder fleet,
    Like thunder rattling at the noon of day,
On Algar's shield the arrow did assay,
    There through did pierce, and stick into his groin;
In griping torments on the field he lay,
    Till welcome death came in and closed his eyne.
Distort with pain he lay upon the borne,
Like sturdy elms by storms in uncouth writhings torn.   290

Alrick, his brother, when he this perceived,
    He drew his sword, his left hand held a spear;
Towards the duke he turned his prancing steed,
    And to the God of heaven he sent a prayer,
Then sent his deadly javelin in the air;
    On Hugh de Beaumont's back the javelin came,
Through his red armour to his heart it tare;
    He fell, and thundered on the place of fame.
Next with his sword he 'sailed the Sieur de Roe,
And burst his silver helm, so furious was the blow.   300

But William, who had seen his prowess great,
    And fearèd much how far his bronde might go,
Took a strong arblaster, and, big with fate,
    From twanging iron sent the fleeting floe.
As Alric hoists his arm for deadly blow,
    Which, had it come, had been de Roeës last,
The swift-winged messenger from William's bow
    Quite through his arm into his side y-past;
His eyes shot fire, like blazing star at night,
He gripped his sword, and fell upon the place of fight.   310

Oh! Alfwold, say, how shall I sing of thee,
  Or tell how many did beneath thee fall?
Not Harold's self more Norman knights did slea,
  Not Harold's self did for more praises call.
How shall a pen like mine then shew it all?
  Like thee, their leader, each Bristolian fought;
  Like thee, their blaze must be canonical;
  For they, like thee, that day revenge y-wrought.
Did thirty Normans fall upon the ground,
Full half a score from thee and they receive their
  fatal wound. 320

  First Fitz-Chivelloys felt thy direful force;
  Naught did his held-out brazen shield avail;
  Eftsoon through that thy driving spear did pierce,
  Nor was it stoppèd by his coat of mail;
  Into his breast it quickly did assail;
  Out ran the blood, like hyger of the tide,
  With purple stainèd all his aventayle.
  In scarlet was his cuish of silver dyed.
Upon the bloody carnage-house he lay,
Whilst his long shield did gleam with the sun's rising
  ray. 330

  Next Fescamp fell. Oh! Christ, how hard his fate
  To die the leckedst knight of all the throng!
  His sprite was made of malice deslavate,
  Nor shoulden find a place in any song.
  The broched keen javelin, hurled from hand so
    strong
  As thine, came thundering on his crested beave;
  Ah! naught availed the brass or iron thong;
  With mighty force his skull in two did cleave;
Falling, he shooken out his smoking brain,
As withered oaks or elms are hewn from off the
  plain. 340

BATTLE OF HASTINGS (II)

Nor, Norcie, could thy might and skilful lore
    Preserve thee from the doom of Alfwold's spear
Could'st thou not know, most skilled astrologer,
    How in the battle it would with thee fare?
When Alfwold's javelin, rattling in the air,
    From hand divine on thy habergeon came,
Out at thy back it did thy heart's blood bear;
    It gave thee death and everlasting fame.
Thy death could only come from Alfwold's arm,
As diamonds only can its fellow-diamonds harm. 350

Next Sieur du Mouline fell upon the ground,
    Quite through his throat the deadly javelin pressed,
His soul and blood came rushing from the wound;
    He closed his eyes and oped them with the blest.
It eannot be I should behight the rest,
    That by the mighty arm of Alfwold fell;
Past by a pen to be count or expressed,
    How many Alfwold sent to heaven or hell.
As leaves from trees shook by derne autumn's hand,
So lay the Normans slain by Alfwold on the strand. 360

As when a drove of wolves with dreary yells
    Assail some flock, nor cares if shepherd ken't,
Scattering destruction o'er the woods and dells,
    The shepherd swains in vain their loss lament;
So fought the Bristol men; nor one crevent,
    Nor one abashed enthoughten for to flee;
With fallen Normans all the plain besprent,
    And, like their leaders, every man did slea.
In vain on every side the arrows fled,
The Bristol men still raged, for Alfwold was not dead. 370

Many meanwhile by Harold's arm did fall,
  And Leofwine and Gurth increased the slain;
'Twould take a Nestor's age to sing them all,
  Or tell how many Normans pressed the plain.
But of the earls whom record not hath slain,
  Oh Truth! for good of after-times relate,
That, though they're dead, their names may live again,
  And be in death, as they in life were, great.
So after-ages may their actions see,
And, like to them, eternal alway strive to be.   380

Adhelm, a knight, whose holy deathless sire
  For ever bended to St Cuthbert's shrine,
Whose breast for ever burned with sacred fire,
  And e'en on earth he might be called divine;
To Cuthbert's church he did his goods resign,
  And left his son his God's and fortune's knight.
His son the Saint beheld with look adigne,
  Made him in gemot wise, and great in fight;
Saint Cuthbert did him aid in all his deeds,
His friends he lets to live, and all his foemen bleeds.   390

He married was to Kenewalcha fair,
  The finest dame the sun or moon adave;
She was the mighty Aderedus' heir,
  Who was already hasting to the grave;
As the blue Briton, rising from the wave,
  Like sea-gods seem in most majestic guise,
And round about the rising waters lave,
  And their long hair around their bodies flies:
Such majesty was in her port displayed,
To be excelled by none but Homer's martial maid,   400

BATTLE OF HASTINGS (II)

White as the chalky cliffs of Britain's isle,
    Red as the highest-coloured Gallic wine,
Gay as all nature at the morning-smile,
    Those hues with pleasure on her lips combine ;
Her lips more red than summer-evening skyne,
    Or Phœbus rising in a frosty morn ;
Her breast more white than snow in fields that lain,
    Or lily lambs that never have been shorn,
Swelling like bubbles in a boiling well,
Or new-burst brooklets gently whispering in the dell.   410

Brown as the filbert dropping from the shell,
    Brown as the nappy ale at Hoektide game,
So brown the crooked rings, that featly fell
    Over the neck of the all-beauteous dame.
Grey as the morn before the ruddy flame
    Of Phœbus ehariot rolling through the sky ;
Grey as the steel-horned goats Conyan made tame,
    So grey appeared her featly sparkling eye ;
Those eyes, that oft did mickle pleasèd look
On Adhelm, valiant man, the virtues' doomsday-book.   420

Majestic as the grove of oaks that stood
    Before the abbey built by Oswald king ;
Majestic as Hibernia's holy wood,
    Where saints, for souls departed, masses sing ;
Such awe from her sweet look forth issuing
    At once for reverence and love did call ;
Sweet as the voice of thrushes in the spring,
    So sweet the words that from her lips did fall ;
None fell in vain ; all shewèd some entent ;
Her wordies did display her great entendèment.   430

BATTLE OF HASTINGS (II)

    Taper as candles laid at Cuthbert's shrine,
      Taper as elms that Goodrick's abbey shrove,
    Taper as silver chalices for wine,
      So taper was her arms and shape y-grove.
    As skilful mine-men by the stones above
      Can tell what metal is y-lach'd below,
    So Kenewalcha's face, y-made for love,
      The lovely image of her soul did shew;
Thus was she outward formed; the sun, her mind,
Did gild her mortal shape, and all her charms
    refined.   440

    What blazours then, what glory shall he claim,
      What doughty Homer shall his praises sing,
    That left the bosom of so fair a dame
      Uncalled, unasked, to serve his lord the king?
    To his fair shrine good subjects ought to bring
      The arms, the helmets, all the spoils of war,
    Through every realm the poets blaze the thing,
      And travelling merchants spread his name to far:
The stout Norwegians had his anlace felt,
And now among his foes death-doing blows he
    dealt.   450

    As when a wolfin, getting in the meads,
      He rageth sore, and doth about him slea,
    Now here a talbot, there a lambkin bleeds,
      And all the grass with clotted gore doth stree;
    As when a riv'ette rolls impetuously,
      And breaks the banks that would its force restrain,
    Along the plain in foaming rings doth flee,
      'Gainst walls and hedges doth its course maintain;
As when a man doth in a corn-field mow,
With ease at one fell stroke full many is laid low. 460

BATTLE OF HASTINGS (II)

So many, with such force, and with such ease,
    Did Adhelm slaughter on the bloody plain;
Before him many did their heart's blood lease,
    Oft times he fought on towers of smoking slain.
Angillian felt his force, nor felt in vain;
    He cut him with his sword athur the breast,
Out ran the blood and did his armour stain,
    He closed his eyën in eternal rest;
Like a tall oak, by tempest borne away,
Stretched in the arms of death upon the plain he lay.   470

Next through the air he sent his javelin fierce
    That on De Clearmounde's buckler did alight,
Through the vast orb the sharp pheon did pierce,
    Rang on his coat of mail and spent its might.
But soon another winged its airy flight,
    The keen broad pheon to his lungs did go;
He fell, and groaned upon the place of fight,
    Whilst life and blood came issuing from the blow,
Like a tall pine upon his native plain,
So fell the mighty sire, and mingled with the slain.   480

Hugh de Longeville, a forcie doutremere,
    Advancèd forward to provoke the dart,
When soon he found that Adhelm's pointed spear
    Had found an easy passage to his heart;
He drew his bow, nor was of death astart,
    Then fell down breathless to increase the corse.
But, as he drew his bow devoid of art,
    So it came down upon Troyvillian's horse;
Deep through his hatchments went the pointed floe;
Now here, now there, with rage bleeding he round doth go.   490

Nor does he heed his master's known commands,
  Till, growèn furious by his bloody wound,
Erect upon his hinder feet he stands,
  And throws his master far off to the ground.
Near Adhelm's feet the Norman lay astound,
  Scattered his arrows, loosened was his shield ;
Through his red armour, as he lay enswooned,
  He pierced his sword, and out upon the field
The Norman's bowels steamed, a deadly sight ;
He oped, and closed his eyes in everlasting night. 500

Caverd, a Scot, who for the Normans fought,
  A man well skilled in sword and sounding string,
Who fled his country for a crime enstrote,
  For daring with bold word his loyal king ;
He at earl Adhelm with great force did fling
  An heavy javelin, made for bloody wound ;
Along his shield askance the same did ring,
  Pierced through the corner, then stuck in the ground ;
So when the thunder rattles in the sky,
Through some tall spire the shafts in a torn clevis fly. 510

Then Adhelm hurled a crooked javelin strong
  With might that none but such great champions know ;
Swifter than thought the javelin passed along,
  And hit the Scot most fiercely on the prow ;
His helmet bursted at the thundering blow,
  Into his brain the trembling javelin steck ;
From either side the blood began to flow,
  And run in circling ringlets round his neck ;
Down fell the warrior on the deadly strand,
  Like some tall vessel wrecked upon the tragic sand. 520

BATTLE OF HASTINGS (II)

Where fruitless heaths and meadows clad in grey,
  Save where sad hawthorns rear their humble head,
The hungry traveller upon his way
  Sees a huge desert all around him spread,
The distant city scarcely to be sped,
  The curling force of smoke he sees in vain,
'Tis too far distant, and his only bed,
  Y-wimpled in his cloak, is on the plain,
Whilst rattling thunder forrey o'er his head,
And rains come down to wet his hard uncouthlie bed;   530

A wondrous pile of rugged mountains stands,
  Placed on each other in a drear array,
It not could be the work of human hands,
  It not was rearèd up by men of clay.
Here did the Britons adoration pay
  To the false god whom they did Tauran name,
Dighting his altar with great fires in May,
  Roasting their victual round about the flame,
'Twas here that Hengist did the Britons slea,
As they were met in council for to be.   540

Near, on a lofty hill, a city stands,
  That lifts its shafted head unto the skies,
And kingly looks around on lower lands,
  And the long brown plain that before it lies.
Hereward, born of parents brave and wise,
  Within this vylle first a-drew the air,
A blessing to the earth sent from the skies;
  In any kingdom naught could find his peer.
Now, ribbed in steel, he rages in the fight,
And sweeps whole armies to the realms of night.   550

So when sad autumn with his sallow hand
  Tears the green mantle from the lymèd trees,
The leaves, besprengèd on the yellow strand,
  Fly in whole armies from the blatant breeze;

BATTLE OF HASTINGS (II)

All the whole field a carnage-house he sees,
    And souls unknellèd hovered o'er the blood ;
From place to place on either hand he sleas,
    And sweeps all near him like a furious flood ;
Death hung upon his arm ; he slew so maynt,
'Tis past the pencil of a man to paint.   560
    Bright sun in haste hath drove his fiery wain
        A three-hours' course along the whited skyne,
    Viewing the swarthless bodies on the plain,
        And longèd greatly to plunge in the brine.
    For as his beamès and far-stretching eyne
Did view the pools of gore in purple sheen,
        The wolsomme vapours round his locks did twine,
    And did disfigure all his semlykeene ;
Then to hard action he his wain did rouse,
In hissing ocean to make glair his brows.   570
    Duke William gave command : each Norman knight
        That bare war-token in a shield so fine
    Should onward go, and dare to closer fight
        The Saxon warrior, that did so entwine,
        Like the nesh bryon and the eglantine,
        Or Cornish wrestlers at a Hocktide game.
    The Normans, all enmarshalled in a line,
        To the ourt array of the thight Saxons came.
There 'twas the whapèd Normans, on a par,
Did know that Saxons were the sons of war.   580
    Oh Turgot ! wheresoe'er thy sprite doth haunt,
        Whether with thy loved Adhelm by thy side,
    Where thou mayst hear the swotie night-lark chant,
        Or with some mocking brooklet sweetly glide,
        Or rolling fiercely with fierce Severn's tide,
        Where'er thou art, come and my mind enleme
    With such great thoughts as did with thee abide,
        Thou sun, of whom I oft have caught a beam,

BATTLE OF HASTINGS (II)

Send me again a drybblette of thy light,
That I the deeds of Englishmen may write. 590
 Harold, who saw the Normans to advance,
  Seized a huge bill, and laid him down his spear,
 So did each wight lay down the pointed lance,
  And groves of bills did glitter in the air.
 With shouts the Normans did to battle steer.
  Campynon, famous for his stature high,
 Fiery with brass, beneath a shirt of lere,
  In cloudy day he reached into the sky;
Near to king Harold did he come along,
And drew his steel morglaïen sword so strong. 600
 Thrice round his head he swung his anlace wide,
  On which the sun his visage did agleeme,
 Then, straining as his members would divide,
  He struck on Harold's shield in manner breme;
 Along the field it made a horrid cleme,
  Cutting king Harold's painted shield in twain;
 Then in the blood the fiery sword did steam,
  And then did drive into the bloody plain.
So when in air the vapours do abound,
Some thunderbolt tears trees, and drives into the
  ground. 610
 Harold upreared his bill, and furious sent
  A stroke, like thunder, at the Norman's side;
 Upon the plain the broken brass besprent
  Did not his body from death-doing hide;
 He turnèd back and did not there abide;
  With stretched out shield he ayenward did go,
 Threw down the Normans, did their ranks divide,
  To save himself, left them unto the foe.
So elephants, in kingdom of the sun,
When once provoked, doth through their own troops
  run. 620

Harold, who knew he was his army's stay,
  Needing the rede of general so wise,
Bid Alfwold to Campynon haste away ;
  As through the army ayenward he hies,
Swift as a feathered arrow Alfwold flies,
  The steel bill blushing o'er with lukewarm blood.
Ten Kenters, ten Bristolians for th' emprise
  Hasted with Alfwold where Campynon stood,
Who ayenward went, whilst every Norman knight
Did blush to see their champion put to flight. 630

As painted Briton, when a wolfin wild,
  When it is cold, and blustering winds do blow,
Enters his bordel, taketh his young child,
  And with his blood bestreynts the lily snow,
He thórough mountain high and dale doth go,
  Through the quick torrent of the swollen Ave,
Through Severn rolling o'er the sands below
  He skims aloft, and blents the beating wave,
Nor stints, nor lags the chase, till 'fore his eyne
In pieces he the murdering thief doth chine. 640

So Alfwold, he did to Campynon haste ;
  His bloody bill awhaped the Norman's eyne ;
He fled, as wolves when by the talbots chased,
  To bloody battle he did not incline.
Duke William struck him on his brigandine,
  And said—'Campynon, is it thee I see ?
Thee ? who didst acts of glory so bewryen,
  Now poorly come to hide thyself by me ?
Away ! thou dog, and act a warrior's part,
Or with my sword I'll pierce thee to the heart !' 650

Between earl Alfwold and duke William's bronde
  Campynon thought that naught but death could be,
Seized a huge sword morglaïen in his honde,
  Muttering a prayër to the Virginè.

So hunted deer the driving hounds will slea,
    When they discover they cannot escape ;
And fearful lambkins, when they hunted be,
    Their infant hunters do they oft awhape.
Thus stood Campynon, great but heartless knight,
When fear of death made him for death to fight.   660

Alfwold began to dight himself for fight.
    Meanwhile his men on every side did slea ;
When on his lifted shield with all his might
    Campynon's sword in burlie-brande did dree.
Bewopen, Alfwold fell upon his knee ;
    His Bristol men came in him for to save ;
Eftsoon upgotten from the ground was he,
    And did again the towering Norman brave.
He grasped his bill in such a drear array,
He seemed a lion catching at his prey.   670

Upon the Norman's brazen adventayle
    The thundering bill of mighty Alfwold came ;
It made a dentful bruise and then did fail.
    From rattling weapons shot a sparkling flame.
Eftsoon again the thundering bill y-came,
    Pierced through his adventayle and skirts of lare ;
A tide of purple gore came with the same,
    As out his bowels on the field it tare.
Campynon fell, as when some city-wall
In doleful terrors on its miners fa.l.   680

He fell, and did the Norman ranks divide ;
    So when an oak, that shot into the sky,
Feels the broad axes piercing his broad side,
    Slowly he falls and on the ground doth lie,
Pressing all down that is with him anigh,
    And stopping weary travellers on the way ;
So stretched upon the plain the Norman high,
*   *   *   *   •   *

Bled, groaned, and died; the Norman knights
    astound
To see the bawsyn champion pressed upon the
    ground.   690
  As when the hyger of the Severn roars,
    And thunders ugsom on the sands below,
  The sound rebounds to Wedëcester's shore,
    And sweeps the black sand round its hoary prow ;
  So furious Alfwold through the war did go.
  His Kenters and Bristolians slew each side,
    Betreinted all along with bloodless foe,
    And seemed to swim along with bloody tide.
From place to place, besmeared with blood, they went,
And round about them swarthless corse besprent. 700
  A famous Norman, who, y-clept Aubene,
    Of skill in bow, in tilt, and hand-sword fight,
  That day in field had many Saxons slain,
    For he, in soothen, was a man of might.
  First did his sword on Adelgar alight,
    As he on horseback was, and pierced his groin,
  Then upward went ; in everlasting night
  He closed his rolling and dim-sighted eyne.
Next Eadlyn, Tatwyn, and famed Adelred,
By various causes sunken to the dead.   710
  But now to Alfwold he opposing went,
    To whom compared, he was a man of stre,
  And with both hands a mighty blow he sent
    At Alfwold's head, as hard as he could dree ;
  But on his painted shield so bismarlie
    Aslant, his sword did go into the ground.
  Then Alfwold him attacked most furiously,
    And through his gaberdine he did him wound ;
  Then soon again his sword he did upryne,
  And clove his crest, and split him to the eyne.   720
          *   *   *   *   *   *

THE ROMAUNTE OF THE CNYGHTE

BY JOHN DE BURGHAM

THE sun into Virginè was gotten,
The flowers all around onspryngede,
The woddie grass blanched the fen,
The yellow flag arised from bed.
Sir Knight did mount upon a steed,
No cart-horse, not little of make,
Then went forth for hardy deed
With morglaie his foemen to make bleed;
Eke, quickly as wind trees, their hearts to shake.

All down in a dell, a dark gloomy dell,   10
Where coppice eke thighe trees there be,
There did he perchance to see
A damsel asking for aid on her knee;
A knight uncourteous did by her stand,
He held her fast by her hand.
'Discourteous knight, I do pray now thou tell
Why doest thou be so to the damsel?'
The knight him answered eftsoons,
' It beeth no matter of thine,
Begone, for I wait not thy boons'.   20

The knight said, ' I prove on the gaberdine'.
Alyche boars enchafed to fight they flies.
The discourteous knight be strong, but stronger the
   right,
The sound be heard a mile for fury in the fight
Till the false knight y-falleth and dies.

'Damsel', quoth the knight, 'Now come thou with me'.
'I wot well', quoth she, 'I need thee not fear,
The knight y-fallen bad would I should be,
But lo, he is dead, may it speed heavenwere'.

THE ROMANCE OF THE KNIGHT

MODERNISED BY CHATTERTON

The pleasing sweets of spring and summer past,
The falling leaf flies in the sultry blast,
The fields resign their spangling orbs of gold,
The wrinkled grass its silver joys unfold,
Mantling the spreading moor in heavenly white,
Meeting from every hill the ravished sight.
The yellow flag uprears its spotted head,
Hanging regardant o'er its watery bed;
The worthy knight ascends his foaming steed,
Of size uncommon, and no common breed.   10
His sword of giant make hangs from his belt,
Whose piercing edge his daring foes had felt.
To seek for glory and renown he goes,
To scatter death among his trembling foes;
Unnerved by fear, they trembled at his stroke;
So cutting blasts shake the tall mountain oak.

Down in a dark and solitary vale,
Where the cursed screech-owl sings her fatal tale,
Where copse and brambles interwoven lie,
Where trees entwining arch the azure sky,   20
Thither the fate-marked champion bent his way,
By purling streams to lose the heat of day.

THE ROMANCE OF THE KNIGHT

A sudden cry assaults his listening ear,
His soul's too noble to admit of fear.
The cry re-echoes: with his bounding steed
He gropes the way from whence the cries proceed.
The arching trees above obscured the light,
Here 'twas all evening, there eternal night.
And now the rustling leaves and strengthened cry
Bespeaks the cause of the confusion nigh; 30
Through the thick brake the astonished champion sees
A weeping damsel bending on her knees;
A ruffian knight would force her to the ground,
But still some small resisting strength she found.
(Women and cats, if you compulsion use,
The pleasure which they die for will refuse.)
The champion thus: 'Desist, discourteous knight,
Why dost thou shamefully misuse thy might?'
With eye contemptuous thus the knight replies,
'Begone! whoever dares my fury dies!' 40
Down to the ground the champion's gauntlet flew,
'I dare thy fury, and I'll prove it too'.
Like two fierce mountain-boars enraged they fly,
The prancing steeds make echo rend the sky,
Like a fierce tempest is the bloody fight,
Dead from his lofty steed falls the proud ruffian knight.
The victor, sadly pleased, accosts the dame,
'I will convey you hence to whence you came'.
With look of gratitude the fair replied,
'Content: I in your virtue may confide. 50
But', said the fair, as mournful she surveyed
The breathless corse upon the meadow laid,
'May all thy sins from heaven forgiveness find
May not thy body's crimes affect thy mind!'

ECLOGUE THE FIRST

ROBERT *and* RAUFE

WHEN England, smoking from her deadly wound,
From her galled neck did pluck the chain away,
Knowing her lawful sons fall all around,
(Mighty they fell, 'twas honour led the fray);
Then in a dale, by eve's dark mantle gray,
Two lonely shepherds did abrodden fly,
(The rustling leaf doth their white hearts affray),
And with the owlet trembled and did cry;
First Robert Neatherd his sore bosom stroke,
Then fell upon the ground and thus y-spoke.   10

Rob.   Ah, Raufe! if thus the hours do come along,
If thus we fly in chase of farther woe,
Our foot will fail, albeit we be strong,
Nor will our pace swift as our danger go.
To our great wrongs we have enhepèd moe.
The Barons war! Oh, woe and well-a-day!
I haveth life, but have escapèd so,
That life itself my senses do affray.
Oh Raufe, come list, and hear my dernie tale,
Come hear the baleful doom of Robin of the
    Dale.   20

Raufe.   Say to me naught; I know thy woe in mine.
Oh! I've a tale that Sabalus might tell.
Sweet flowerets, mantled meadows, forests
    digne;
Gravots, far-seen, around the hermit's cell,
The sweet ribible sounding in the dell,
The joyous dancing in the hoastrie court;
Eke the high song and every joy, farewell!
Farewell, the very shade of fair disport;

ECLOGUE THE FIRST

Annoying trouble on my head do come,
Nor one kind saint to ward the aye-increasing doom. 30

Rob. Oh! I could wail my kingcup-deckèd mees,
My spreading flocks of sheep of lily white,
My tender applynges, and embodyde trees,
My parker's grange, far-spreading to the sight,
My tender cows, my bullocks strong in fight,
My garden whitened with the comfreie plant,
My flower Saint-Mary shooting with the light,
My store of all the blessings heaven can grant;
I am duressèd unto sorrow's blow,
Accustomed to the pain, will let no salt tear flow. 40

Raufe. Here I will abide until death do 'pear,
Here, like a foul empoisoned deadly tree,
Which slayeth every one that cometh near,
So will I, fixèd unto this place, gre.
I to lament haveth more cause than thee;
Slain in the war my much-loved father lies;
Oh! joyous I his murderer would slea,
And by his side for aye enclose mine eyes.
Cast out from every joy, here will I bleed,
Fell is the 'cullis-gate of my heart's castle-stead. 50

Rob. Our woes alike, alike our fate shall be.
My son, my only son, y-storven is;
Here will I stay, and end my life with thee;
A life like mine a burden is, I wis.

144 ECLOGUE THE SECOND

Now from e'en lodges fled is happiness,
Minsters alone can boast the holy saint.
Now doeth England wear a bloody dress,
And with her champions' gore her face depeyncte,
Peace fled, disorder sheweth her dark rode,
And thórough air doth fly, in garments stained
    with blood.   60

ECLOGUE THE SECOND

NIGEL

'SOULS of the blest', the pious Nigel said,
' Pour out your pleasure on my father's head.
Richard of lion's heart to fight is gone,
    Upon the broad sea do the banners gleam ;
The amenusèd nations be aston
    To see so large a fleet, so fine, so breme.
The barkìs heasods cut the glassy stream ;
    Waves sinking, waves upon the hard oak rise ;
The water-trumpets, with a swotye cleme,
    Conteke the sounding air, and reach the skies. 10
Souls of the blest, on golden thrones astedd,
Pour out your pleasure on my father's head.

The red depeyncted oars from the black tide,
    Carved with devices rare, do shimmering rise ;
Upswelling do they shew in drierie pride,
    Like gore-red estells in the eve-dark skies ;
The name-depcynctèd shields, the spears arise,
    Alyche tall rushes on the water-side ;
Along from bark to bark the bright sheen flies ;
    Short-lived delights do on the water glide. 20

ECLOGUE THE SECOND

Souls of the blest, and every saint y-dead,
Pour out your pleasure on my father's head.

> The Saracen looks out; he doëth fear,
>   That England's furious sons do cut the way;
> Like hunted bucks, they runneth here, and there,
>   Onknowlachynge in what place to obaie.
> The banner glisters on the beam of day,
>   The mighty cross Jerusalem is seen,
> Thereof the sight their courage do affray,
>   In woeful dole their faces be y-wreene.   30

Souls of the blest, and every saint y-dead,
Pour out your pleasure on my father's head.

> The bollengers and cottes, so swift in fight,
>   Upon the sides of every bark appear;
> Forth to his office leapeth every knight,
>   Eftsoon his squire, with his shield and spear.
> The joining shields do shimmer and much glare,
>   The dashing oar do make united din;
> The running foemen, thinking if to dare,
>   Boun the dark sword, they seek affray, they
>   blyn.   40

Souls of the blest, and every saint y-dead,
Pour out your pleasure on my father's head.

> Now come the warring Saracens to fight:
>   King Richard, like a lyoncelle of war,
> In shining gold, like fiery meteors, dight,
>   Shaketh aloft his hand, and seen afar.
> So haveth I espied a greater star
>   Among the smaller ones to shine full bright;
> So the sun's wain with amayled beams do bar
>   The silver moon or estells to give light.   50

Souls of the blest, and every saint y-dead,
Pour out your pleasure on my father's head.

Distraught affray, with locks of blood-red dye,
   Terror, emburlèd in the thunder's rage,
Death, linkèd to dismay, doth ugsomme fly,
   Encouraging every champion war to wage.
Spears bevyle spears, swords upon swords engage ;
   Armour on armour sounds, shield upon shield ;
Nor death of thousands can the war assuage ;
   But falling numbers blacken all the field.   60
Souls of the blest, and every saint y-dead,
Pour out your pleasure on my father's head.

   The foemen fall around, the cross waves high ;
      Stainèd in gore, the heart of war is seen ;
   King Richard, thórough every troop, doth fly
      And beareth many Turks unto the green ;
   By him the flower of Asia's men is slain ;
      The waylynge moon doth fade before his sun ;
   By him his knights be formed to actions digne,
      Doing such marvels, strangers be aston.   70
Souls of the blest, and every saint y-dead,
Pour out your pleasure on my father's head.'

   The fight is won : king Richard master is ;
      The English banner kisseth the high air ;
   Full of pure joy the army is, I wis,
      And every one haveth it on his bayre.
Again to England come, and worshipped there,
   Pulled into loving arms, and feasted eft ;
In every eye a-reading naught of weere,
   Of all remembrance of past pain bereft.   80
Souls of the blest, and every saint y-dead,
Such pleasures pour upon my father's head.'

   So Nigel said, when from the blue-y sea
      The swollen sail did dance before his eyne ;
   Swift as the wish, he to the beach did flee,
      And found his father stepping from the brine.

Let thyssen men, who haveth soul of love,
Bethink unto themselves how might the meeting
   prove!

ECLOGUE THE THIRD

A MAN, A WOMAN, SIR ROGER

WOULD'ST thou know nature in her better part?
  Go, search the huts and bordels of the hind;
If they have any, it is rough-made art,
  In them you see the naked form of kind;
Haveth your mind a liking of a mind?
  Would it know everything, as it might be?
Would it hear phrase of the vulgar from the hind,
  Without wiseacre words and knowledge free?
If so, read this, which I disporting penned,
If naught beside, its rhyme may it commend.   10

Man. But whither, fair maid, do you go?
    O where do you bend your way?
  I will know whither you go,
    I will not be answered nay.
Woman. To Robin and Nell, all down in the dell,
    To help them at making of hay.
Man. Sir Roger, the parson, have hired me there,
    Come, come, let us trip it away,
  We'll work and we'll sing, and we'll drink of
    strong beer,
  As long as the merry summer's day.   20
Woman. How hard is my doom to wurch!
    Much is my woe:
    Dame Agnes, who lies in the church
      With birlette gold,
    With gilded aumeres, strong, untold,
    What was she more than me, to be so?

ECLOGUE THE THIRD

Man.   I see Sir Roger from afar,
       Tripping over the lea;
       I ask why the loverd's son
       Is more than me.   30

Sir Roger.   The sultry sun doth hie apace his wain,
       From every beam a seed of life do fall;
       Quickly scille up the hay upon the plain,
       Methinks the cocks beginneth to grow tall.
       This is alyche our doom; the great, the small,
       Must wither and be dried by deathis dart.
       See! the sweet floweret hath no sweet at all;
       It with the rank weed beareth equal part.
       The coward, warrior, and the wise be blent,
       Alyche to dry away with those they did lament.   40

Man.   All-a-boon, Sir Priest, all-a-boon!
       By your priestship, now say unto me;
       Sir Gaufrid the knight, who liveth hard by,
       Why should he than me be more great,
       In honour, knighthood, and estate?

Sir Roger.   Attourne thine eyes around this hayèd mee;
       Carefully look around the chaper dell
       An answer to thy barganette here see,
       This withered floweret will a lesson tell;
       Arist, it blew, it flourished, and did well, 50
       Looking disdainfully on the neighbour green;
       Yet with the deigned green its glory fell,
       Eftsoon it shrank upon the day-burnt plain,

ECLOGUE THE THIRD

Did not its look, whilèst it there did stand,
To crop it in the bud move some dread hand?
 Such is the way of life; the loverd's ente
  Moveth the robber him therefor to slea;
 If thou hast ease, the shadow of content,
  Believe the truth, there's none more haile than thee.
 Thou workest; well, can that a trouble be? 60
  Sloth more would jade thee than the roughest day.
 Could'st thou the hidden part of soulès see,
  Thou would'st eftsoon see truth in what I say.
But let me hear thy way of life, and then
Hear thou from me the lives of other men.

Man. I rise with the sun,
  Like him to drive the wain,
 And ere my work is done,
  I sing a song or twain.
I follow the plough-tail,   70
With a long jubb of ale.
 But of the maidens, oh!
  It lacketh not to tell;
 Sir Priest might not cry woe,
  Could his bull do as well.
I dance the best heideignes,
And foil the wisest feygnes.
 On every saint's high-day
  With the minstrel am I seen,
 All a-footing it away   80
  With maidens on the green.
But oh! I wish to be more great
In glory, tenure, and estate.

150   ECLOGUE THE FOURTH

Sir Roger. Hast thou not seen a tree upon a hill,
    Whose unlist branches reachen far to sight?
    When furious tempests do the heaven fill,
      It shaketh dire, in dole and much affright;
    Whilst the dwarf floweret, with humility dight,
      Standeth unhurt, unquashèd by the storm.
    Such is a picte of life; the man of might   90
      Is tempest-chafed, his woe great as his form;
    Thyself, a floweret of a small account,
      Wouldst harder feel the wind, as thou didst higher mount.

ECLOGUE THE FOURTH

ELINOURE *and* JUGA

On Rudborne bank two pining maidens sat,
    Their tears fast dripping to the water clear;
Each one lamenting for her absent mate,
    Who at Saint Alban's shook the murdering spear.
The nut-brown Elinoure to Juga fair
Did speak acroole, with languishment of eyne,
Like drops of pearly dew, glistened the quivering brine.

Elin. O gentle Juga! hear my sad complaint,
    To fight for York, my love is dight in steel;
    O may no sanguine stain the white rose paint,   10
    May good Saint Cuthbert watch Sir Robert wele;
    Much more than death in phantasy I feel;

ECLOGUE THE FOURTH

See, see! upon the ground he bleeding lies;
Infuse some juice of life, or else my dear love dies.

Juga. Sisters in sorrow, on this daisied bank,
    Where melancholy broods, we will lament,
  Be wet with morning dew and even dank;
    Like blasted oaks in each the other bent,
    Or like forsaken halls of merriment,
Whose ghastly ruins hold the train of fright,   20
Where deadly ravens bark, and owlets wake the night.

Elin. No more the bagpipe shall awake the morn,
    The minstrel-dance, good cheer, and morris-play;
  No more the ambling palfrey and the horn
    Shall from the forest rouse the fox away.
    I'll seek the forest all the livelong day;
All night among the graved churchyard will go,
And to the passing sprites relate my tale of woe.

Juga. When murky clouds do hang upon the leme
    Of leden moon, in silver mantles dight;   30
  The tripping fairies weave the golden dream
    Of happiness, which flieth with the night.
    Then (but the saints forbid!) if to a sprite
Sir Richard's form is lyped, I'll hold, distraught,
His bleeding clay-cold corse, and die each day in thought.

Elin. Ah! woe-lamenting words! what words can shew?
    Thou glassy river, on thy bank may bleed
  Champions, whose blood will with thy waters flow,
    And Rudborne stream be Rudborne stream indeed!
    Haste, gentle Juga, trip it o'er the mead, 40

To know, or whether we must wail again,
Or with our fallen knights be mingled on the plain.
So saying, like two lightning-blasted trees,
  Or twain of clouds that holdeth stormy rain,
They movèd gently o'er the dewy mees,
  To where Saint Alban's holy shrines remain.
There did they find that both their knights were slain.
Distraught, they wandered to swoll'n Rudborne's side,
Yellèd their deadly knell, sank in the waves, and died.

THE STORIE OF WILLIAM CANYNGE

AGAINST a brooklet as I lay reclined,
  Listening to hear the water glide along,
Minding how thórough the green mees it twined,
  Awhilst the caves responsed its muttering song,
At distant rising Avon to be sped,
Mingled with rising hills, did shew its head.

Engarlandèd with crowns of osier weeds
  And wreaths of alders of a bercie scent,
And sticking out with clod-agested reeds,
  The hoary Avon shewed dire semblament,   10
Whilst blatant Severn, from Sabrina cleped,
Roars flemie o'er the sandès that she heaped.

These eynegears quickly bringeth to my thought
  Of hardy champions knowen to the flood,
How on the banks therof brave Ælla fought,
  Ælla descended from Merce kingly blood,
Warden of Bristol town and castle-stead,
Who ever and anon made Danes to bleed.

Methought such doughty men must have a sprite
   Dote in the armour-brace that Michael bore, 20
When he with Satan, king of hell, did fight,
   And earth was drenchèd in a mere of gore;
Or, soon as they did see the worldìs light,
Fate had wrote down, this man is born to fight.

'Ælla', I said, or else my mind did say,
   'Why is thy actions left so spare in story?
Were I to dispose, there should liven aye
   In earth and heaven's rolls thy tale of glory;
Thy acts so doughty should for aye abide,
And by their test all after-acts be tried'. 30

Next holy Wareburghus filled my mind,
   As fair a saint as any town can boast,
Or be the earth with light or dark y-wrynde,
   I see his image walking through the coast;
Fitz-Harding, Bithrickus, and twenty moe
In vision 'fore my phantasy did go.

Thus all my wandering faytour thinking strayed,
   And each digne builder dequaced on my mind,
When from the distant stream arose a maid,
   Whose gentle tresses moved not to the wind; 40
Like to the silver moon in frosty neet,
The damoisel did come, so blithe and sweet.

No broided mantle of a scarlet hue,
   No shoe-peaks plaited o'er with riband gear,
No costly paraments of woaden blue,
   Naught of a dress but beauty did she wear;
Naked she was, and lookèd sweet of youth,
All did bewrayen that her name was Truth.

STORIE OF WILLIAM CANYNGE

The easy ringlets of her nut-brown hair
  What not a man should see did sweetly hide,   50
Which on her milk-white bodykin so fair
  Did show like brown streams fouling the white tide,
Or veins of brown hue in a marble cuarr,
Which by the traveller is seen from far.

Astounded mickle, there I silent lay,
  Still scauncing wondrous at the walking sight;
My senses, forgard, not could run away,
  But was not forstraught when she did alight
Anigh to me, dressed up in naked view,
Which might in some adulterous thoughts a-brew.   60

But I not did once think of wanton thought;
  For well I minded what by vow I hete,
And in my pocket had a crouchee brought,
  Which in the blossom would such sins anete;
I looked with eyes as pure as angels do,
And did the every thought of foul eschew.

With sweet semblance and an angel's grace
  She 'gan to lecture from her gentle breast;
For Truthès words are in her mindès face,
  False oratories she did aye detest;   70
Sweetness was in each word she did y-wreene,
Though she strove not to make that sweetness sheen.

She said, 'My manner of appearing here
  My name and slighted mindbruch may thee tell;
I'm Truth, that did descend from heavenwere,
  Goulers and courtiers do not know me well;
Thy inmost thoughts, thy labouring brain I saw,
And from thy gentle dream will thee adawe.

Full many champions and men of lore,
  Painters and carvellers have gained good name, 80
But there's a Canynge to increase the store,
  A Canynge, who shall buy up all their fame.
Take thou my power, and see in child and man
What truly nobleness in Canynge ran'.

As when a cottager on easy bed,
  Tired with the labours maynt of sultry day,
In sleepis bosom layeth his deft head,
  So, senses sunk to rest, my body lay;
Eftsoon my soul, from earthly bands untied,
Mingled in flanchèd air with Truth aside. 90

Straight was I carried back to times of yore,
  Whilst Canynge swathèd yet in fleshly bed,
And saw all actions which had been before,
  And all the scroll of fate unravellèd;
And when the fate-marked babe a-come to sight,
I saw him eager gasping after light.

In all his shepen gambols and child's play,
  In every merrymaking, fair, or wake,
I saw a purpled light of wisdom's ray;
  He ate down learning with the wastle-cake. 100
As wise as any of the aldermen,
He'd wit enow to make a mayor at ten.

As the soft downy beard began to gre,
  So was the well-thight texture of his lore;
Each day enheeding mockler for to be,
  Great in his counsel for the days he bore.
All tongues, all carols did unto him sing,
Wondering at one so wise, and yet so yinge.

Increasing in the years of mortal life,
  And hasting to his journey into heaven, 110
He thought it proper for to choose a wife,
  And use the sexes for the purpose given.

He then was youth of comely semelikeede,
And he had made a maiden's heart to bleed.

He had a father (Jesus rest his soul!)
    Who lovèd money as his cherished joy;
He had a brother (happy man be's dole!)
    In mind and body his own father's boy.
What then could Canynge wissen as a part
To give to her who had made chop of heart?   120

But lands and castle-tenures, gold and bighes,
    And hoards of silver rusted in the ente,
Canynge and his fair sweet did that despise;
    To change of truly love was their content.
They lived together in a house adigne,
Of good sendaument, comëly and fine.

But soon his brother and his sire did die,
    And left to William 'states and renting-rolls,
And at his will his brother John supply.
    He gave a chantry to redeem their souls,   130
And put his brother into such a trade,
That he lord mayor of London town was made.

Eftsoon his morning turned to gloomy night,
    His dame, his second self, gave up her breath,
Seeking for eterne life and endless light,
    And fled good Canynge; sad mistake of death!
So have I seen a flower in summer-time
Trod down and broke, and wither in its prime.

Next Redcliff church (oh, work of hand of heaven,
    Where Canynge sheweth as an instrument!)   140
Was to my bismarde eyesight newly given;
    'Tis past to blazon it to good content!
You that would fain the fetive building see,
Repair to Redcliff, and contented be.

I saw the myndbruche of his noble soul
  When Edward menacèd a second wife,
I saw what pheryons in his mind did roll ;
  Now fixed from second dames a priest for life.
'This is the man of men', the vision spoke ;
Then bell for evensong my senses woke.   150

ON OUR LADY'S CHURCH

As on a hill one eve sitting,
At Our Lady's church much wondering,
The cunning handiwork so fine
Had well nigh dazzelèd mine eyne.
Quoth I : 'Some cunning fairy hand
Y-reared this chapel in this land ;
Full well I wot so fine a sight
Was not y-reared of mortal wight '.
Quoth Truth : ' Thou lackest knowledging ;
Thou, forsooth, not wottest of the thing.   10
A reverend father, William Canynge hight,
Y-rearèd up this chapel bright,
And eke another in the town
Where glassy bubbling Trym doth run '.
Quoth I : 'No doubt, for all he's given,
His soul will certès go to heaven '.
'Yea', quoth Truth, ' Then go thou home,
And see thou do as he hath done '.
Quoth I : 'I doubt, that cannot be,
I have not gotten markès three '.   20
Quoth Truth : ' As thou hast got, give almsdeeds so ;
Canynges and Gaunts could do no moe '.
                                   T. R.

ON THE SAME

[OUR LADY'S CHURCH]

STAY, curious traveller, and pass not by,
Until this fetive pile astound thine eye.
  Whole rocks on rocks with iron joined survey,
And oaks with oaks entremèd disposed lie.
  This mighty pile, that keeps the winds at bay,
Fire, lightning and the murky storm defy,
That shoots aloft into the realms of day,
Shall be the record of the builder's fame for aye.

  Thou seest this mastery of a human hand,
The pride of Bristol and the western land;   10
  Yet is the builder's virtues much more great,
Greater than can by Rowlie's pen be scanned.
  Thou seest the saints and kings in stony state,
That seemed with breath and human soul dispande;
As 'pared to us enseem these men of slate,
Such is great Canynge's mind when 'pared to God elate.

  Well mayst thou be astound; but view it well,
Go not from hence before thou see thy fill,
  And learn the builder's virtues and his name;
Of this tall spire in every county tell,   20
  And with thy tale the lazing rich men shame;
Shew how the glorious Canynge did excel,
How he, good man, a friend for kings became,
And glorious paved at once the way to heaven and fame.

ON THE DEDICATION OF OUR LADY'S CHURCH

Soon as bright sun along the skies
    Had sent his ruddy light,
And fairies hid in oxlip cups
    Till wished approach of night,
The matin-bell with shrilly sound
    Re-echoed through the air,
A troop of holy friars did
    For Jesus' mass prepare;
Around the high unsainted church
    With holy relics went,   10
And every door and post about
    With godly things besprent.
Then Carpenter, in scarlet dressed,
    And mitred holily,
From Master Canynge his great house
    With rosary did hie.
Before him went a throng of friars
    Who did the mass-song sing,
Behind him Master Canynge came,
    Tricked like a barbèd king;   20
And then a row of holy friars
    Who did the mass-song sound;
The procurators and church-reeves
    Next pressed upon the ground.
And when unto the church they came,
    A holy mass was sang,
So loudly was their swotie voice,
    The heaven so high it rang.
Then Carpenter did purify
    The church to God for aye.   30

With holy masses and good psalms,
    Which he did therein say.
Then was a sermon preachèd soon
    By Carpenter holy,
And after that another one
    Y-preached was by me.
Then all did go to Canynge's house,
    An interlude to play,
And drink his wine and ale so good,
    And pray for him for aye.   40

THE PARLYAMENTE OF SPRYTES

WRITTEN BY T. ROWLEIE AND J. ISCAM

INTRODUCTION BY QUEEN MAB. (BY ISCAM)

When from the earth the sun's hulstrèd,
    Then, from the flowerets straught with dew,
My liege men make ye awhapèd,
    And witches their wychencref do.
Then rise the sprites terrible and rou,
And take their walk the churchyard through.

Then do the sprites of valorous men
    Agleam along the barbèd hall,
Pleasant the mouldering banners ken,
    Or sit around in honoured stall.   10
Our sprites attourne their eyes to-night,
And look on Canynge his church bright.

In sooth, in all my bismarde round,
    Truly the thing must be bewryen,
In stone or wooden work is found
    Naught so fair-welcome to mine eyne
As is good Canynge his church of stone,
Which blatauntlie will show his praise alone.

TO JOHN CARPENTER, BISHOP OF WORCESTER
(BY ROWLEIE)

To you, good bishop, I address my say,
   To you, who honoureth the cloth you wear;
Like precious jewels in gold of best allay,
   Each one doth make the other seem more fair.
Other than you, where could a man be found
So fit to make a place be holy ground?

The saints in stone so neatly carvellèd,
   They scarcely are what they enseem to be,
By fervent prayer of yours might rear their head,
   And chant out masses to our Virginè.
Were every prelate like a Carpenter,
The church would not blush at a Winchester.

Learned as Beauclerc, as the Confessor
   Holy in life, like Canynge charitable,
Busy in holy church as Vavasour,
   Slack in things evil, in all good things stable,
Honest as Saxons was, from whence thou'rt sprung,
Though body weak, thy soul for ever young.

Thou knowest well thy conscience free from stain,
   Thy soul her rode no sable 'batements have;
Y-clenchèd o'er with virtue's best adaygne,
   A day eterne thy mind does aye adave.
No spoilèd widows, orphyäns distressed,
Nor starving priests distract thy nightly rest.

Here then to thee let me, for one and all,
   Give laud to Carpenter and commendation,
For his great virtues; but, alas! too small
   Is my poor skill to shew you his just blation,
Or to blaze forth his public good alone,
And all his private good to God and him is known.

THE PARLYAMENTE OF SPRYTES

Spirit of Nimrod speaketh. (BY ISCAM)

  Soon as the morn, but newly 'wake,
    Spied night y-storven lie,   50
  On her corse did dewdrops shake,
    Then 'fore the sun upgotten was I.

The ramping lion, fell tigère,
  The buck that skips from place to place,
The elephant and rhinocère,
  Before me through the greenwood I did chase.

Nimrod, as Scripture calls my name,
  Baal, as jetted stories say;
For rearing Babel of great fame
  My name and renown shall lyven for aye.   60

But here I spy a finer rearing,
  'Gainst which the cloudès doth not fight,
On which the stars do sit, to appearing;
  Weak men think it reaches the kingdom of light.

Oh! where is the man that builded the same,
  Expending worldly store so well?
Fain would I change with him my name,
  And stand in his chance not to go to hell.

Sprites of Assyrians sing

  When, to their caves eterne abest,
  Then waters have no more distressed   70
    The world so large;
    But did discharge
  Themselves into their bed of rest;

  Then men, besprengèd all abroad,
  No more did worship the true God;
    But did create
    High temples great
  Unto the image of Nimrod.

THE PARLYAMENTE OF SPRYTES

But now the Word of God is come,
Born of Maid Mary, to bring home 80
  Mankind, his sheep;
  Them for to keep
In the fold of his heavenly kingdòm.

This church which Canynge he did rear,
To be usèd in praise and prayer,
  Men's souls to save
  From 'vouring grave,
And purify them heaven-were.

Sprites of ELLE, BYTHRYCKE, FITZ-HARDYNGE, FRAMPTON, GAUNTES, SEGOWEN, LANYNGETON, Knightes Templars, *and* BYRTONNE. (BY ROWLEIE)

Sprite of BYTHRYCKE *speaketh*

Ellè, thy Bristol is thy only care,
  Thou art like dragon vigilant of its good; 90
No loving dames, too kind, more love can bear,
  Nor Lombards over gold more vigilant brood.

Sprite of ELLE *speaketh*

Quickly, ye sprites, forsake the swollen flood,
  And browke a sight with me, a sight enfyne;
Well have I vended mine for Danish blood,
  Since this great structure greets my 'mazèd eyne.
Ye that have builded on the Radclefte side,
Turn there your eyes, and see your works outvied!

Sprite of BYTHRYCKE *speaketh*

What wondrous monument! what pile is this,
  That binds in wonder's chain entendèment? 100
That doth aloft the airy skyën kiss,
  And seemeth mountains, joinèd by cement,

From God His great and wondrous storehouse sent.
Full well mine eyes conceive it cannot be,
That man could rear of such a great extent
   A church so bawsyn handsome as we see.
The 'frighted clouds, disparted, from it fly,
'Twill be, I wis, to all eternity.

        ELLE'S *sprite speaketh*
Were I once more cast in a mortal frame,
   To hear the chantry-song sound in mine ear,   110
To hear the masses to our holy dame,
   To view the cross-aisles and the arches fair!
Through the half-hidden silver-twinkling glare
   Of yon bright moon in foggy mantles dressed;
I must content the building to aspere,
   Whilst broken clouds the holy sight arrest;
Till, as the nights grow old, I fly the light.
Oh! were I man again, to see the sight!

There sit the canons; cloth of sable hue
   Adorn the bodies of them every one;   120
The chanters white with scarfs of woaden blue,
   And crimson chappeaus for them to put on,
With golden tassels, glittering in the sun;
   The dames in kirtles all of Lincoln green,
And knotted shoe-peaks, of brave colours done.
   A finer sight in sooth was never seen.

        BVRTONNE'S *sprite speaketh*
In tilts and tournics was my dear delight,
   For man and God His warfare had rennome,
At every tilting-yard my name was hight,
   I bear the bell away where'er I come.   130
Of Redcliff church the building new I done,
   And did full many holy place endow,
Of Mary's house made the foundation,
   And gave a threescore marks to John his too.

Then closed mine eyes, on earth to ope no moe,
Whilst six-month's mind upon my grave was doe.
  Full glad am I my church was pullèd down,
    Since this brave structure doth agreete mine eye.
  This building rare, most noble of the town,
    Like to the donor's soul, shall never die.   140
  But if, percase, time, of his dire envý,
    Shall beat it to rude walls and heaps of stone,
  The wandering traveller, that passes by,
    Will see its ruined ancient splendour shewn
In the old arches and the carvelling,
And pillars their green heads to heaven rearing.

Sprite of SEGOWEN *speaketh*
  Deceiving gold was once my only toy,
    With it my soul within the coffer lay,
  It did the mastery of my life employ,
    By night my mistress, and my jubb by day.   150
  Once, as I dozing in the witch-hour lay,
    Thinking how to benym the orphan's bread,
  And from the helpless take their goods away,
    I from the skyën heard a voice, which said:
'Thou sleepest; but lo! Satan is awake,
Some deed that's holy do, or he thy soul will take'.

  I quickly was upryst, with fear astound,
    Methought in mirk was playing devils felle;
  Straight did I number twenty aves round,
    Thinking full soon for to go to hell.   160
  In the morn my case to a good priest did tell,
    Who did counsel me to y-build that day
  The church of Thomas, then to pieces fell.
    My heart expanded into heaven lay:
Soon was the silver to the workmen given,
'Twas best bestowed, a karynte gave to heaven.

But well, I wot, thy causalles were not so,
   'Twas love of God that set thee on the rearing
Of this fair church, Oh! Canynge, for to do
   This noble building of so fine appearing;   170
This church, our lesser buildings all out-daring,
   Like to the moon with stars of little light;
And after-times, the handsome pile revering,
   The prince of churches' builders thee shall hight;
Great was the cause, but greater was the effect,
So all will say who do this place prospect.

Sprite of FITZ-HARDYNGE *speaketh*

From royal parents did I have retaining,
   The red-haired Dane confessed to be my sire;
The Dane who, often through this kingdom draining,
   Would mark their way athrowgh with blood and fire.   180
As stoppèd rivers always rise more higher,
   And rammed stones by opposures stronger be,
So they, when vanquishèd, did prove more dire,
   And for one countryman did threescore slea.
From them, of Denmark's royal blood, came I,
Well might I boast of my gentility.

   The pipes may sound and bubble forth my name,
      And tellen what on Radclefte-side I did;
   Trinity College should not grudge my fame,
      The fairest place in Bristol y-buildèd.   190
   The royal blood that through my veinès slid
      Did tinge my heart with many a noble thought;
   Like to my mind the minster y-rearèd
      With noble carvèd workmanship was wrought;
High at the daïs, like a king on's throne,
Did I take place, and was myself alone.

But thou, the builder of this pleasant place,
   Where all the saints in sweet adjunction stand,
A very heaven for its beauteous grace,
   The glory and the wonder of the land, 200
That shews the builder's mind and former's hand
   To be the best that on the earth remains,
At once for wonder and delight command,
   Shewing how much he of the god retains :
Canynge, the great, the charitable, and good,
Noble as kings, if not of kingly blood.

Sprite of FRAMPTONE *speaketh*

Bristol shall speak my name, and Radclefte too,
   For here my deeds were godly every one,
As Owden's minster by the gate will shew,
   And John's at Bristol what my works have done, 210
Besides another house I had begun.
   But mine, compared to this one, is a groffe,
Not to be mentioned or lookèd upon,
   A very punelstre or very scoff.
Canynge, thy name shall living be for aye,
Thy name not with the church shall waste away.

Sprite of GAUNTES *speaketh*

I did full many reparations give,
   And the Bonne-Hommès did full rich endow,
As touring to my God on earth did live,
   So all the Bristol chronicles will shew. 220
But all my deeds will be as nothing now
   Since Canynge has this building finishèd,
Which seemeth to be the pride of Bristow,
   And by no building to be overmatched :
Which aye shall last and be the praise of all,
And only in the wreck of nature fall.

A Knight Templar's sprite speaketh

In holy ground, where Saracens defile
 The ground whereon our Saviour did go;
And Christ His temple make to mosquès vile,
 Wordies of despite 'gainst our Saviour throw;   230
There 'twas that we did our warfarage do,
 Guarding the pilgrims of the Christian fay;
And did our holy arms in blood embrue,
 Moving like thunder-bolts in drear array,
Our strokes, like lightning tearing the tall tree,
Our God our arm with deadly force did dree.

Maint tenures fair, and manors of great wealth,
 Green woods, and brooklets running through the lea,
Did men us give for their dear soul her health;
 Gave earthly riches for goods heavenly.   240
Nor did we let our riches useless be,
 But did y-build the Temple Church so fine;
The which is wrought about so bismarlie,
 It seemeth camoys to the wondering eyne.
And ever and anon when bells ringèd,
 From place to place it moveth its high head:
But Canynge from the sweat of his own brows
Did get his gold and raise this beauteous house.

LANYNGETON'S sprite speaketh

Let all my faults be buried in the grave;
 All obloquies be rotted with my dust;   250
Let him first carpen that no wemmes have;
 'Tis past man's nature for to be aye just.
But yet, in soothen, to rejoice I must,
 That I did not immeddle for to build;
Since this quaintissed place so glorious,
 Seeming all churches joinèd in one guild,

Has now supplied for what I had [not] done,
Which, to my candle, is a glorious sun.

   ELLE'S *sprite speaketh*

Then let us all do jointly reverence here ;
 The best of men and bishops here do stand, 260
Who are God's shepherds and do take good care
 Of the good sheep He putteth in their hand ;
Not one is lost, but all in well likand
 Await to hear the General Bishop's call,
When Michael's trump shall sound to inmost land,
 Affright the wicked, and awaken all ;
Then Canynge rises to eternal rest,
And finds he chose on earth a life the best.

ON THE MINSTER

ATTRIBUTED TO JOHN, SECOND ABBOT OF SAINT AUSTIN'S MINSTER

WITH hasty step religion, dight in grey,
 Her face of doleful hue,
Swift as an arrow through bright heaven took her way,
 And oft and ere anon did say,
 'Ah me ! What shall I do?
See Bristol city, which I now do ken,
 Arising to my view,
Thick thronged with soldiers and with traffic-men ;
 But saintès I see few '.

Fitz-Hardynge rose—he rose like bright sun in the
    morn, 10
  ' Fair dame, adryne thine eyne,
  Let all thy grief be mine ;
For I will rear thee up a minster high,
The top whereof shall reach into the sky;
And will a monk be shorn '.
Then did the dame reply,
  ' I shall not be forlorn ;
Here will I take a comfortable rest,
And spend my days upon Fitz-Hardynge's breast '.

FRAGMENT ON RICHARD I.

ATTRIBUTED TO JOHN, SECOND ABBOT OF SAINT AUSTIN'S MINSTER

HEART of lion ! Shake thy sword,
  Bare thy murdering stainèd hand,
Quash whole armies to the queed,
  Work thy will in burlie brande,
Barons here on cushions 'broidered,
  Fight in furs against the cale,
Whilest thou in thundering armès
  Warriketh whole cities' bale.
Heart of lion ! Sound the beme,
  Sound it into inner lands ; 10
Fear flies sporting in the cleme,
  In thy banner terror stands.

THE WARRE

ATTRIBUTED TO JOHN, SECOND ABBOT OF SAINT
AUSTIN'S MINSTER

OF war's glum pleasure do I chant my lay,
   Truth tips the pencil, wisdom marks the line,
Whilst hoar experience telleth what to say,
   And blasted husbandry with bleary eyne,
   Standeth and woe laments ; the trickling brine
Running adown his cheeks which doeth shew,
Like his unfruitful fields, long strangers to the plough.

Say, Gloucester, when, besprenged on every side,
   The gentle, hyndlette, and the villein fell ;
When smoking blood did flow like to a tide,   10
   And sprites were damnèd for the lack of knell,
   Diddest thou know no likeness to an hell,
Where all were misdeeds doing like unwise,
Where hope unbarred and death eftsoon did shut their
     eyes?

Ye shepherd swains who ribible ken,
   End the tight dance, nor look upon the spear ;
In ugsommnesse war must be clothed to men,
   Unhappiness attendeth honour-were ;
   Quaff your sweet vernage and atreted beer.

THE WORLD: AN INTERLUDE

FATHER, SON, *and* MINSTRELS

Father. To the world new and its bestoykenynge way,
 This coistrel son of mine is all my care ;
 Ye minstrels, warn him how with rede he stray
 Where gilded vice doth spread his mascilled snare ;
 To getting wealth I would he should be bred,
 And crowns of ruddy gold, not glory, round his head.

1 *Min.* My name is Interest, 'tis I
 Do into all bosoms fly :
 Each one's hidden secret's mine ;
 None so worthy, good, and digne,   10
 But will find it to their cost,
 Interest will rule the roast.
 I to every one give laws,
 Self is first in every cause.

2 *Min.* I am a faytour flame
  Of lemmies melancholy,
 Love some behight my name,
  Some do anemp me Folly.
 In sprites of melting mould
  I set my burning seal ;   20
 To me a gouler's gold
  Doth not a pin avail ;

THE WORLD: AN INTERLUDE

  I prey upon the health,
  And from God's counsel flee;
 The man who would get wealth
  Must never think of me.

3 *Min.* I be the Queed of Pride, my 'spiring head
  Must reach the clouds, and still be rising high.
 Too little is the earth to be my bed,
  Too hannow for my breathing-place, the sky. 30
 Daynous I see the world beneath me lie.
  But to my betters I so little 'gree,
  Beneath a shadow of a shade I be;
 'Tis tó the small alone that I can multiply.

4 *Min.* I am the Queed of Goulers; look around,
  The airs about me thieves do represent;
 Bloodstainèd robbers spring from out the ground,
  And airy visions swarm around my ente.
 Oh! save my monies, it is their intent
  To nymme the red god of my frighted sprite; 40.
 What joy can goulers have, or day or night?

5 *Min.* Vice be I hight, on gold full oft I ride,
  Full fair unto the sight for aye I seem;
 My ugsomness with golden veils I hide,
  Laying my lovers in a silken dream.
 But when my untrue pleasures have been tried,
  Then do I shew all filthiness and rou,
 And those I have in net would fain my grip eschew.

6 *Min.* I be great Death; all know me by the name,
 But none can say how I do loose the sprite;   50
 Good men my tardying delay doeth blame,
 But most rich goulers from me take a flight;
 Mickle of wealth I see, where'er I came,
 Doëth my terror mickle multiply,
 And maketh them afraid to live or die.

Father. How! villain minstrels, and is this your rede?
 Away, away! I will not give a curse.
 My son, my son, of this my speech take heed,
 Nothing is good that bringeth not to purse.

IN IMITATION OF OUR OLD POETS

ONE CANTO OF AN ANCIENT POEM, CALLED
THE UNKNOWN KNIGHT; OR, THE TOURNAMENT

The mattin-bell had sounded long,
The cocks had sang their morning song,
When lo! the tuneful clarions' sound,
(Wherein all other noise was drowned)
Did echo to the rooms around,
And greet the ears of champions strong;
' Arise, arise from downy bed,
For sun doth 'gin to shew his head!'

Then each did don in seemly gear,
What armour each beseemed to wear,
And on each shield devices shone,
Of wounded hearts and battles won.

All curious and nice each one ;
With many a tasselled spear ;
And, mounted each one on a steed,
Unwote, made ladies' hearts to bleed.

Heralds each side the clarions wound,
The horses started at the sound ;
The knights each one did point the lance,
And to the combats did advance ;
From Hiberne, Scotland, eke from France ;
Their prancing horses tare the ground ;
All strove to reach the place of fight.
The first to exercise their might—

O'Rocke upon his courser fleet,
Who, swift as lightning were his feet,
First gained the lists and gat him fame ;
From West Hibernee Isle he came,
His might depictured in his name.
All dreaded such an one to meet ;
Bold as a mountain-wolf he stood,
Upon his sword sat grim death and blood.

But when he threw down his asenglave,
Next came in Sir Botelier bold and brave,
The death of many a Saracen ;
They thought him a devil from hell's black pen,
Not thinking that any of mortal men
Could send so many to the grave.
For his life to John Rumsee he rendered his thanks,
Descended from Godred, the King of the Manks.

Within his sure rest he settled his spear,
And ran at O'Rocke in full career ;
Their lances with the furious stroke
Into a thousand shivers broke,

Even as the thunder tears the oak,
And scatters splinters here and there :
So great the shock, their senses did depart,
The blood all ran to strengthen up the heart.

Sir Botelier Rumsie first came from his trance,
And from the marshal took the lance ;
O'Rocke eke chose another spear,
And ran at Sir Botelier [in] full career ;
His prancing steed the ground did tear :
In haste he made a false advance ;
Sir Botelier seeing, with might amain,
Felled him down upon the plain.

Sir Pigotte Novlin at the clarions' sound,
On a milk-white steed with gold trappings around,
He couched in his rest his silver-point spear,
And fiercely ran up in full career ;
But for his appearance he paid full dear,
In the first course laid on the ground ;
Besmeared in the dust with his silver and gold,
No longer a glorious sight to behold.

Sir Botelier then having conquered his twain,
Rode conqueror off the tourneying plain ;
Receiving a garland from Alice's hand,
The fairest lady in the land.
Sir Pigotte this viewed, and furious did stand,
Tormented in mind and bodily pain.
Sir Botelier crowned, most gallantly stood,
As some tall oak within the thick wood.

Awhile the shrill clarions sounded the word ;
Next rode in Sir John, of Adderleigh lord,
Who over his back his thick shield he did bring,
In checkee of red and silver shining,

With steed and gold trappings beseeming a king,
A gilded fine adder twined round his sword.
De Bretville advanced, a man of great might,
And couched his lance in his rest for the fight.   80

Fierce as the falling waters of the lough,
That tumble headlong from the mountain's brow,
Even so they met in dreary sound;
De Bretville fell upon the ground,
The blood from inward bruisèd wound
Did out his stainèd helmet flow;
As some tall bark upon the foamy main,
So lay De Bretville on the plain.

Sir John, of the Dale, or Compton, hight,
Advancèd next in lists of fight;   90
He knew the tricks of tourneying full well,
In running race no man could him excel,
Or how to wield a sword better tell,
And eke he was a man of might:
On a black steed with silver trappings dight
He dared the dangers of the tourneyed fight.

Within their rests their spears they set,
So furiously each other met,
That Compton's well-intended spear
Sir John his shield in pieces tare,   100
And wounded his hand in furious geir;
Sir John's steel asenglave was wet:
Sir John then to the marshal turned,
His breast with mickle fury burned.

The 'tenders of the field came in,
And bade the champions not begin;
Each tourney but one hour should last,
And then one hour was gone and past.

* * *

THE BRODER OF ORDERYS WHYTE

THERE was a brother of orders white,
He sung his masses in the night ;
   Ave Maria, Jesu Maria.
The nuns all sleeping in the dorture,
Thought him of all singing friars the flower.
   Ave Maria, Jesu Maria.

Sister Agnes loved his singing well,
And sung with him too, the soothen to tell :
   Ave Maria, etc.
But be it not said by old or young   10
That ever they otherwise did sing
   Than Ave Maria, etc.

This brother was called everywhere,
To Kenshamm and to Bristol nonnere ;
   Ave Maria, etc.
But singing of masses did work him so low,
Above his skin his bones did grow.
   Ave Maria, etc.

He eaten beef and dishes of mows,
And haunted every knightés house   20
   With Ave Maria, etc.
And being once more in good lyken,
He sang to the nuns and was poren again ;
   With Ave Maria, etc.

DIALOGUE

Between MASTER PHILPOT *and* WALWORTH, Cockneies

PHILPOT

GOD ye God den, my good neighbour, how d'ye
 ail?
How does your wife, man! what never assole?
Cum rectitate vivas, verborum mala ne cures.

WALWORTH

Ah, Master Philpot, evil tongues do say,
That my wife will lyën down to-day :
'Tis not twain months since she was mine for aye.

PHILPOT

*Animum submittere noli rebus in advresis,
Nolito quædam referenti semper credere.*
But I pity you, neighbour, is it so?

WALWORTH

Quæ requirit misericordiam mala causa est. 10
Alack, alack, a sad doom mine, in fay,
But oft with citizens it is the case ;
*Honesta turpitudo pro bonâ
Causâ mori,* as ancient pensmen says.

PHILPOT

Home news well let alone and Latin too,
 For me a memory doth 'gin to fail;
Say, Master Walworth, what good news have you,
 Pray have you hearden of the stones of hail?

WALWORTH

I have, and that it with reddour did 'sail;
  Some hailstones were like cherries rege and
    great,   20
And to the ground there did the trees prevail.
But goodman Philpot, what do you ahete
'Bout goods of Lamington, now held by you,
For certain monies' store to you for chattels due?

PHILPOT

Ah, I have nymd him special; for his wine
  Have ta'en at once twelve pounds; for dainty
    cheer,
Though the same time my wife with him did dine,
  Been paid a mark—non-extra of the beer;
But when his sinking purse did 'gin to wear,
  I lent him full six marks upon his faie;   30
And he, poor custrel, having naught to spare,
  Favoured a clear and now doth run away.
His goods I down at Bristol town will sell,
For which I will get forty shining marks full well.

WALWORTH

Tide life, tide death, I will with thee go down,
And sell some goods too in brave Bristol town.

THE MERRIE TRICKES OF LAMYNGETOWNE

BY MAISTRE JOHN A ISCAM

Lam. A rigorous doom is mine, upon my fay,
  Before the parent-star, the lightsome sun,
    Hath three times lighted up the cheerful day,
      To other realms must Lamington be gone,

TRICKES OF LAMYNGETOWNE

    Or else my flimsy thread of life is spun.
    And shall I hearken to a coward's rede,
    And from so vain a shade as life is, run?
        No! fly all thoughts of running to the queed;
    No! here I'll stay, and let the cockneys see
    That Lamington the brave will Lamington still be.   10

    To fight, and not to flee, my sabatans
        I'll don, and gird my sword unto my side;
    I'll go to ship, but not to foreign lands,
        But act the pirate, rob in every tide;
    With cockneys' blood shall Thamysis be dyed.
        Their goods in Bristol market shall be sold,
    My bark the loverde of the waters ride,
        Her sails of scarlet and her stere of gold;
    My men the Saxons, I the Hengist, be,
    And in my ship combine the force of all their three.   20

    Go to my trusty men in Selwood's chase
        That through the lesselle hunt the burlèd boar;
    Tell them how stands with me the present case,
        And bid them revel down at Watchet's shore,
    And saunt about in hawlkes and woods no more;
        Let every auntrous knight his armour brace,
    Their meats be man's flesh, and their beverage gore,
    Hancele, or hanceled from, the human race.

> Bid them, like me their leader, shape their mind
> To be a bloody foe, in arms 'gainst all mankind. 30

Ralph. I go my boon companions for to find.
[*Exit* RALPH.

Lam. Unfaithful cockney dogs! your god is gain.
When in your town I spent my great estate,
What crowds of cits came flocking to my train,
What shoals of tradesmen caten from my. plate!
My name was always Lamington the great.
But when my wealth was gone, ye knew me not,
I stood in ward, ye laughéd at my fate,
Nor cared if Lamington the great did rot.
But know, ye curriedowes ye soon shall feel, 40
I've got experience now, although I bought it weel!

> You let me know that all the world are knaves,
> That lords and cits are robbers in disguise;
> I and my men, the cockneys of the waves,
> Will profit by your lessons and be wise;
> Make you give back the harvest of your lies;
> From deep-fraught barks I'll take the miser's soul,
> Make all the wealth of every [man] my prize,
> And, cheating London's pride, to digner Bristol roll.

*   *   *   *   *   *

LAMINGTON, PHILPOTT, *and* ROBYNNE

Lam. Thou sayest, man, that thou would'st go with me, 50
'And bear a part in all my men's emprise;
Think well upon the dangers of the sea,
And guess if that will not thee recradize,

When through the skies the lightning brandë flies,
 And lightnings sparkle in the whited oundes,
Seeming to rise at lepestones to the skies,
 And not contented be with its set bounds.
Then rolls the bark and tosses to and fro ;
Such dreary scenes as this will cast thy blood, I trow.

Think, when with bloody axes in our hands, 60
 We are to fight for gold and silver too,
Our neighbour's myndbruch life no one then stands,
 But all his aim and end is—death to do.

Rob. I've thought on all, and am resolved to go ;
 Fortune ! no more I'll be thy taunted slave,
Once I was great, now plunged in want and woe,
 I'll go and be a pick-hatch of the wave.
Goods I have none, and life I do disdain,
 I'll be a victor, or I'll break my galling chain.
I'll wash my hands in blood and deal in death, 70
Our ship shall blow along with winds of dying breath.

Lam. I like thy courage, and I'll tell thy doom,
 Thou wilt hereafter a brave captain be ;
Go thou to Bristol, stay until we come,
 For there we shall, haply, have need of thee ;
And for a tight and shapely warehouse see
 Wherein to put the chattels we shall bring,
And know if there two cockney knaves may be,
 Philpott and Walworth ; so report doth sing ;

If so, I'll trounce the usurer, by my fay ! So
There's monies, man, for thee—Ralph ! take
  the things away
Which we from Watchet town have taken now ;
In the bark's bottom see the same thou stow.
Ralph. Master of mine, I go as you do say.
Rob. And I to Bristol town will haste away.

SONGE OF SEYNCTE BALDWYNNE

WHEN Norrurs and his men of might,
Upon this bridge dared all to fight,
Forslagen many warriors lay,
And Dacians well-nigh won the day.
When doughty Baldwinus arose,
And scattered death among his foes ;
From out the bridge the purling blood
Embollèd high the running flood.
Death did upon his anlace hang,
And all his arms were *gutte de sanguc*.   10
His doughtiness wrought such dismay,
The foreign warriors ran away.
Earl Baldwinus regarded well
How many men forslagen fell ;
To heaven lift up his holy eye,
And thankèd God for victory ;
Then threw his anlace in the tide,
Lived in a cell, and hermit died.

SONGE OF SEYNCTE WARBURGHE

    When king Kynghill in his hand
    Held the sceptre of this land,
    Shining star of Christès light,
    The murky mists of pagan night
        'Gan to scatter far and wide.
    Then Saint Warburghe he arose,
    Doffed his honours and fine clothes;
    Preaching his Lord Jesus' name,
    To the land of Wessex came,
        Where black Severn rolls his tide.   10

    Strong in faithfulness, he trod
    O'er the waters like a god,
    Till he gained the distant hecke,
    In whose banks his staff did stick,
        Witness to the miracle.
    Then he preachèd night and day,
    And set many in right way.
    This good staff great wonders wrought,
    More than guessed by mortal thought,
        Or than mortal tongue can tell.   20

    Then the folk a bridge did make
    O'er the stream unto the hecke,
    All of wood eke long and wide,
    Pride and glory of the tide;
        Which in time did fall away.
    Then earl Leof he bespedde
    This great river from his bed,
    Round his castle for to run;
    'Twas in truth an ancient one,
        But war and time will all decay.   30

Now again, with bremie force,
Severn, in his ancient course,
Rolls his rapid stream along,
With a sable swift and strong,
    Moreying many an oaky wood.
We, the men of Bristol town,
Have y-reerd this bridge of stone,
Wishing each that it may last
Till the date of days be past,
    Standing where the other stood.   40

IN IMITATION OF OUR OLD POETS
ON OURE LADYES CHIRCH

(Acknowledged by Chatterton as his work, and consequently printed without alteration)

In auntient dayes, when Kenewalchyn King
  Of all the borders of the sea did reigne,
Whos cutting celes, as the Bardyes synge,
  Cut strakyng furrowes in the foamie mayne,
Sancte Warbur cast aside his Earles estate,
As great as good, and eke as good as great.
Tho blest with what us men accounts as store,
Saw something further, and saw something more.

  Where smokyng Wasker scours the claiey bank,
    And gilded fishes wanton in the sunne,   10
  Emyttynge to the feelds a dewie dank,
    As in the twyning path-waye he doth runne;

Here stood a house, that in the ryver smile
Since valorous Ursa first wonne Bryttayn Isle ;
The stones in one as firm as rock unite,
And it defyde the greatest Warriours myghte.

Around about the lofty elemens hie,
   Proud as their planter, reerde their greenie crest,
Bent out their heads, whene'er the windes came bie
   In amorous dalliaunce the flete cloudès kest.   20
Attendynge Squires dreste in trickynge brighte,
   To each tenth Squier an attendynge Knyghte,
The hallie hung with pendaunts to the flore,
A coat of nobil armes upon the doore ;

Horses and dogges to hunt the fallowe deere,
   Of pastures many, wide extent of wode,
Faulkonnes in mewes, and, little birds to teir,
   The Sparrow Hawke, and manie Hawkies gode.
Just in the prime of life, when others court
   Some swottie Nymph, to gain their tender hand,   30
Greet with the Kynge and trerdie greet with the Court
   And as aforesed mickle much of land . . .

*   *   *   *   *   *

A CHRONYCALLE OF BRYSTOWE

WROTE BIE RAUFE CHEDDER, CHAPPMANNE, 1356

IN former days, as story says,
    In famous Bristol town
There livèd knights, doughty in fights,
    Of marvellous renown.
A Saxon bold, renowned of old
    For death and cruel deed,
Maint Tanmen slone, the bridge upon,
    I-causing them to bleed.
Baldwin his name, rolls say the same,
    And give him glory great,   10
He livèd near the Ellynteire,
    All by Saint Leonard's Gate.
A mansion high, made bismarlie,
    Was rearèd by his hand,
When he y-sterve, his name unkerve,
    In Baldwin Street do stand.
One Ælla then, of Mercian men,
    As many pencils blase,
In castle-steed made doleful deed,
    And did the Danes arrase.   20
One Leëfwync, of kingly line,
    In Bristol town did live,
And to the same for his good name
    The Ackman Gate did give.
Hammon, a lord of high accord,
    Was in the street named Brede;
So great his might, so strong in fight,
    On battle he did feed.

Fitz Lupous digne, of gentle line,
  On Radcliffe made his bay,   30
In muddy ground, the which upon
  Both sedge and rushes lay.

There Radcliffe street of mansions meet
  In seemly gear do stand,
And Canynge great of fair estate
  Bringeth to Trading land.

Harding did come from long kingdom
  In Knyvesmyth Street to line,
Robert, his son, much good things done,
  As abbotts to blasynne.   40

Robert the earl, no conquered churl,
  In castle-steed did fray;
Young Henry too in Bristol true
  As hydelle did obaic.

A mayor there be, and I am not he,
  But an ungentle wight;—
Saint Mary tend each amnie friend
  By holy taper light.

ON HAPPIENESSE

BY WILLIAM CANYNGE

May happiness on earthès bounds be had?
  May it adyghte in human shape be found?
Wote ye, was it with Eden's bower bestadde,
  Or quite erasèd from the scaunce-layed ground,
  When from the secret founts the waters did abound?

Does it affrighted shun the bodied walk,
Live to itself and to its echoes talk?
    All hail, content, thou maid of turtle-eyne,
        As thy beholders think thou art y-wreene,
    To ope the door to happiness is thine,   10
        And Christ His glory doth upon thee sheene ;
    Doer of the foul thing ne'er hath thee seen ;
In caves, in woods, in woe, and sad distress,
Whoe'er hath thee hath gotten happiness.

THE GOULER'S REQUIEM

BY WILLIAM CANYNGE

My lovèd entes, adieu ! No more the sight
    Of golden mark shall meet my joyous eyne,
No more the silver noble, shining bright,
    Shall fill my hand with weight to speak it fine ;
No more, no more, alas ! I call you mine.
    Whither must you, ah ! whither must I go?
I know not either. Oh, my emmers digne,
    To part with you will work me mickle woe.
I must be gone, but where I dare not tell ;
Oh storthe unto my mind ! I go to hell.   10

    Soon as the morn did dight the ruddie sun,
        A shade of thieves each streak of light did seem ;
    When in the heaven full half his course was run,
        Each stirring neighbour did my heart afleme ;
    Thy loss, or quick or sleep, was aye my dream ;
        For thee, O gold, I did the law y-crase ;
    For thee I gotten, or by wiles or breme ;
        In thee I all my joy and good did place ;
But now to me thy pleasure is no moe,
I know not but for thee I to the queed must go.   20

ONN JOHNE A DALBENIE
BY WILLIAM CANYNGE

JOHNE makes a jarre 'bout Lancaster and Yorke ;
Be still, good man, and learn to mind thy work.

HERAUDYN
A Fragment

YOUNG Heraudyn all by the green wood sat,
    Hearing the sweet chelandrie and the oue,
Seeing the marked enamelled flowerets neat,
    Ensyngynge to the birds his love song true.
Sir priest came by and forth his bead-roll drew,
    Five Aves and a Pater must be said ;
Twain song : the one his song of willow rue,
    The other one——
    *   *   *   *   *   *

EPITAPH ON ROBERT CANYNGE

THIS morning-star of Redcliff's rising ray,
    A true man, good of mind, and Canynge hight,
Beneath this stone lies mouldering into clay,
    Until the dark tomb shine an eterne light.
Third from his loins the present Canynge came ;
    Hollow are wordès for to tell his due ;
For aye shall live his heaven-recorded name,
    Nor shall it die when time shall be no more.
When Michael's trump shall sound to rise the soul,
He'll wing to heaven with kin and happy be their
    dole.

THE ACCOUNTE OF W. CANYNGE'S FEAST

THROUGH the hall the bell hath sound ;
Welcoming doth the mayor beseem ;
The aldermen do sit around,
And snuffle up the savoury steam,
Like asses wild in desert waste
Sweetly the morning air do taste.

So keen they ate ; the minstrels play,
The din of angels do they keep,
High style. The guests have nought to say,
But nod their thanks, and fall asleep.   10
Thus every day be I to dine,
If Rowley, Iscam, or Tib. Gorges be not seen.

FRAGMENT

ATTRIBUTED TO ELMAR, BISHOP OF SELSEIE

TRANSLATED BY ROWLEY

Now may all hell open to gulp thee down,
Whilst azure darkness, mingled with the day,
Shew light on darkened pains to be more roune ;
Oh ! mayëst thou die living deaths for aye !
May floods of sulphur bear thy sprite anon
Sinking to depths of woe ! May lightning-brands
Tremble upon thy pain-devoted crown,
And singe thy all-in-vain-imploring hands !
May all the woes that Goddès wrath can send
Upon thy head alight, and there their fury spend !   10

FRAGMENT

ATTRIBUTED TO ECCA, BISHOP OF HEREFORD
A.D. 557

TRANSLATED BY ROWLEY

When azure skies is veiled in robes of night,
  When glimmering dewdrops 'stound the traveller's eyne,
When flying clouds, betinged with ruddy light,
  Doth on the brindling wolf and wood-boar shine;
When even-star, fair herald of the night,
  Spreads the dark dusky sheen along the mees,
The writhing adders sends a gloomy light,
  And owlets wing from lightning-blasted trees;
Arise, my sprite, and seek the distant dell,
And there to echoing tongues thy raptured joys y-tell. 10

*   *   *   *   *

When spring came dancing on a floweret bed,
  Dight in green raiment of a changing kind,
The leaves of hawthorn budding on his head,
  And white primroses cowering to the wind,
Then did the shepherd his long alban spread
  Upon the greeny bank, and danced around,
Whilst the soft flowerets nodded on his head,
  And his fair lambs besprengèd on the ground;
Aneath his foot the brooklet ran along,
Which strollèd round the vale to hear his joyous song. 20

NOTES TO VOLUME I.

PAGE I. AFRICAN ECLOGUES.—Chatterton published seven eclogues, or pastoral poems. Three, here printed, he called 'African Eclogues', and four are to be found with the Rowley Poems, at vol. ii., pages 142-152. The incidents and names are all imaginary.

PAGE 11. THE REVENGE.—This play, as printed, differs from the copies to be found in other editions. It was first issued, in 1795, as a separate publication, which previous editors appear to have followed. The MS. is said to have been lost soon after, and no subsequent editor mentions that he has seen it. Whatever its earlier history may have been the MS. was bought for the British Museum in 1841, at the sale of Bishop Butler's collection. Its number is Additional MSS. 12050. It is, unfortunately, not complete. The copy, from a transcript of which the present reprint has been made, seems to have been used for acting purposes, as it is lavishly scored, and contains many stage directions. There are also corrections in the text in another handwriting than that of Chatterton, although the author himself has made alterations and additions. The version now printed for the first time, so far as the present editor is aware, has been carefully collated with the MS. The lines now printed are those of Chatterton, differing from the other editions, which have issued the burletta as revised by another hand. This revision was most probably done by Mr. Atterbury, then the proprietor of the Marylebone Gardens, to whom Chatterton sold the MS. on 6th July 1770 for the sum of five guineas. It is said to have been acted in 1770, in the Marylebone

Gardens, but there is no record of the fact beyond the statement on the title-page of the first issue. The plot is broad and the words are not the most refined, but it is a spirited piece of work and emphasises the wonderful versatility of the author. There is in the British Museum (Additional MSS. 5766 B) another manuscript, or rather fragment, entitled 'Amphitryon', which is probably the first draft of what was eventually this burletta. The present editor is not aware that it has ever been printed.

PAGE 39. THE WOMAN OF SPIRIT.—This is only a fragment. Whether more than two scenes were ever written is not known.

PAGE 42. ON MR. ALCOCK, OF BRISTOL.

Line 1. This is a reference to the nine muses, and occurs frequently in these poems. The phrase *Chorded shell* is probably taken from Dryden's 'When Jubal struck the chorded shell'. Literally it means a shell strung with musical chords or strings. The reference occurs several times in the poems.

PAGE 44. TO MISS BUSH, OF BRISTOL.—Chatterton wrote this poem when he was hoping to obtain a position as ship's doctor on a vessel trading to Africa. 'I intend going abroad as a ship's surgeon', he wrote. He had no diploma, it is true, but neither had many an 'experienced' ship's surgeon of those days! The song, 'Fanny of the Hill', vol. i., page 49, was probably also addressed to Miss Bush.

PAGE 45. TO MISS C.—The Miss C. here referred to was most likely Miss Sally Clarke. Compare line 3 of the next poem but one, 'Acrostic on Miss Sally Clarke', vol. i., page 46.

PAGE 48. A NEW SONG, TO MR. G. CATCOTT.—A brother of the Rev. Alexander Catcott, he was a partner of Mr. Burgum, the pewterer, who was hoaxed by Chatterton with a bogus pedigree. George Catcott himself was also taken in by Chatterton's Rowley forgeries. He is satirized in the poem 'Happiness', vol. i., page 166. It was as a bibliomaniac, who boasted that none of his books were less than a hundred years old, that he became interested in the works of Rowley. To his interest in the matter, and his copies taken from

Chatterton's own manuscripts, we are indebted for the preservation of so many of these productions to the present day, including 'Ælla'.

Line 5 is an allusion to Broderip, the organist of St Mary's, Redcliffe.

PAGE 49. FANNY OF THE HILL.—Probably Miss Fanny Bush; see also poem on vol. i., page 44.

PAGE 50. TO MRS. HAYWOOD. — Mrs. Haywood lived from about 1693 to 1756. She was the author of a considerable number of novels, mostly of a questionable character, particularly the earlier ones. Pope satirized her in the 'Dunciad'. Her works enjoyed a great vogue in Chatterton's time, but are practically unknown now.

PAGE 50. TO MR. HOLLAND.—Charles Holland (1733-69) was a popular actor of Chatterton's day. Although belauded by Chatterton, he was satirized by Churchill. There is a monument to him in Chiswick Church, with an inscription written by Garrick.

PAGES 52 to 60. TO THE BEAUTEOUS MISS HOYLAND, etc.—Miss Eleanor Hoyland was the *fiancée* of one of Chatterton's old schoolfellows, Baker by name, who had emigrated to Charlestown, South Carolina. It would appear that the latter had asked Chatterton to oblige him with a few poems which he could pass off to his inamorata as his own. Chatterton was complaisant, as the following nine poems show. See also the poem 'To a friend' [Baker] printed on vol. i., page 65.

PAGE 60. THE COMPLAINT. — Possibly addressed to a Miss Love. This poem is attributed to Chatterton both by Professor Skeat and Dr. Maitland. It appeared first in the *Universal Magazine* for November 1769.

PAGE 62. TO MR. POWEL. — William Powel, the actor, who was an understudy to Garrick, lived from 1735 to 1769. He built the theatre in King Street, Bristol (1764-66). His death at the age of thirty-four was universally lamented. Chatterton also refers to him in his poem 'Clifton', printed at vol. i., page 211, lines 77 *et seq.*

NOTES TO VOL. I.

PAGE 62. THE ADVICE.—Miss Rumsey, to whom this poem is addressed, was at one time a sweetheart of Chatterton. When it was written she was engaged to be married to Jack Forster, the Bristol poet, whom Chatterton frequently satirizes, *e.g.* in the 'Journal Sixth', vol. i., page 90, lines 33 and 150, and under the name of *Pitholeon* in the present poem. The fourth verse refers to Kitty Clive, the actress. This lady, afterwards pensioned by Walpole, bade a farewell to the stage, in an epilogue which the latter had written for her, on 24th April 1769.

PAGE 64. To HORACE WALPOLE.—Chatterton had sent some of the 'Rowley' productions to Walpole. The latter, although at first deceived, had subsequently asked the opinion of some of his friends. The result was that he had accused Chatterton of forging the documents, and advised him to give his attention to his profession until he should have made his fortune. In reply Chatterton affirmed the genuineness of the manuscripts, and asked for their return. Walpole was busy at the time and did not attend to the matter at once. Chatterton thereupon wrote him what Walpole termed 'a singularly impertinent' letter, with the result that the documents were returned to Chatterton by Walpole in a rage. The latter has received much undeserved blame for what has been termed his harsh treatment of Chatterton, but one does not see how he could have anticipated that the attorney's apprentice would become famous as a poet. To him he was a detected forger. It must also be remembered that Chatterton did not send Walpole many poems, but prose pieces, which, as a rule, have not the same merit as the poems. Nevertheless Walpole is said to have always regretted his curt behaviour. In his subsequent writings Chatterton was very bitter in any of his references to Walpole. The poem here is a case in point.

Walpole, as is well known, was an irrepressible letter-writer, and also a man who liked the society of the great ones of the earth. Both of these attributes are sneered at by Chatterton in the poem. The query 'Who wrote "Otranto"?' is a fair one, and a palpable hit. Walpole's novel, 'The Castle of Otranto', was first published as a translation of an old black-letter book supposed to have been printed in 1529 at Naples, to have been written by one Onuphrio Muralto, and translated by William Marshall. The authorship was only acknowledged by Walpole when a second edition was called for. Doubtless Chatterton thought that the man who could act thus should not be too hard on another author who, in his opinion, was acting in the same manner with another work.

PAGE 65. TO A FRIEND.—This was his friend Baker, the *fiancé* of Miss Hoyland. See also note relating to this lady on vol. ii., page 196.
Line 2, see note to ' On Mr. Alcock', vol. ii., page 195.

PAGE 67. VERSES TO A LADY IN BRISTOL.— Probably Miss Sally Clarke, see *ante*.

PAGE 69. THE CONSULIAD. — The first draft of this satire is to be seen in the British Museum (Additional MSS. 5766 B), under the title of 'The Constabiliad'. It first appeared in the *Freeholder's Magazine*, for January 1770. The Twitcher referred to was John Montagu, fourth Earl of Sandwich, who took a prominent part in the prosecution of John Wilkes, his former friend. The satire describes an imaginary fight at a political dinner, and is aimed generally at the Grafton ministry. Like many other political satires of previous days, those of Chatterton are not so easy of comprehension at the present time as they were when they were written. It is impossible to identify all the characters mentioned under fictitious names.

PAGE 77. EPISTLE TO THE REVEREND MR. CATCOTT.—The person here satirized is the Rev. Alexander Catcott, vicar of Temple Church, Bristol, and brother of Mr. George Catcott, previously referred to in the note on vol. ii., pages 195-196. He had published a book entitled 'Treatise on the Deluge and Structure of the Earth', of which a second edition was issued in 1768. Chatterton's productions had been criticised by Mr. Catcott, so he returned the compliment by writing the 'Epistle'. He trounces Mr. Catcott severely, and advises him

> 'When you advance new systems, first unfold
> The various imperfections of the old'.

It is a case of *Quis custodiet custodios ipsos?* Chatterton himself falls into several errors. For example, he writes *strata* for *stratum*, and *stratas* for *strata*. In another place he refers to David when he means Joseph.

Although nominally addressed to Mr. Catcott the epistle wanders over a variety of subjects,

> ' Excuse me, Catcott, if from you I stray,
> The muse will go where merit leads the way '.

It attacks the clergy generally, and proclaims with no uncertain voice Chatterton's religious opinions, emphasised more fully in ' The Defence '. Most of the personal remarks are unintelligible to-day. Clogher, mentioned at line 40, was the Bishop of Clogher, whose account of the deluge had been criticised by Catcott. Broughton, whose name appears more than once, was the Rev. Thomas Broughton, vicar of Bedminster, near Bristol, who published, among other works, a ' Dictionary of Religions ', in 1742.

Previously Chatterton had been on friendly terms with the vicar of the Temple Church, but it would seem that he tired of the parson, who might have been something of a bore, with his fossils and his views of the deluge. Chatterton may also have found him wanting in interest in anything outside his own special hobby, and revenged himself for fancied slights by holding up his erstwhile friend to ridicule. Catcott is still more bitterly attacked in the ' Exhibition ' which is too indecent to be fully published here.

PAGE 85. THE EXHIBITION.—Only a few lines of this satire are printed. Professor Wilson, in his ' Life of Chatterton ' says :—

' It has never been published; and it would have been well had it perished, with its evidence that youthful purity had been sullied, and the precocious boy was only too conversant with forbidden things '.

PAGE 89. JOURNAL SIXTH.—Why this title has been chosen is not at all clear. The satire is very rambling in its contents, and contains lines on three distinct subjects, the last one dealing in a scoffing way with Whitfield's manner in the pulpit. The three pieces are all written on the same sheet of paper, folded into four columns. Each succeeds the other without a fresh title, and it seems from the last line that the poem, as printed, is meant to form one whole.

PAGE 101. KEW GARDENS.—This is the longest of the poems which are formally acknowledged by Chatterton as being his own composition. The whole satire, like most of the others from Chatterton's pen, is somewhat discursive, wanders over a variety of subjects, and pillories many different persons. The title is taken from the fact that at Kew Gardens there lived Augusta, the widow of the eldest son of George II. (Frederick, Prince of Wales, who died in 1751), and mother of George III. This royal lady exercised a great influence in politics during the latter part of the eighteenth century, in conjunction with the third Earl of Bute, with whom her name was popularly coupled in more ways than one. See also 'The Whore of Babylon' (vol. i., page 134), and 'Resignation' (vol. i., page 138). The former of these two satires consists mainly of the latter half of the poem we are now dealing with, the lines being differently arranged. Much of it is also to be found in the unpublished 'Exhibition', and several lines appear in 'Sunday'. 'Kew Gardens' is a rambling jumble of politics and personalities, but is a remarkable effusion for a youth of seventeen. It was commenced in 1769, and finished early in 1770, but was not printed in its entirety until 1837. Like the other satires the personalities are hidden from the ken of the modern reader, even where, as is the case in some instances, Chatterton's blanks or rows of asterisks have been filled in with the names of those he lampoons. No attempt has been made in this edition to explain who these persons were. Professor Skeat, in his edition of Chatterton's works, endeavours to do so, although his attempt is incomplete. Advantage has been taken here of some of his suggestions.

PAGE 138. RESIGNATION. — This is one of the most scurrilous of Chatterton's satires. Although nominally addressed to the premier, the Duke of Grafton, it deals principally with the Earl of Bute and the widow of Frederick, Prince of Wales, to whom reference has already been made in 'Kew Gardens' and 'The Whore of Babylon' (see previous note). If Chatterton had wanted to be taken seriously he should have been more careful of his facts. His account of the rise of the Earl of Bute, and of his earlier days, is ludicrous in its absurdity:

> 'Far in the north . . .
> A humble cottage reared its lonely head.
> One narrow entrance opened to the day.
> Here lived a laird, the ruler of his clan',

and so on. Bute is constantly referred to in this and other poems as the 'Thane', and the lady of Kew is dubbed 'The Carlton Sibyl'. Many of the lines are not fit for publication, and must have seemed indecent even in an age of bitter personal satire and great latitude. Grafton resigned the premiership on 28th January 1770.

PAGE 162. THE ART OF PUFFING. — This is not so violent as some of the other satires. It is not possible to identify all the persons named. Edmund Curll incurred the enmity of Pope, and was convicted of printing immoral books. Israel Pottinger was a dramatist and founder of various periodicals. Cooke is probably John Cooke, a London bookseller of the time, who did a good trade in the issue of books in weekly parts. Pasquale de Paoli was a Corsican patriot, a friend of Johnson and Boswell. Bingley was the printer and proprietor of the *Political Register*, and W. G. Edmunds was the editor of the *Middlesex Journal*, a bi-weekly newspaper.

PAGE 163. THE DEFENCE.—This satire is nominally addressed to the same Mr. Smith who is referred to at vol. i., page 198, where an elegy was written to his memory on the wrongful supposition that he was dead. This poem is particularly interesting for Chatterton's avowal that (although his other writings belie him) he was not an atheist:

> 'Fallacious is the charge: 'tis all a lie, . . .
> I own a God, immortal, boundless, wise, ...'.

PAGE 166. HAPPINESS.

Lines 49 *et seq*. The Catcott here referred to is George Catcott, previously mentioned in 'A New Song', vol. i., page 48. He was evidently a person very fond of show, and the poem recalls the fact that, when St Nicholas' Church at Bristol was being rebuilt, he had ascended the spire before it was finished, placing a pewter plate at the top detailing the facts,

He had also been the first person to cross the new bridge at Bristol, also before it was finished.

PAGE 170. CHATTERTON'S WILL.—While he was still apprentice to the attorney Lambert, Chatterton, in a fit of despair, wrote a satirical will, partly in prose, and the remainder in verse. He had asked Burgum, the pewterer, for a loan, and had been refused. The will was left on his desk and there seen by his master, who immediately took steps to cancel the indentures. The remainder of the will being in prose is not printed here.

PAGE 181. ELEGY WRITTEN AT STANTON DREW.—This place is a village about seven miles south of Bristol, containing great megalithic remains, more especially stone circles. In this elegy Chatterton appears to have imagined himself watching a human sacrifice at Stanton Drew in prehistoric times.

PAGE 185. ELEGY ON WILLIAM BECKFORD.—The subject of this elegy was the father of the celebrated author of 'Vathek'. He was the son of a governor of Jamaica, and was born there in 1709. He received his education at Westminster, and afterwards became a successful merchant in London. He was elected alderman of the Billingsgate ward in 1752, and sheriff in 1755. The City returned him three times as its member, and he was twice Lord Mayor of London. He became an ardent Wilkesite, and is famous for having presented the Remonstrance of the City of London to the king. Chatterton conceived the idea of securing the popular chief magistrate as a patron, and the latter had commenced to take an interest in the young poet when he died suddenly on 21st June 1770. His death was a great blow to Chatterton, who, we are told, 'was perfectly frantic and out of his mind, and said that he was ruined'. He had expected great things with Beckford as patron. Two years after his death, in 1772, the City Corporation erected a statue to his memory at a cost of £1,300. It is to be seen in the Guildhall, and shows Beckford in the act of addressing the king. It contains a transcript of his speech.

Chatterton's elegy is somewhat fulsome, but it is also stilted, as if it had not been written from the heart.

Beckford, extolled as the pattern of all the virtues, was the father of a number of illegitimate children, who were, however, provided for under his will.

PAGES 189 to 198. THREE ELEGIES ON THOMAS PHILLIPS' DEATH.—Phillips was an usher at Colston's school, where Chatterton had been a pupil, and was himself something of a poet. A friendship sprung up between the two which was only ended by Phillips' death, towards the end of 1769. Full of his grief Chatterton wrote the elegy commencing 'No more I hail'. Some months later he re-wrote this with some alterations and additional verses. This second elegy is also printed here *in extenso*. There are two versions of the third elegy, but only one is now given. It is addressed 'To Clayfield', a friend and encourager of Chatterton, to whom, in his bogus 'Will', he left 'the sincerest thanks that my gratitude can give'. Michael Clayfield was a distiller, and is referred to in the 'Epistle to the Rev. Mr. Catcott' (vol. i., page 81, lines 149-52), as well as in some of Chatterton's letters.

PAGE 198. ELEGY ON MR. WILLIAM SMITH.— There is a note by Chatterton in the MS. at the British Museum, 'Happily mistaken, having since heard from good authority it is Peter'.

PAGE 199. ELEGY ON THE DEATH OF MR. JOHN TANDEY, SEN.—This gentleman was the father-in-law of William Barrett, the surgeon and Bristol historian, who was so completely deceived by Chatterton regarding the Rowley poems, etc.

PAGE 200. ON THE LAST EPIPHANY. — As Chatterton's first known poem this is most interesting. It was printed when he was only ten years and two months old. The next four poems were written while he was only eleven.

PAGE 209. CLIFTON.
Line 21. The rocks are called St. Vincent's Rocks.
Lines 26 *et seq*. A monument was erected by General Sir William Draper to the memory of those soldiers of the 79th regiment (which he raised himself) who

fell during the various battles in which he and they took part—

> 'And by this tribute, which his pity pays,
> Twines his own virtues with his soldier's praise'.

Line 52. Charles I.

Line 53. Prince Rupert, after capturing Bristol in 1643, surrendered the city to Fairfax in 1645.

Line 79. William Powel, the actor. See note on vol. ii., page 196.

PAGE 216. EPITAPH ON AN OLD MAID.—Professor Skeat published this first as a poem of Chatterton, from a MS. in the possession of Mr. Bell. It is here reprinted by permission.

PAGE 216. SUNDAY.—Several of the lines in this poem are repeated in 'Kew Gardens'.

NOTES TO VOLUME II.

Explanations of archaic and other words in the following poems will be found in the Glossary, page 208, vol. ii.

PAGE 1. EXECUTION OF SIR CHARLES BAWDIN. — In other editions this poem has been printed under the title of 'Bristowe Tragedy', although it is difficult to tell why. It was first published, as a separate work, in 1772. The poem, as printed in Tyrwhitt's edition of the Rowley poems, in 1777, is said to have been checked by a copy made by George Catcott from one in the handwriting of Chatterton. The present edition has followed the earliest printed copy, both as regards text and title. Dean Milles, one of the doughtiest champions of the authenticity of the Rowley poems, thought it the most authentic of the whole collection, and yet Chatterton admitted to his mother and sister that he himself was the author! The style is less archaic than any of the other Rowley poems. It deals with the execution of Sir Baldwin Fulford, a Lancastrian knight, who was put to death by order of Edward IV., in 1461, after a trial by a special commission. Of this commission William Canynge, or

Canynges, Mayor of Bristol, was a member. According to the poem Canynge unsuccessfully appealed to the king's clemency. Edward is said to have watched the procession to the place of execution from a window in St. Ewen's Church.

PAGE 15. ÆLLA. — This is acknowledged to be Chatterton's masterpiece. He himself, writing to Dodsley, the bookseller, says: ' It is a perfect tragedy ; the plot is clear, the language spirited, and the songs (interspersed in it) are flowing, poetical, and elegantly simple '. One cannot but agree with this opinion. While this work has been passing through the press a manuscript, alleged to be the first draft of ' Ælla ', under the title of ' Eldred ', was sold by Messrs. Sotheby for £255 on 6th December 1905.

Line 213. ' As ever clove pin or the basket '. The pin was the centre of the target (in archery), used originally to fasten it to the butt. ' To split the peg which fastened it to the butt ranked as the *ne plus ultra* of his skill ', says Hansard's ' Book of Archery ', p. 112. Also see ' Romeo and Juliet ', act ii., scene 4, ' The very pin of his heart cleft by the blind boy's butt-shaft '.

Line 458. This line is really nonsense as printed. It is given as written by Chatterton, but it is unintelligible, at any rate at the present day. *Morie* means ' marsh '; Chatterton gives *Gronfer* as meaning a meteor; *Drocke* is a water-course; *Druge* means ' dry '. The line translated in respect to these meanings reads ' My shield, like summer marshy meteor dry ', which is meaningless. There are other cases of unintelligible lines in this portion of Chatterton's poems.

Lines 639 and 662. The raven was the sign borne on the Danish standards.

Line 819. Probably means ' to gain as *fair* a prize '.

PAGE 80. ENGLISH METAMORPHOSIS.—The poem is, of course, an imitation of Ovid's ' Metamorphosis ' in the first place, but the inspiration appears to have been more from Canto Nine of the second book of Spenser's ' Faerie Queene '.

PAGE 84. AN EXCELENTE BALADE OF CHARITIE. —In a note to this poem Chatterton says: ' Thomas Rowley, the author, was born at Norton Mal-reward, in Somersetshire, educated at the convent of St. Kenna. at Keynesham, and died at Westbury, in Gloucestershire'.

PAGE 87. TO JOHNE LADGATE.—Chatterton has made another mistake here. He evidently means to speak of John Lydgate, who became a Benedictine monk at Bury St Edmunds. He was an imitator of Chaucer, and died *circa* 1450, aged about eighty years. It has been suggested that the Stowe, mentioned on line 5, should be Stone, a famous Bristol preacher, and member of the Carmelite Order.

PAGE 90. THE TOURNAMENT.—Chatterton also produced a life of Sir Simon de Burton, the hero of this poem. Incidentally, too, he used it to further mistify worthy Burgum, the pewterer, by introducing as a character Sir Johan de Berghamme, a supposed ancestor of Burgum.

Line 88. This is a recognised form of challenge. See also line 21 of the 'Romaunte of the Cnyghte', vol. ii., p. 139.

PAGES 98-138. BATTLE OF HASTINGS.—Chatterton wrote two versions of this poem. The first he gave to Barrett as the work of Turgot the Monk, in the tenth century (he surely meant the eleventh!), translated by Rowley. He was later on asked to show Barrett the original, when he confessed that he had written the poem himself 'for a friend'. He had, however, so he said, another poem on the same subject, an original by Rowley, here printed as No. II. Of the second version lines 531 and onward were supplied some time after the other lines were given to Barrett.

PAGE 139. THE ROMAUNTE OF THE CNYGHTE. —This Chatterton ascribes to John de Burgham, the 'manufactured' ancestor for Burgum the Bristol pewterer. When Chatterton sent this poem to the worthy Burgum he included a paraphrase which is printed after it here, although in other editions it is placed with the acknowledged poems. It has been thought better to place it with the original, so that they can be the more easily compared.

PAGE 142. ECLOGUE THE FIRST.
Line 34. The 'parker's grange' means the park-keeper's farm.

NOTES TO VOL. II.

PAGE 152. THE STORIE OF WILLIAM CANYNGE.—In addition to this poem there is also a Rowley *prose* account of Canynge. This person is mentioned several times in these poems, *e.g.* see note on vol. ii., page 204, 'Execution of Sir Charles Bawdin'. For a fuller account see Pryce's 'Memorials of the Canynge's family'. See also 'Accounte of W. Canynge's Feast', vol ii., p. 192.

PAGE 157. ON OUR LADY'S CHURCH.—St. Mary's Church, Redcliffe.

PAGE 160. THE PARLYAMENTE OF SPRYTES.—The joint author of this production, according to Chatterton, was John Iscam, a canon at St Augustine's monastery, Bristol.

Line 38. Chatterton translates this as meaning 'The complexion of thy soul is free from the black marks of sin'.

PAGE 178. THE BRODER OF ORDERYS WHYTE.—There are in the British Museum a few lines relating to a brother of orders black, but they are unprintable.

PAGE 186. ON OURE LADYES CHIRCH.—This is printed in some editions under the title of 'Sancte Warbur', but it is here given as printed in Southey's edition of 'Chatterton's Works'. It is an acknowledged imitation.

GLOSSARY

Note.—Wherever Chatterton has, in a note, explained the meaning of any archaic word, his alternative is given either in the text or below. In other cases the presumed meaning has been given from other sources. No attempt has been made to give the correct spelling of the following words; as a rule they are given as written in the original. H. D. R.

Abest, Brought down
Aborde, Went on
Aborne, Burnished
Abound, Avail
Abounc, Make ready
Abrodden, Abruptly
Acale, Chill
Accaie, Assuage
Acheke, Choke
Achments, Achievements
Acome, Had come
Acroole, Faintly
Adave, Enjoy, awakened
Adawe, Awake
Adaygne, Worth
Adeene, Worthily
Adente, Annex, fasten
Aderne, Cruel
Adigne, Noble
Adradde, Afraid
Adrames, Churls
Adryne, Dry
Adventayle, Armour; that part of a helmet that admits the air
Adyghte, Clad

Adygne, Kind, worthy
Affear, Terrify
Affraie, The fray
Affray, To frighten, to join in the fight, fear
Affynd, Akin
Afleme, Frighten
Agested, Heaped up
Agguylte, Offended
Agleeme, Shine
Agreete, Greet
Agroted, Bursting
Ahete, Propose
Aidens, Help
Alans, Hounds
Alatche, Call out
Alban, A white robe
All-a-boone, Favour
Allay, Stop
Alleyne, Alone
Aluste, Release
Alyche, Like
Alyne, Across one's shoulders
Alyse, Allow, set free, release

GLOSSARY

Amate, Abate, destroy, lessen
Amayled, Enamelled
Amenused, Lessened
Ametten, Met
Amield, Enamelled
Amnie, Dear
Aneath, Beneath
Anemp, Name
Anente, Against
Anere, Another, another time
Anete, Annihilate
Anlace, Sword
Applynges, Grafted trees
Arblaster } Cross-bow
Arcublaster }
Arcublastries, Cross-bowmen
Ardurous, Burning
Argent, White
Arist, Arisen, arose
Armlace, Armlet
Armour-brace, Suit of armour
Arrase, Pluck up, erase
Asenglave, Lance, hilt of a lance; sometimes a steel glove
Askaunted, Looked
Aslee, Slide
Aspere, Look at
Assay, Attempt
Assayled, Essayed
Assole, Answer
Asswaie, Cause
Astart, Afraid
Astedd, Seated
Astende, Astonish
Asterte, Neglected
Aston } Astonished,
Astound } Stunned
Astrodde, Astride
Athorowe, And through
Athrow, Throughout
Athrowgh, Through

Atreted, Extracted from corn
Attend, Defend
Attoure, Around, turn
Attourne, Turn around
Atturne, Turn
Aumere, Robe, apparel
Auntrous, Adventurous
Aunture, Adventure
Autremete, Loose white robe, worn by priests
Ave, River Avon
Awhaped, Amazed
Ayenward, Backward

Bane, Curse
Banted, Cursed
Barbed, Hung with banners or armour
Barganette, Song
Barrows, Burial mounds
Bataunt, A musical instrument
Battayles, Boats
Batten, Beat
Battent, Loudly
Battentlie, Recklessly
Bawsyn, Large, bulky, mighty
Bayre, Brow
Beave, Beaver
Behight, Name, call
Behylte, Commanded
Behyltren, Hidden
Belent, Stopped
Beme, Trumpet
Benned, Cursed, tormented
Benym, Take away
Bercie, Meaning obscure
Berne, Bairn, child
Berten, Venomous
Bespedde, Turned away
Besprenged } Scattered
Besprent }

GLOSSARY

Bestadde } Lost
Bestanne }
Bested, Fought, contended
Bestoykenynge, Betraying, deceitful
Bestreynts, Bestrews
Betreinted, Besprinkled
Bevyle, Break
Bewopen, Astonished
Bewrate, Treachery
Bewrayen } Declare
Bewree }
Bewreene, Express, disclose
Bewryen, Expressed, discover
Bighes, Jewels
Birlette, Hood, coif
Bismarde, Curious
Bismarlie, Steadfastly, curiously
Blake, Naked
Blase, Proclaim
Blasynne, Record
Blatant, Loud, bawling
Blatauntlie, Loudly
Blation, Praise
Blazours, Praisers
Blent, Blended
Blents, Turns back
Blethe, Bleed
Blyn } Cease
Blynge }
Bodykyn, Substance
Bollenger, A sailing vessel
Boots, Matters
Bordel, Cottage
Bordelyer, Cottager
Borne, Burnishing
Borne, Field, bank
Boune, Make ready, draw
Bourne, Cliff
Bourne, Kept within bounds
Bowke, Bulk, body

Brace, Suit
Braste, Break
Brayd, Displayed
Brayde, Embroider
Breastis, Breasts
Brede, Broad
Breme } Strong, furious
Bremie } force, strength
Brend, Burn
Brigandine, Armour, coat of mail
Brindling, Spotted
Broched, Pointed
Bronde, Fury
Brondeynge, Furious
Browded, Embroidered
Brynnynge, Declaring
Brystowans, Men of Bristol
Burled, Armed
Burlie - brande, Armed fury
Bysmare, Meandering
Bysmarelie, Steadfastly

Cale, Cold, chill
Camoys, Crooked
Carnes, Cairn, stones
Carvelled, Carved
Carvellers, Carvers, sculptors
Carvelling, Carving
Castle-stere, Castle stair
Caties, Dainty victuals
Causalles, Motives
Caytysned, Captive
Celes, Keels
Celness, Coldness
Champion, Challenge
Chaper, Dry, thirsty
Chapournette, Small hat
Chappeau, Hat
Chelandree, Goldfinch
Cherisaunei } Comfort
Cherysauncys }
Chevyced, Preserved

GLOSSARY

Chine, To cut through to the backbone
Chirckynge, Chattering
Chop, Change
Chough, Raven
Church-glebe-house, The grave
Cleme, Clamour, sound
Cleped, Called
Clerche, Clergy
Clergyond, Taught
Clevis, Cleft, piece of rock
Cleyne, Sound
Clinie, Movement
Clocke, Hour
Coistrel, Young
Comfreie, A herb
Compheere, Companion, equal
Conteke, Complaint, contend with
Corse, Corpse
Corven, Picture
Cotte, A small boat
Couraciers, Coursers
Coyen, Shy
Crevent, Craven
Cross-stone, Monument
Crouche, Crucifix
Croucheynge, Winding
Crowen, Crows
Cuarr, Quarry
Cuishes, Thigh armour
Curriedowes, Flatterers
Custrel, Servant

Dacians, Danes
Daised, Seated on a dais
Damoiselle, Damsel
Dareygne, Attempt
Daynous, Disdainful
Dead-wounded, Wounded to death
Declynie, Stooping posture
Deere, Dire, dreadful
Defayte, Decay

Defs, Vapours
Deft, Trim
Deigned, Disdained
Demasing, Considering
Dente, Fasten, fix
Denwere, Doubt
Depeyncte, Paints
Depycte, Painted
Depyctures, Drawings
Dequaced, Dashed, rushed
Dere, Hurt, injury
Derne } Cruel, woeful,
Dernie } sad,
Deslavate, Foul, lecherous
Deslavatie, Lecherousness
Difficile, Difficult
Dight, Clad, deck
Digne, Kind, worthy, noble, gentle
Dispande, Disposed
Dispent, Expended
Divinistre, A divine
Doe, Done
Dole, Lot, portion, dismay, lamentation
Doled, Sad
Dolt, Foolish
Dorture, Dormitory
Dote, Dressed
Doutremere, Foreigner
Dree, Drive, endure rush
Drented, Drenched
Drierie, Dreadful
Droke, Dry
Drybblette, Small, trivial
Duressed, Hardened
Dynneth, Soundeth
Dyspendynge, Expending
Dysperpellest, Scatterest
Dysportysment, Enjoyment
Dysregate, Renounce

Eft, Often, even
Eftsoon, Soon, quickly
Eke, Even, also

GLOSSARY

Elmen, Elm-tree
Elocation, Elocution
Émarschalled, Emblazoned
Emblanched, Whitened
Embodyde, Stout
Embollen, Swelled, swelling
Embower, Lodge
Emburled, Armed
Emmate, Lessen
Emmers, Money
Emmertleynge, Glittering
Emprise, Enterprise
Encaled, Chilled
Enchafed, Furious
Encheered, Encouraged
Enfyne, Full, fine
Enheal, Heal
Enheeding, Taking care
Enheped, Added
Enjoyous, Enraptured
Enleme, Enlighten
Enlowed, Aflame
Enrone, Unsheath
Enseem, Appear
Enshone, Displayed
Enstrote, Deserving punishment
Enstroughted, Stretched
Enswolters, Sucks in
Enswote, Sweeten
Ensyngynge, Singing
Ensyrke, Encircle
Ente, Purse, treasury
Entendement, Intelligence, understanding
Entent, Meaning
Enthoghteynge, Intending
Enthought, Thought of
Entremed, Mingled
Erlies, Earl's
Estells, Stars
Estroughted, Stretched
Ethe, Ease. easily

Eve-spect, Speckled with evening dew
Everiche } Every,
Everychone } every one
Ewbryce, Adultery
Even } Eyes
Eyne }
Eynegears, Objects
Fage, Tale
Faie, Faith
Fair, Chaste
Fay, Faith
Faytour, Treacherous, wandering
Feignes, Feints
Felle, Many
Fetive, Handsome, neat, dexterous
Fetyvelie, Neatly
Flaiten, Scaring
Flanched, Arched
Fleme } Frighten
Flemie }
Flemynge, Affrighting
Floes, Arrows
Flotting, Flying
Fonnis } Devices
Fons }
Forcie, Mighty
Forgard, Lose, lost
Forlorn, Deprived
Forloyne, Retreat
Forrey, Destroy
Forslagen, Slain
Forslege, Slay
Forstraught, Distracted
For-weltrynge, Blasting
Forwyned } Dried,
Foryned } withered
Fote, Foot
Freme, Grief
Fremed, Strange
Fructuous, Fertile

Gaberdine { A piece of armour, a cloak

GLOSSARY

Gare, Cause
Geare, Guise
Geason, Strange
Geer, Twist
Geir, Fury
Gemot, Assembly
Gemote, Assemble
Geven, Give
Glair, Clear
Glare, Shine
Gledes, Glides
Gloure, Glory
Goe, Gone
Gouler, Usurer
Gratch, Apparel, dress
Gravots, Groves
Gre, Grow
Greave, Leg armour; but is used at "Hastings," (2), line 276, to mean breast-plate
Groffe, Laughing stock, a poor thing
Groffyshe, Rudely
Gron, Fen or moor
Gronfer, Fen fire, meteor
Grore, Meaning obscure
Grossile, Grovelling
Groted, Bursting
Gutte de sangue, Drops of blood
Guylde, Tax
Gye, Guide
Gyte, Robe

Habergeon, Breast-armour
Haile } *Hailie* } Happy
Halceld, Defeated
Hallie, Hall
Halline, Joy, gladness
Hancele, Cut off
Hanne, Had, have, gained
Hannow, Narrow
Hantoned, Hunted
Harried, Tossed

Hartys, Heart's
Hatch, Lock
Hatched, Covered with hatchments
Hatchment, Coat of arms, caparison
Hawlkes, Valleys
Heasod, Head
Heaven-were, Heavenward
Hecke, Height
Hecket, Wrapped
Heideignes, Country dances
Hele, Help
Hent, Grasp
Hentylle, Custom
Herehaughtes, Heralds
Hest, Order
Hete, Promised
Hie, Hasten
Hight, Called, named
Hillis, Hill's
Hilt, Hide, secrete, shield
Hoastrie, Hostlery
Holtred, Hidden
Hommageres, Retainers
Honde, Hand
Honde-poyncte, Moment
Honour - were, Honour - wards
Hopelen, Hopelessness
Horrowe, Disagreeable, horrid
Hulstred, Hidden
Hydelle, Person in sanctuary
Hyger, The flowing tide of the Severn; a tidal wave
Hyghte, Called
Hylte, Hid, hide
Hyndlette, Peasant

Impleasaunce, Annoyance
Investing, Covering

GLOSSARY

Jape, Short surplice worn by friars of an inferior class, and by secular priests
Jetted, Devised, fabled
Jubb, Bottle

Karynte, Loan
Ken, Know, knowledge
Kende, Spied
Kenters, Men of Kent
Keppened, Sharpened
Kest, Kissed
Kind, Nature
Kiste, Coffin
Knightis, Knights
Knowlached, Known
Knowlaching, Knowing

Lackest, Wantest
Lackynge, Yearning, wishing
Ladden, Lay
Lare, Leather
Lease, Lose
Lechemanne, Physician
Leckedst, Most dispraised
Lecturnyes, Lectures, warnings
Leden, Languishing, waning
Leech, Physician
Leege, Homage
Leffed, Left
Leman, Mistress
Leme } Gleam, light,
Lemmie } flash, ray
Lemed, Lighted
Lepestones, Leaps
Lere, Leather
Lesselle, A bush, hedge, or arbour
Lethlen, Still, dead
Lette, Hinder
Levynde, Lightning-struck
Levynn, Lightning
Liefe, Choice

Likand, Liking, pleasure
Limitour, A licensed begging friar
Line, Stay, linger
List, Pleasure
Loaste, Loss
Lode, Praise
Lordynge, Standing on hind legs
Loverde, Lord
Lowing, Flame
Lurdanes, Lazy fellows
Lyken, Health
Lymed, Polished
Lynge, Linger, long
Lyoncelle, Young lion
Lyped, Wasted away
Lysse, Sport
Lyssed, Turned
Lyven, Live

Maie, Great
Maint, Many
Mancas, Mancuses; pieces of gold
Manchyn, Sleeve
Mascilled, Full of meshes
Maugre, In spite of
Maynt, Many
Mead, Meadow
Meed, Reward
Mees, Meadows
Meeten, Meet
Meint, Many
Memuine, Command
Menged, Mingled
Merce, Mercian
Mere, Lake
Metten, Met
Mewes, Cages
Meynte, Many, great numbers
Mickle, Really means little, but seems to be used throughout to mean " muckle," great

GLOSSARY

Mindbruch, Worship
Mirk, Darkness
Mitte, Mighty
Mockler, More
Moe, More
Moke }
Mokie } Dark
Mollock, Wet
Moreying, Rooting up
Morglaien, Deadly
Morie, Marshy
Morthe, Death
Mows, Boiled corn
Myndbruche, Hurt honour

Ne, Not
Nee, Nothing
Neet, Night
Nesh, Tender
Nightys, Night's
Nillynge, Unwilling
Nonnere, Nunnery
Noyance, Destruction
Nymd, Caught
Nymme, To steal

Obaie, Abide
Onflemed, Undismayed
Onknowlachynge, Not knowing
Onlyghte, Obscure
Onspryngede, Became faded
Ore, Other
Ouched, Garlanded
Oue, Black-bird
Ounde, A wave, flood
Oundynge, Bounding
Ourt, Open
Overest, Uppermost

Parament, Royal apparel
'Pared, Compared
Parties, Parts
Passent, Leisurely
Paves, Shields, daggers

Peene, Punishment
Pencte, Painted
Pendaunts, Pennons
Penne, Hill
Perdie, Par Dieu
Persante, Sharply
Pete, Raze
Pheere, Equal
Pheon } The barbed
Pheryon } head of a dart or arrow
Pick hatch, Thief
Picte, Picture
Port, Carriage
Poyntelle, Pencil
Proto-slain, First-slain
Prow, Forehead
Puerilitie, Boyhood
Punelstre, Empty boast
Pyghte, Pluck, place, torture

Quaced, Vanquished
Quaintissed, Curiously devised, quaint
Queed, The devil
Quent, Quaint

Receivure, Receipt
Recendize, Cowardice
Recradize, Make coward
Recreand, Recreant, coward
Reddour, Violence, vehemence
Rede, Intelligence, wit, counsel, advice
Reded, Wise
Redeynge, Wisdom
Rege, Huge
Regrate, Favour, esteem
Rele, Wave
Rennome, Honour, reputation
Reyne, Run
Reytes, Water flags

Ribible, Fiddle
Riv'lette, River
Rode, Face, complexion
Rodeynge, Ruling
Rou, Horrid, ugly
Roune, Terrific
Royn, Spoil
Royners, Spoilers
Rudborne, Red water
Rynde, Ruined
Ryne, Run
Rynge, To fix

Sabalus, The devil
Sabatans, Boots
Sabbataners, Foot soldiers
Sable, Sand, darkness
Saunt, Saunter
Sayne, Said
Scath, Damage
Scathe, Scarce
Scaunce-layed, Uneven
Scauncing, Looking
Scethe, Damage
Scille, Gather
Scond, Shun
Seck, Suck
Seere, Search
Semblament, Appearance
Semelikeede ⎫ Counte-
Semlykeene ⎭ nance
Sendaument, Semblance, appearance
Shappe, Fate, destiny
Sheene, Shine
Shente, Brake
Shepen, Innocent
Shrove, Shrouded
Siker, Surer
Skyne, Skies
Slea, Slay
Sleave, Floss silk
Sled, Hurdle
Sleen, Slain
Slone, Slew
Slowelie, Sluggish

Smethe, Smoke
Smore, Smothered
Soothen, Truth
Spar, A bar of wood
Sped, Reached
Sprenge, Scatter, besprinkle
Sprite, Spirit, soul
Steck, Stuck
Steeked, Stole
Stente, Stained
Stere, Hold, rudder
Steynced, Mingled
Storthe, Dread
Storven, Dead
Stowe, Place
Straught, Stretched
Stre, Straw
Stree, Strew
Stroke, Struck
Stroven, Striven
Summertons, Somerset men
Sunnis, Sun's
Sussers, Men of Sussex
Swangs, Swings
Swarthe, A shadow
Swarthless, Lifeless
Swarthynge, Dying
Swote ⎫ Sweet
Swotie ⎭
Swythe, Quickly
Synge, Sing
Sythe ⎫ Since
Sythence ⎭

Talbot, Species of dog
Tanmen, Danes
Teir, Tear
Tend, Attend
Tene, Sorrow
Tere, Muscle, healthy
Thamysis, Thames
Thighe, Close together
Thight, Joined
Thorowe, Through

GLOSSARY

Thoughten, Thought
Thyssen, Those
Tochelod, Endowed
Treynted, Dealt
Trym, A stream, joining the Avon below Bristol
Twaie, Twain
Twight, Pulled
Tyde, Betide
Tyngue, Tongue

Ugsom, Terribly
Ugsomme, Terrible, loathsome, ugly
Ugsomness, Terror
Unaknelled, No knell rung
Uncouthlie, Uncomfortable
Uncted, Anointed
Undevise, Explain
Unespryte, Spiritless
Unken'd, Unknown
Unkerve, Uncarven
Unliart, Unforgiving
Unlist, Unbounded
Unlydgefulle, Disloyal
Unplayte, Explain
Untentyff, Uncared for
Unthewes, Rudeness, barbarity
Unwote, Unknown
Unweere, Tempest
Upryne, Lift up
Upryst, Risen up

Val, Helmet
Vernage, Wine
Vert, Leaf
Volunde, Will
Vylle, Town, city

Wanhope, Despair
Ward, Guard, keep off
Warriketh, Worketh
Wastle-cake, Fine wheat cake
Waylynge, Waning
Wayte, Assist
Weal, Commonwealth
Weed, Dress
Weere, Grief
Wele, Well
Welke, Course
Wemmes, Faults
Whaped, Astonished, amazed
Wind, Sound
Wis, Think, consider
Wissen, Wish
Wite, Reward
Woaden, Coloured with woad
Woddie, Wrinkled
Wolfin, Wolf
Wolsomme, Loathsome
Wordeynge, Praying
Wordie, Worthy
Wote, Think
Wotted, Knew
Wrynne, Declare
Wurch, Work
Wurchys, Works
Wychencref, Witchcraft

Yaped, Laughable
Y-bereynge, Bearing
Y-blent, Blinded
Y-borne, Born one
Y-brende, Burn
Y-brent, Burnt
Y-broched, Horned
Y-brogten, Brought
Y-clenched, Covered
Y-clept, Called
Y-corne, Engraved
Y-corven, Mould
Y-crase, Break, distract
Y-dronks, Drinks up
Y-grove, Formed
Yinge, Young
Y-lach'd, Contained
Ynutile, Useless

Y-readen, Made ready
Y-reerd, Reared
Y-spedde, Despatched
Y-spende, Consider
Y-spoke, Spake
Y-storven, Dead
Y-wielde, Wield

Y-wimpled, Muffled, covered
Y-wreene } Covered,
Y-wrynde } concealed

Zabalus, The devil

INDEX OF FIRST LINES

	PAGE
A rigorous doom is mine, upon my fay, (II.)	180
Accept, fair nymph, this token of my love, (I.)	58
Against a brooklet as I lay reclined, (II.)	152
Ah blame me not, Catcott, if from the right way (I.)	48
Almighty Framer of the skies! (I.)	201
Amidst the wild and dreary dells, (I.)	59
As Elinor by the green lesselle was sitting, (II.)	27
As on a hill one eve sitting, (II.)	157
As spring now approaches with all his gay train, (I.)	46
Ascend, my muse, on sorrow's sable plume, (I)	198
Assist me, powers of heaven! what do I hear? (I.)	193
Away to the woodlands, away! (I.)	36
Bacchus, ever smiling power, (I.)	35
Before I seek the dreary shore (I.)	44
Before yon ruddy sun has drove his wain (II.)	19
Begin, my muse, the imitative lay, (I.)	177
Behold! just coming from above, (I.)	200
Burgum, I thank thee, thou hast let me see (I.)	170
Clifton, sweet village! now demands the lay, (I.)	209
Count all the flowers that deck the meadow's side, (I.)	56
Enchanting is the mighty power of love; (I.)	58
Far distant from Britannia's lofty isle, (I.)	52
Far from the reach of critics and reviews, (I.)	172
Farewell, Bristolia's dingy piles of brick, (I.)	221
Go, gentle muse, and to my fair one say, (I.)	57
God ye God den, my good neighbour, how d'ye ail? (II.)	179
Had Israel's monarch, when misfortune's dart (I.)	45
Hail Kew! thou darling of the tuneful nine, (I.)	101
Hail resignation! hail ambiguous dame, (I.)	138
Harold! (II.)	72
Haste, haste! ye solemn messengers of night, (I.)	179

INDEX OF FIRST LINES

	PAGE
Having with much attention read, (II.)	89
Heart of lion! Shake thy sword, (II.)	170
Here lies, her debt of nature paid, (I.)	216
Hervenis, harping on the hackneyed text, (I.)	216
I swear by Styx, this usage is past bearing; (I.)	11
I tell you, Lady Tempest— (I.)	39
If gentle love's immortal fire (I.)	49
In auntient dayes, when Kenewalchyn King, (II.)	186
In days of old, when Wesley's power, (I.)	205
In former days, as story says, (II.)	188
In Virginè the sweltry sun 'gan sheene, (II.)	84
Interest, thou universal god of men, (I.)	175
Johne makes a jarre 'bout Lancaster and York; (II.)	191
Joyless I hail the solemn gloom, (I.)	181
Joyless I seek the solitary shade, (I.)	182
Let Sappho's name be heard no more, (I.)	50
Love, lawless tyrant of my breast, (I.)	60
Lucy, since the knot was tied, (I.)	38
Marriage, dear M[ason], is a serious thing; (I.)	65
May happiness on earthès bounds be had? (II.)	189
Morals, as critics must allow, (I.)	86
Mounted aloft in Bristol's narrow streets, (I.)	208
My lovèd entes, adieu! No more the sight (II.)	190
No more, dear Smith, the hackneyed tale renew; (I.)	163
No more I hail the morning's golden gleam, (I.)	189
Now may all hell open to gulp thee down, (II.)	192
O'erwhelmed with pleasure at the joyful news, (I.)	65
Of warring senators, and battles dire, (I.)	69
Of war's glum pleasure do I chant my lay, (II.)	171
Oh Christ, it is a grief for me to tell (II.)	98
O God, Whose thunder shakes the sky, (I.)	218
Oh! sing unto my roundelay, (II.)	53
Oh thou, or what remains of thee, (II.)	88
Oh truth! immortal daughter of the skies, (II.)	115
On Rudborne bank two pining maidens sat (II.)	150
On Tiber's banks, Tiber, whose waters glide (I.)	1

INDEX OF FIRST LINES

	PAGE
Once more the muse to beauteous Hoyland sings; (I.)	53
'Recite the loves of Narva and Mored', (I.)	8
Revolving in their destined sphere, (I.)	62
Say, O my soul, if not allowed to be (I.)	219
Says Tom to Jack, ' "Tis very odd ', (I.)	207
Seraphic virgins of the tuneful choir, (I.)	46
Sharp was the frost, the wind was high, (I.)	202
Since happiness was not ordained for man, (I.)	166
Since short the busy scene of life will prove, (I.)	54
Since we can die but once, what matters it, (I.)	218
Some cherisaunei 'tis to gentle mind, (II.)	18
Soon as hright sun along the skies (II.)	159
Souls of the blest, the pious Nigel said, (II.)	144
Stay, curious traveller, and pass not by, (II.)	158
Strange doom it is, that, in these days of ours, (II.)	16
Sweet are thy charming smiles, my lovely maid, (I.)	56
Tell me, god of soft desires, (I.)	55
The budding flowerets blushes at the light, (II.)	25
The feathered songster chanticleer (II.)	1
The mattin-bell had sounded long, (II.)	174
The night was cold, the wind was high, (I.)	204
The pleasing sweets of spring and summer past, (II.)	140
The sun into Virginè was gotten, (II.)	139
The sun revolving on his axis turns, (I.)	213
The tournament begins; the hammers sound, (II.)	90
There was a brother of orders white, (II.)	178
This morning-star of Redcliffe's rising ray, (II.)	191
This truth of old was sorrow's friend, (I.)	134
This truth, this mighty truth—if truth can shine, (I.)	85
Though happiness be each man's darling aim, (I.)	220
Through the hall the bell hath sound; (II.)	192
'Tis mystery all, in every sect (I.)	89
'Tis sung by minstrels, that in ancient time, (II.)	15

INDEX OF FIRST LINES

	PAGE
To Clayfield, long renowned the muse's friend, (I.)	197
To sing of Clarke my muse aspires, (I.)	45
To the world new and its bestoykenynge way, (II.)	172
To use a worn-out simile, (I.)	67
Turn thee to thy shepherd swain, (II.)	22
Versed by experience in the subtle art, (I.)	162
Walpole, I thought not I should ever see, (I.)	64
Weep on, ye Britons—give your general tear; (I.)	185
Well, then, good John, since it must needs be so, (II.)	87
What gentle youth, my lovely fair one, say, (I.)	214
What is war and all its joys? (I.)	36
What language, Powel! can thy merits tell, (I.)	62
What numbers, Holland, can the muses find, (I.)	50
What strange infatuations rule mankind! (I.)	77
When azure skies is veiled in robes of night, (II.)	193
When England, smoking from her deadly wound, (II.)	142
When freedom, dressed in blood-stained vest, (II.)	79
When from the earth the sun's hulstrèd, (II.)	160
When king Kynghill in his hand, (II.)	185
When Norrurs and his men of might, (II.)	184
When Scythians, savage as the wolves they chased, (II.)	80
Where the rough Caigra rolls the surgy wave, (I.)	5
Whilom by writers much ungentle name (II.)	71
Why blooms the radiance of the morning sky? (I.)	183
With hasty step religion, dight in grey, (II.)	169
Would'st thou know nature in her better part? (II.)	147
Ye nine, awake the chorded shell, (I.)	42
Ye virgins of the sacred choir, (I.)	199
Ye, who high in murky air, (II.)	36
Yes! I am caught, my melting soul (I)	215
Young Colin was as stout a boy, (I.)	207
Young Heraudyn all by the green wood sat, (II.)	191
Young Strephon is as fair a swain (I.)	37

Printed in Great Britain
by Amazon